The Next Systemic Financial Crisis – Where Might it Come From?

Institute for Law and Finance Series

Edited by
Theodor Baums
Andreas Cahn

Volume 27

The Next Systemic Financial Crisis – Where Might it Come From?

Financial Stability in a Polycrisis World

Edited by
Andreas Dombret
Patrick S. Kenadjian

DE GRUYTER

ISBN 978-3-11-134085-2
e-ISBN (PDF) 978-3-11-134093-7
e-ISBN (EPUB) 978-3-11-134103-3

Library of Congress Control Number: 2023944014

Bibliographic information published by the Deutsche Nationalbibliothek
The Deutsche Nationalbibliothek lists this publication in the Deutsche Nationalbibliografie;
detailed bibliographic data are available on the Internet at http://dnb.dnb.de.

Foreword

By Davide Taliente, Global Chair, Public Sector, Oliver Wyman

We are pleased to introduce the proceedings of the Institute for Law and Finance 11th Conference on the Future of the Financial Sector on "The Next Systemic Financial Crisis – Where Might it Come From?: Financial Stability in a Polycrisis World."

The world economy has clearly entered a new phase: geopolitics is challenging the highly globalised and interconnected economic systems that had developed since the early 90s. The consensus view is that economic systems are migrating towards greater "strategic autonomy" within major regional blocks, as evidenced by the plethora of policy initiatives in the US (e.g., IRA), EU (e.g., Next Gen EU), and China (micro-chip and rare earth industry development). The knock-on effects include supply chain breakdowns, labour shortages, inflation, widening health disparities, on top of which climate change has the potential to accentuate migrant and refugee crises.

This "polycrisis" world is therefore the new reality and will require human ingenuity to rise to a new level: investment in green technology and new power systems will accelerate a transition to a more sustainable economy; COVID-19 exposed many fault lines in our socioeconomic systems, accelerating trends, but also helped illustrate where we should spend time and energy to build more resilience into our economy and healthcare systems; artificial intelligence will fundamentally reshape our economic system and labour markets, and should be used as a catalyst to rethink our education systems, skills training and government service models.

Recognizing that we are in this new reality implies taking a step back, acknowledging a necessary shift in our outlook, and making the appropriate plans and investments to achieve better outcomes. This requires us to learn from the past and invest differently in our resiliency and risk management approaches.

This book can help us make these necessary reflections. The financial services industry is entering a period of uncertainty and convergence with the "big tech" industry. Discussions around the future of banking and money are crucial. The contributions in this book from leaders of financial institutions, central bankers, regulators, supervisors, and public officials are now more important than ever and we thank the authors for sharing their perspectives. We would like to express our gratitude to Patrick Kenadjian, Dr. Andreas Dombret, and the Institute for Law and Finance for their partnership and their dedication to arranging this conference and furthering the conversation.

https://doi.org/10.1515/9783111340937-202

Preface

The Future of the Financial Sector Series

This book is the eleventh in the series on the future of the financial sector sponsored by the Institute for Law and Finance (ILF) at Johann Wolfgang Goethe University in Frankfurt and published by De Gruyter, Berlin. Each book corresponds to a day long conference held by the ILF at which leading representatives from the public sector, industry and academia met to examine key issues of the day concerning the future of the financial sector. Together they trace the arc of our concerns for the sector following the Great Financial Crisis.

The first three volumes, as well as the seventh, concern themselves with the resolution of financial institutions, as well as other potential solutions to the "too big to fail" dilemma in the wake of the crisis, and show the remarkable progress we have made in Germany and in Europe on that topic. The first volume was based on a conference held in November 2010, a point at which the term bank resolution was so unfamiliar in Germany that we felt it best to call the conference "Brauchen wir ein Sonderinsolvenzrecht für Banken?", do we need a special insolvency law for banks. For the book, which appeared in 2012, we stuck in Too Big to Fail in the title. Contributors included Andreas Dombret, John Douglas, former General Counsel of the Federal Deposit Insurance Corporation, Thomas Huertas, member of the Executive Committee at the UK Financial Services Authority and Alternate Chair of the European Banking Authority (EBA), Martin Hellwig, Director at the Max Planck Institute for Research on Collective Goods and Charles Randell, who was soon to become external member of the UK Prudential Regulation Committee and later Chair of the UK Financial Conduct Authority.

By May 2012 we were already able to discuss what was then being called the EU Crisis Management Directive, although the actual text itself had been delayed and was only published after the conference. By the time the book appeared in 2013 we were able to call it by its definitive name, the Bank Recovery and Resolution Directive, and actually deal with the text itself. It was clear that by then resolution had been adopted by the EU as its preferred solution to too big to fail, although its complexities were still being sorted through, especially the topic of "living wills" and the then very controversial "bail-in tool". Contributors included Eva Hüpkes, advisor to the Financial Stability Board, Thomas Huertas, Charles Randell and Paul Tucker, Deputy Governor of the Bank of England.

By January 2014 we were considering more radical proposals, as the recommendations of the Liikanen Commission joined the Volcker Rule and the conclusions of the Vickers Commission in the United Kingdom in pointing towards a variety of so-called structural reforms, separating various kinds of banking services. So we asked

https://doi.org/10.1515/9783111340937-203

"Should We Break Up the Banks?" Contributors included Paul Achleitner, Chairman of the Supervisory Board of Deutsche Bank, Jan Krahnen, member of the High level Expert Group on Structural Reforms of the EU Banking Sector and Adam Posen, President of the Peterson Institute for International Economics. At the end of the day, most contributors ended up advocating or conceding that, without a credible bank resolution system, structural proposals to break up the banks would not suffice to solve too big to fail.

We returned to the question of resolution in the spring of 2018 with our program entitled "Resolution in Europe: The Unresolved Questions", the fourth in our series on too big to fail, in which we narrowed our focus to Europe but broadened our scope to include insurance and central counterparties (CCPs). The book was published in 2019 with contributions by José Manuel Campa, the future Chair of the EBA, Benoît Cœuré, member of the Executive Board of the European Central Bank (ECB), Adam Farkas, Executive Director of the EBA, Levin Holle, Director General, Financial Markets Policy Department, German Federal Ministry of Finance, Felix Hufeld, President of the German Federal Financial Supervisory Authority, Elke König, Chair of the Single Resolution Board, Steven Maijoor, Chair of the European Securities and Markets Authority, Fausto Parente, Executive Director of the European Insurance and Occupational Pensions Authority and Sir Paul Tucker. The contributors concluded that significant progress had been made on bank resolution, although significant open issues remained, especially with respect to cross-border cases, but that less progress had been made on insurance and that CCP resolution required significant additional attention.

In March 2015 we turned our attention from the past to the future to consider the European Capital Markets Union in response to the European Commission's Green Paper in a session where we questioned whether it was a viable concept and a real goal. The book appeared, in the same year, with contributions from Benoît Cœuré, Sir Jon Cunliffe, Deputy Governor for Financial Stability of the Bank of England, Philipp Hildebrand, Vice Chairman of BlackRock, Anshu Jain, Co-chief Executive Officer of Deutsche Bank and Wim Mijs, Chief Executive Officer of the European Banking Federation. There was a broad consensus on the desirability of the project, but considerable reservations on the tactics being pursued to accomplish it.

In November 2015 – 2015 was a busy year for us – we turned our attention back to one of the nagging questions left over from the Great Financial Crisis: to what extent was the crisis due to culture and could we hope to restore public confidence in financial institutions without tackling the issue of ethics. "Getting the Culture and the Ethics Right, Towards a New Age of Responsibility in Banking" appeared in 2016, with contributions from Lorenzo Bini Smaghi, Chairman of Société Générale, John Cryan, Chief Executive Officer of Deutsche Bank, Georg Fahrenschon, President of the German Savings Banks Association, Douglas Flint, Group Chairman of HSBC Holdings,

John Griffith-Jones, Chairman of the UK Financial Conduct Authority, Danièle Nouy, Chair of the Supervisory Board of the ECB Single Supervisory Mechanism, Jean-Claude Trichet, Chairman of the Group of Thirty, Sir Paul Tucker and Axel Weber, Chairman of the Board of UBS Group. There was unanimity among the contributors as to the importance of culture and ethics, but less clarity on whether the goals could best be reached through external pressure from regulation and supervision or bankers' codes, or internally through boards of directors and structural changes.

We had intended to hold a conference in 2016 on the final Basel III accord, scheduled for finalization by year end. When the negotiations collapsed we pushed our session back to December 2017 and the book, "Basel III: Are We Done Now?" appeared in 2019 with contributions from Claudio Borio, Head of the Monetary and Economics Department, Bank for International Settlements, William Coen, Secretary General of the Basel Committee on Banking Supervision, Andrea Enria, Chairperson of the EBA, Charles Goodhart, Emeritus Professor at the London School of Economics, Levin Holle, Stefan Ingves, Governor of the Swedish Riksbank and Chairman of the Basel Committee for Banking Supervision, Sabine Lautenschläger, Member of the Executive Board of the ECB, Christian Ossig, Chief Executive of the Association of German Banks, Isabel Schnabel, Member of the German Council of Economic Experts and Shunsuke Shirakawa, Vice Commissioner for International Affairs, Financial Services Agency of Japan, The contributors emphasized both the magnitude of the accomplishment Basel III represented and the issues which still remained to be resolved in the implementation of the accord as well as those items about which no agreement had been reached.

In 2019 we tackled the questions standing in the way of completing the European Banking Union. The book, entitled "EDIS, NPLs, Sovereign Debt and Safe Assets", appeared in 2020 with contributions by Andrea Enria, Chair of the Supervisory Board of the ECB, Edouard Fernandez-Bollo, Secretary General, French Prudential Supervision and Resolution Authority, Martin Hellwig, Levin Holle, Dominique Laboureix, Director of Resolution Planning at the Single Resolution Board, Christian Ossig, Fabio Panetta, Senior Deputy Governor of the Bank of Italy, Isabel Schnabel, Joachim Wuermeling, member of the Executive Board of the Deutsche Bundesbank and Jeromin Zettelmeyer, Deputy Director in the Strategy and Policy Review Department at the International Monetary Fund.

In 2021 we opened up our aperture to tackle the global issues concerning climate change, operating for the first time on a fully virtual basis, with an audience of over 1,000 who were treated to an inspiring keynote address by Christine Lagarde, President of the European Central Bank. The resulting book, entitled, "Green Banking and Green Central Banking", was published to coincide with COP26 in Glasgow in November 2021 with contributions from John Berrigan, Director General in DG FISMA, Günther Bräunig, CEO of KfW, José Manuel Campa, Chairperson of the

European Banking Authority, Wiebe Draijer, Chairman of the Managing Board, Rabobank, Christian Edelmann, Managing Partner Europe at Oliver Wyman, Sylvie Goulard, Second Deputy Governor of the Banque de France, Philipp Hildebrand, Vice Chairman of Blackrock, Werner Hoyer, President, EIB, Otmar Issing, President of the Center for Financial Studies, Christine Lagarde, Valentin von Massow, Vice President of the Board of WWF International, Wim Mijs, Chief Executive Officer of the European Banking Federation, Daniel Mminele, former Deputy Governor of the South African Reserve Bank, Ted Moynihan, Managing Partner and Global Head of Industries at Oliver Wyman, Sirpa Pietikäinen, Member of the European Parliament, Deputy General Manager, BIS, Günther Thallinger, Member of the Board of Management of Allianz SE and Jens Weidmann, President, Deutsche Bundesbank.

In 2022 we turned the challenges of data, digitalization, decentralized finance and central bank digital currencies, asking ourselves what each of these might mean for the future of banking and money. This was our second virtual conference and we beat our attendance record from 2021. Over 1,200 participants from 66 countries signed up to hear Agustin Carstens, General Manager of the Bank for International Settlements give the keynote address in which he cogently made the case for central bank digital currencies. The resulting book, entitled "Data, Digitalization, Decentralized Finance and Central Bank Digital Currencies" appeared in 2023 with contributions from Ashley Alder, Chief Executive Officer of the Securities and Futures Commission of Hong Kong, John Berrigan, Director General in DG FISMA of the European Commission, Ulrich Bindseil, Director General, Market Infrastructure and Payments at the European Central Bank, Markus K. Brunnermeier, the Edward S. Sanford Professor in the economics department at Princeton University, Stephen G. Cecchetti, Rosen Family Chair in International Finance at Brandeis University, Barry Eichengreen, the George C. Pardee and Helen N. Pardee Professor of Economics and Professor of Political Science at the University of California, Berkeley, Michael J. Hsu, Acting Comptroller of the Currency of the United States, Stefan Ingves, Governor of Sveriges Riksbank, Bernd Leukert, member of the Deutsche Bank Management Board, Andréa Maechler, member of the Swiss National Bank's Governing Board, Wim Mijs, Chief Executive Officer of the European Banking Federation, Mu Changchun, Director General of the Digital Currency Institute of the People's Bank of China and Randal Quarles, former Vice Chairman for Supervision of the Board of Governors of the Federal Reserve System.

The full list of the titles and contributors is set forth below. We are very grateful for all of them for the efforts they put into these volumes, which we hope have contributed to advancing thinking in Europe on the various topics we covered.

Andreas Dombret
Patrick Kenadjian   Frankfurt Main, April 2023

Institute for Law and Finance Series;
Titles on the Future of the Financial Sector

Vol. 9: *Too Big To Fail – Brauchen wir ein Sonderinsolvenzrecht für Banken?*
Ed. Patrick S. Kenadjian (2012)
Authors: Dirk H. Bliesener, Andreas Dombret, John L. Douglas, Martin Hellwig, Thomas F. Huertas, Patrick S. Kenadjian, Wolfgang M. Nardi, Klaus Pannen, Carl Pickerill, Leo Plank, Matthias Raphael Prause, Wolfgang M. Nardi, Charles Randell, Christoph Thole.

Vol. 13: *The Bank Recovery and Resolution Directive: Europe's Solution for*
"Too Big to Fail?", Ed. Andreas Dombret and Patrick S. Kenadjian,
De Gruyter Recht Berlin (2013)
Authors: Andreas Cahn, Dirk H. Bliesener, Andreas Dombret, Randall D. Guynn, Thomas F. Huertas, Eva Hüpkes, Patrick S. Kenadjian, Simon Gleeson, Mathias Otto, Charles Randell, Paul Tucker.

Vol. 16: *Too Big to Fail III: Structural Reform Proposals Should We Break Up the*
Banks? Ed. Andreas Dombret and Patrick S. Kenadjian, De Gruyter Recht Berlin
(2015)
Authors: Paul Achleitner, Andreas Dombret, Douglas J. Elliott, Simon Gleeson, Randall D. Guynn, Patrick S. Kenadjian, Jan P. Krahnen, Adam S. Posen, Miguel de la Mano, Debra Stone.

Vol. 17: *The European Capital Markets Union A viable concept and a real goal?*
Ed. Andreas Dombret and Patrick S. Kenadjian, De Gruyter Recht Berlin (2015)
Authors: Cyrus Ardalan, Andrew Bosomworth, Benoît Cœuré, Sir Jon Cunliffe, Andreas Dombret, Alexandra Hachmeister, Philipp Hildebrand, Anshu Jain, Patrick S. Kenadjian, Wim Mijs, Christian Ossig, Dirk Schoenmaker.

Vol. 20: *Getting the Culture and the Ethics Right Towards a New Age of*
Responsibility in Banking and Finance, Ed. Patrick S. Kenadjian and Andreas
Dombret, De Gruyter Recht, Berlin (2016)
Authors: Lorenzo Bini Smaghi, John Cryan, Andreas Dombret, Georg Fahren-schon, Leonhard H. Fischer, Douglas Flint, Simon Gleeson, John Griffith-Jones, Klaus J. Hopt, Patrick S. Kenadjian, Jan P. Krahnen, Sylvie Matherat, Wim Mijs, Alberto G. Musalem, Danièle Nouy, Dominik Treeck, Jean-Claude Trichet, Sir Paul Tucker, Axel A. Weber.

Vol. 21: *Basel III: Are We Done Now? Ed. Andreas Dombret and Patrick S. Kenadjian, De Gruyter Recht Berlin (2019)*
Authors: Claudio Borio, William Coen, Andreas Dombret, Douglas J. Elliott, Andrea Enria, Michael S. Gibson, C.A.E. Goodhart, Stuart Graham, Paul Hilbers, Levin Holle, Stefan Ingves, Patrick S. Kenadjian, Sabine Lautenschläger, Laurie Mayers, Martin Merlin, Sandie O'Connor, Christian Ossig, Shunsuke Shirakawa, Isabel Schnabel.

Vol. 22: *Resolution in Europe: The Unresolved Questions, Ed. Andreas Dombret and Patrick S. Kenadjian, De Gruyter Recht Berlin (2019)*
Authors: José Manuel Campa, Benoît Cœuré, Andreas Dombret, Wilson Ervin, Joachim Faber, Adam Farkas, Helmut Gründl, Levin Holle, Thomas F. Huertas, Felix Hufeld, Patrick S. Kenadjian, Elke König, Daniel Maguire, Steven Maijoor, Fausto Parente, Giulio Terzariol, Sir Paul Tucker, Mark E. Van Der Weide, James von Moltke.

Vol. 23: *EDIS, NPLs, Sovereign Debt and Safe Assets, Ed. Andreas Dombret and Patrick S. Kenadjian, De Gruyter Recht Berlin (2020)*
Authors: Klaus Adam, Roland Boekhout, Thiess Büttner, Rebecca Christie, Andreas Dombret, Colin Ellis, Andrea Enria, Edouard Fernandez-Bollo, Martin Hellwig, Joachim Hennrichs, Georg Huber, Thomas F. Huertas, Patrick S. Kenadjian, Nikki Kersten, Slawek Kozdras, Jan P. Krahnen, Dominique Laboureix, Álvaro Leandro, Nicoletta Mascher, Sylvie Matherat, Wim Mijs, Arthur J. Murton, Charles Nysten, Christian Ossig, Fabio Panetta, Jörg Rocholl, Karl-Peter Schackmann-Fallis, Isabel Schnabel, Anita van den Ende, Nicolas Véron, Klaus Wiedner, Joachim Wuermeling, Jeromin Zettelmeyer.

Vol 24: *Green Banking and Green Central Banking, Ed. Andreas Dombret and Patrick S. Kenadjian, De Gruyter Recht Berlin (2021)*
Authors: John Berrigan, Jean Boivin, Günther Bräunig, José Manuel Campa, Andreas Dombret, Wiebe Draijer, Christian Edelmann, Ed Fishwick, Sylvie Goulard, Philipp Hildebrand, Werner Hoyer, Andreas Dombret, Otmar Issing, Patrick Kenadjian, Matthias Kopp, Christine Lagarde, Valentin von Massow, Wim Mijs, Daniel Mminele, Ted Moynihan, Simona Paravani-Mellinghoff, Sirpa Pietikäinen, Christian Sewing, Luiz Awazu Pereira da Silva, Jessica Tan, Günther Thallinger, Bouke de Vries, Jens Weidmann.

Vol. 25: *Data, Digitalization, Decentralized Finance and Central Bank Digital Currencies: The Future of Banking and Money, Ed. Andreas Dombret and Patrick S. Kenadjian, De Gruyter Recht Berlin (2023)*
Authors: Ashley Ian Alder, John Berrigan, Ulrich Bindseil Markus K. Brunnermeier, Agustin Carstens, Stephen G. Cecchetti, Andreas Dombret, Christian Edelmann,

Barry Eichengreen, Michael J. Hsu, Stefan Ingves, Patrick Kenadjian, Jean-Pierre Landau, Bernd Leukert, Andréa M. Machler, Steven Maijoor, Wim Mijs, Ted Moynihan, Mu Changchun, Randal K. Quarles, Kermit L. Schoenholz, Oliver Wuensch.

Contents

I. Macroeconomic Factors

II. Crypto Assets and Cybersecurity

Introduction

The 11th Conference on the future of the financial sector at the Institute for Law and Finance (ILF) took place on January 24, 2023. It was the first to be held with physical presence since 2020 and was held in a hybrid format. Hybrid formats are particularly challenging to organize and we are particularly grateful for the support of the ILF staff, our knowledge partner Oliver Wyman and the support from Amazon Web Services as well as the 26 other speakers who generously donated their time to prepare for and speak at the conference.

At it we asked where the next systemic financial crisis might come from and pondered the question of financial stability in a poly crisis world. We chose the topic because we all know there will be another financial crisis, we just don't know when or what will trigger it. But we also know that fortune favors the prepared mind, so we divided the day into four areas for deep dives into possible causes: macroeconomic factors; crypto assets and cyber security; non-bank financial institutions (NBFIs); and regulated financial service providers. We discussed each of the sectors separately, keeping in mind that each sector can interact with the others to produce a cluster of risks with compounding effects such that the overall impact exceeds the sum of the parts. Hence the reference to the "poly crisis", which the Financial Times recently named its buzzword of the year and the World Economic Forum adopted for its recent Global Risks Report.

Writing these lines in April 2023 there is a hint that the next crisis might come from the sector which, on January 24 it is fair to say we considered the least likely source, the regulated banking sector, which we considered in Panel 4, and that the trigger might be the rapid interest rate increases carried out by the central banks to combat inflation, which we considered in Panel 1.

However, as Chou En Lai is reputed to have told Henry Kissinger, who asked him whether the Chinese Revolution had been a success, "it is too early to tell." In any case, the events triggered by the collapse of a California based regional bank in early March 2023 did have repercussions as far away as Switzerland where the country's second largest bank had to be taken over to prevent its collapse. But, thanks to the prompt and decisive reactions by supervisors, regulators and the treasuries in the US and in Switzerland, they have not so far resulted in a systemic crisis. Rather, as of now, we might speak of a warning shot against complacency in supervision and regulation in even what we consider to be the safest parts of the financial sector and a call to reexamine what we know about the causes and prevention of bank runs, what constitutes good supervision and the function and extent of deposit insurance.

We were honored to start the day with a keynote address providing an overview of the issues presented by Klaas Knot, chair of the Financial Stability Board

https://doi.org/10.1515/9783111340937-205

(FSB) and President of De Nederlandische Bank, who gave us an excellent sense of what issues relating to financial stability were top of mind at the FSB and consequently on the international regulatory agenda, covering both current cyclical problems and more far-reaching structural shifts being mapped, measured and monitored by the FSB as part of its efforts to increase resilience of the financial system through identifying key vulnerabilities.

The first panel, moderated by Lisa Quest, partner of Oliver Wyman, was devoted to all those factors outside the financial sector which are largely beyond the control of actors within the sector, but which could trigger the next crisis. The views of the panelists were sobering. They considered that our economies were facing a set of challenges unprecedented since World War II, including war, more persistent inflation, a crisis of the global commons in the absence of global frameworks to deal with cyber crime, pandemics and climate change, in a context of rising inequality. The panelists emphasized the need to build global structures for cooperation in the areas of climate and technology similar to the ones we have built for the financial sector, at a time when some politicians seem intent on building walls. The panel also touched on the topic of Panel 3, the dangers which may arise from NBFIs, providing a useful introduction to that panel.

Panel 2 was preceded by an illuminating discussion of cyber risks between Chad Woolf, Vice President, Security of Amazon Web Services and Andreas Dombret, ranging widely from the known knowns and known unknowns of our current cyber challenges to the new challenges presented by machine learning and quantum computing.

The panel itself was introduced by an excellent keynote from Mike Hsu, Acting US Comptroller of the Currency, who challenged us to push beyond the known knowns of recession, credit deterioration and market dysfunctions and the known unknowns of cyber, operational resilience and crypto on to unknown unknowns, asking us to reflect on how mindsets may change as a result of digitalization and what blind spots of private actors merit the attention of the financial stability community.

Panel 2 was moderated by Maria Tsani of Amazon Web Services and focused on the crypto market, its inherent structural limitations and the sense of urgency for authorities to act. Banning crypto, isolating it from the rest of the financial sector (making it a niche activity) and regulation were considered as alternative approaches. The third approach was seen as the most promising, although it is far from simple to accomplish. While the social value of crypto was viewed as yet to be established, the value of the technology was viewed as having more promise as a basis for new economic activity.

Panel 3 was moderated by Patrick Kenadjian and focused on two specific areas of the vast NBFI field, money market mutual funds (MMFs) and other open ended bond funds, which have been the subject of significant attention by the FSB and national regulators resulting in reform proposals from the FSB and US regulators. We were lucky to have one of the US regulators on the panel, who gave us a comprehensive overview of the US approach to the area. The discussion ranged widely from deep dives into the design and operation of these funds, to the extent to which regulated financial institutions might provide an alternative to NBFIs, to the question of whether it was the nature of the markets these NBFIs operate in, in particular the government securities markets, which needs reforming as much as the NBFIs themselves.

Panel 4 was moderated by Andreas Dombret and covered the regulated financial sector. As noted above, this was the sector we had considered the least likely to be the source of a systemic crisis and the panelists largely confirmed this view, although they did see a danger in short term liquidity tensions, coupled with leverage and with connections among financial institutions, both in the regulated and non-bank sectors. The panel followed the known versus unknown risk pattern of inquiry used by Panel 2. Liquidity risk recurred in the analysis of the panelists as among the likeliest triggers for a crisis. It was also mentioned as one of the three supervisory priorities of the European Central Bank for 2023, together with digitalization and climate. The panelists noted that "zero failure" is not possible to achieve in the financial sector and that the goal of supervision and regulation thus had to be to achieve orderly failures.

The afternoon wrapped up with concluding remarks by Dominik Weh of Oliver Wyman who called for bold policy making in the face of the global and polycrisis nature of the risks we are facing, reminding us that while the next crisis will surely come, it is unlikely to come from the same direction as the last crisis.

Andreas Dombret
Patrick Kenadjian   Frankfurt, April 2023

The Authors

Tobias Adrian

Tobias Adrian is the Financial Counsellor and Director of the Monetary and Capital Markets Department of the International Monetary Fund (IMF). In this capacity, he leads the IMF's work on financial sector surveillance, monetary and macroprudential policies, digital money, financial regulation, bank resolution, sovereign debt, capital markets, and climate finance. He also oversees capacity building activities in IMF member countries with regard to the supervision and regulation of financial systems, bank resolution, central banking, monetary and exchange rate regimes, central bank digital currency, and debt management.

Prior to joining the IMF, Mr. Adrian was a Senior Vice President of the Federal Reserve Bank of New York and the Associate Director of the Research and Statistics Group. At the Federal Reserve, he contributed to monetary policy, to financial stability policies, and to crisis management.

Mr. Adrian has published extensively in economics and finance journals. His research spans macro-finance, monetary policy, and financial stability, with a focus on aggregate consequences of capital market developments. He has taught at Princeton University and New York University. He is member of the editorial boards of the International Journal of Central Banking and the Annual Review of Financial Economics.

Mr. Adrian holds a Ph.D. from the Massachusetts Institute of Technology in Economics, an MSc from the London School of Economics in Econometrics and Mathematical Economics, a Diplom from Goethe University Frankfurt and a Maîtrise from Dauphine University Paris. He received his Abitur in Literature and Mathematics from Humboldtschule Bad Homburg.

Torry Berntsen

Torry Berntsen is CEO, Europe & Americas at Standard Chartered.

He was appointed Regional CEO, Europe and Americas and CEO Europe and UK in January 2021. He was previously CEO and Head of Corporate and Institutional Banking for the Americas, Standard Chartered and was responsible for developing and delivering the Bank's strategy in the Americas and led on all aspects of regulatory, governance and financial performance.

Torry has over 35 years of banking and financial services experience Prior to Standard Chartered, he was the President and a Director of Independent Bank Group (IBG), where he was involved in all aspects of the Company's operations, including spearheading its investor relations efforts as well as managing all of its financial institutions relationships and partnerships. He spent 25 years in various senior management roles at The Bank of New York Mellon (BNY Mellon). His last position in BNY

https://doi.org/10.1515/9783111340937-206

Mellon was Senior Executive Vice President, Sector Head, Global Client Management. In his role as CEO Europe and Americas he is responsible for the Corporate & Institutional Banking, Private and Retail Banking businesses in the US, Latin America, UK, Jersey, Falklands, Germany, France, Nordics, Ireland and Turkey.

Claudio Borio
Head of the Monetary and Economic Department

Claudio Borio was appointed Head of the Monetary and Economic Department on 18 November 2013.

At the BIS since 1987, Mr Borio has held various positions in the Monetary and Economic Department (MED), including Deputy Head of MED and Director of Research and Statistics as well as Head of Secretariat for the Committee on the Global Financial System and the Gold and Foreign Exchange Committee (now the Markets Committee).

From 1985 to 1987, he was an economist at the OECD, working in the country studies branch of the Economics and Statistics Department. Prior to that, he was Lecturer and Research Fellow at Brasenose College, Oxford University. He holds a DPhil and an MPhil in Economics and a BA in Politics, Philosophy and Economics from the same university. Claudio is author of numerous publications in the fields of monetary policy, banking, finance and issues related to financial stability.

Edward Bowles
Edward Bowles is Global Director of Public Policy at Meta Financial Technologies. He started his career as a barrister, where he practiced law as a Crown Prosecutor for 8 years, before joining the U.K. Ministry of Justice, heading human rights policy, the private offices of two Ministers and the Permanent Secretary. Edward then joined Standard Chartered Bank one month before the financial crisis, and spent 12 years on banking regulation and trade policy, before joining Facebook, as it then was, in 2019. In 2021 he joined the team responsible for Libra/Diem, payments and digital innovation.

Sarah Breeden
Term of appointment: 2 August 2021–1 August 2024

Sarah is the Executive Director for Financial Stability Strategy and Risk and a member of the Financial Policy Committee (FPC). The FPC is the United Kingdom's 'macroprudential' authority. It is tasked by Parliament with guarding against the financial system damaging the wider economy. Sarah is responsible for the Bank of England's work to deliver that objective.

Sarah also leads the Bank of England's work on climate change, domestically and internationally, a role she has held since 2016. She has been a Steering Group member of the international central bank and supervisors' Network for Greening the Financial System (NGFS) since its inception in 2017, and chaired its macrofinancial workstream from 2018 until early 2022.

Prior to her current role, Sarah was the Executive Director for UK Deposit Takers Supervision, responsible for the supervision of the UK's banks, building societies and credit unions and before that, she was Executive Director for International Banks Supervision, where having joined the directorate in 2015, she was responsible for supervision of the UK operations of international banks.

Before moving into supervision, Sarah was a Director in the Bank's Financial Stability Strategy and Risk Directorate, where she focused on developing the UK's macroprudential policy making framework and supporting the Financial Policy Committee. Previously she was head of the division that assessed risks to financial stability from financial markets, the non-bank financial sector, and the real economy.

José Manuel Campa

José Manuel Campa is the Chairperson of the European Banking Authority (EBA). He was appointed in March 2019 and is serving a renewable five-year term. He represents the Authority and by chairing the meetings of the Board of Supervisors and of the Management Board, he steers the strategic direction of the Authority.

From 2015 and prior to this appointment, Campa served as Global Head of Regulatory Affairs, for the Grupo Santander. Prior to that, he was Professor of Finance and Economics at IESE Business School.

Between 2009 and 2011, Campa served as Secretary of State for the Economy in the Ministry of Economy and Finances of Spain. He was a member of the Financial Stability Board, the board of the European Financial Stability Facility, the Economic and Financial Committee and alternate governor in multilateral financial institutions. He has served in the Expert Group, chaired by Mr. Erkki Liikanen, evaluating policy recommendations on structural reforms for the European Banking industry.

He has also taught at the Stern School of Business of New York University and at Columbia University. He has been Research Associate at the National Bureau of Economic Research and Research Fellow at the Center for Economic Policy Research. Mr. Campa has also been a consultant to a large number of international organizations, including the International Monetary Fund, the Inter-American Development Bank, the Bank of International Settlements in Basel, and the European Commission.

He has served on the boards of Prime Collateralised Securities (PCS) Europe, Bruegel, and General de Alquiler de Maquinaria.

José Manuel Campa holds a Ph.D. and a master degree in economics from Harvard University and a Licenciatura in law and in economics from the Universidad de Oviedo.

Alice Carr

Alice Carr is Executive Director for Public Policy at the Glasgow Financial Alliance for Net Zero (GFANZ), which is working at pace to ensure that the global financial system can deliver on commitments to support economic transition to net zero by 2050 in line with 1.5 degrees. This includes working to ensure that global and national regulatory frameworks support transition finance and leading GFANZ work to support the Just Energy Transition Partnerships. Prior to this, Alice had a two-decade career in central banking, most recently leading the Bank of England's international strategy and policy division during the UK's G7 presidency and Covid crisis.

Joanna Cound

Joanna Cound, Managing Director, is Head of BlackRock's Global Public Policy Group (GPPG), which engages with policy makers and regulators at the global, regional, and national levels to help address financial services policy challenges and to bring the voice of the end investor to the table. The team delivers data driven thought leadership to policy makers, clients, and industry peers, across the spectrum of financial policy issues impacting savers and investors. She is a member of BlackRock's European Executive Committee, BlackRock's Global Operating Committee and the BlackRock Group Limited (BGL) Enterprise Risk Management Committee. She co-chairs the EMEA External Affairs Committee and is a member of the Global External Affairs Operating Committee.

Prior to moving to this role, Ms. Cound was International COO for BlackRock's Cash Management Group. Ms. Cound's service with the firm dates to 1996, including her years with Merrill Lynch Investment Managers (MLIM), which merged with BlackRock in 2006. Prior to joining MLIM in 1996, Ms. Cound worked for Fidelity as head of European product development and as a marketing manager for Citibank retail bank in Germany.

Ms. Cound earned a BA degree in European studies from Loughborough University and a masters in European studies from the College of Europe in Bruges, Belgium. She also has an MBA from the London Business School.

Ms. Cound is Deputy Chair of the Chatham House Council and member of the Human Resources Committee of Loughborough University.

Andreas Dombret

Dr Andreas Dombret was born in the USA to German parents. He studied business management at the Westfälische Wilhelms University in Münster and was awarded his PhD by the Friedrich-Alexander University in Erlangen-Nuremberg.

From 1987 to 1991, he worked at Deutsche Bank's Head Office in Frankfurt, from 1992 to 2002 at JP Morgan in Frankfurt and London, from 2002 to 2005 as the Co-

Head of Rothschild Germany located in Frankfurt and London, before serving Bank of America as Vice Chairman for Europe and Head for Germany, Austria and Switzerland between 2005 and 2009.

From May 2010 to May 2018, he has been a member of the Executive Board of the Deutsche Bundesbank with responsibility for Financial Stability, Statistics, Markets, Banking and Financial Supervision, Economic Education, Risk Controlling and the Bundesbank's Representative Offices abroad. He was also responsible for the IMF (Deputy of the Bundesbank), Financial Stability Commission (Member), Supervisory Board of the SSM (Member), Basel Committee on Banking Supervision (BCBS) (Member) and has been a member of the Board of Directors at the Bank for International Settlements (BIS), Basel, until the end of 2018. Since 2009, Andreas holds a professorship at the European Business School in Wiesbaden and teaches, as Adjunct Senior Fellow, at Columbia University in New York since May 2018.

Stuart Graham

Stuart Graham – Senior Partner, Autonomous Research LLP

Stuart co-founded Autonomous Research, a specialist global financials research firm, in 2009. He was its CEO from 2009–2017, building a business with over 80 staff in Europe, the US and Asia with revenues of $70mn. Prior to founding Autonomous Research, Stuart was the head of European banks equity research at Merrill Lynch. He was the number 1 ranked European bank analyst for six consecutive years. Before joining Merrill Lynch in 2002, Stuart worked at JPMorgan and HSBC (both in banks equity research). He began his career at the Bank of England in 1988 in the Banking Supervision Department. Stuart holds an MA in modern history from Cambridge University.

Michael J. Hsu

Michael J. Hsu is the Acting Comptroller of the Currency and serves as the administrator of the federal banking system and chief executive officer of the Office of the Comptroller of the Currency. The OCC ensures the U.S. federal banking system operates in a safe and sound manner, provides fair access to financial services, treats customers fairly, and complies with applicable laws and regulations.

Kerstin af Jochnick

Kerstin af Jochnick has been an ECB representative to the Supervisory Board since 1 October 2019.

Prior to this she was First Deputy Governor of Sveriges Riksbank, a position she had held since 2012. In that role, she was also an alternate member of the General Council of the European Central Bank from 2015 to 2019. She was also a member of the European Systemic Risk Board from 2015 to 2018.

From 2009 to 2011 Ms af Jochnick was Managing Director of the Swedish Bankers' Association and from 2008 to 2009 she was Chair of the Committee of European Banking Supervisors.

From 1995 to 2007 she was Head of Banking Supervision at Finansinspektionen, the Swedish Financial Supervisory Authority, where she had also worked as a financial analyst from 1991 to 1995.

Her other past roles have included Member of the Board of the Danish Financial Supervisory Authority (2014–18), Member of the IIF Advisory Group on Supervision (2010–11) and Member of the Basel Committee on Banking Supervision (2003–09 and 2013–19).

Patrick Kenadjian

Patrick is currently an Adjunct Professor at the Goethe University in Frankfurt am Main, Germany, where he teaches courses on the financial crisis and financial reform and mergers and acquisitions at the Institute for Law and Finance.

Since 2012, Patrick has co-chaired a series of conferences at the University on financial reform, including the need for and design of resolution regimes for banks, insurance companies and CCPs and other potential solutions for "too big to fail", the proposed European Capital Market Union, the importance of culture and ethics in financial institutions, the final agreement on Basel III and collective action clauses in sovereign debt issues. Since 2015 he has served on the Advisory Council to the Salzburg Global Forum on Finance in a Changing World where he served as Program Director in 2013 and 2014.

Patrick is also Senior Counsel at Davis Polk & Wardwell London LLP. He was a partner of the firm from 1984 to 2010, during which time he opened the firm's Tokyo and Frankfurt offices in 1987 and 1991, respectively and spent over 25 years in its European and Asian offices. He speaks French, German and Italian.

Klaas Knot

Klaas Knot has been President of DNB since 1 July 2011 and has served as Chair of the Financial Stability Board since 2 December 2021. He is also a member of the Governing Council and the General Council of the European Central Bank, member of the European Systemic Risk Board, member of the International Monetary Fund's Board of Governors and a member of the Board of Directors of the Bank for International Settlements.

Klaas holds several secondary positions. Since 2005, he has been professor of economics of central banking at the University of Groningen, and since 2015 he has also been honorary professor of monetary stability at the Economics and Business Department of the University of Amsterdam. Klaas has published a variety of articles in leading Dutch and international journals in the fields of monetary and financial economics. He is also a member of the Group of Thirty, a global body comprised of economic and financial leaders from the public and private sectors and academia.

Before assuming DNB's presidency, Klaas Knot was Deputy Treasurer-General and Director of Financial Markets at the Dutch Ministry of Finance (2009–2011). Earlier, from 1995, he worked for DNB for almost twelve years in various positions including senior economist in the Monetary and Economic Policy Department and Director of the Supervisory Policy Division. At different intervals during this period, he was employed by the International Monetary Fund (1998–1999) and the former Pensions and Insurance Supervisory Authority of the Netherlands (2003–2004).

In 1991, he graduated with honours in economics from the University of Groningen. In 1995, he obtained his PhD in economics.

Martin Moloney

Martin Moloney is currently the Secretary General of IOSCO. He was previously the Director General of the Jersey Financial Services Commission and before that occupied various senior roles in the Central Bank of Ireland, having begun his career in banking. He has been Chair of the Investment Management Standing Committee of ESMA, Chair of an Investment Funds Working Group of the European Systemic Risk Board and Chair of an IOSCO working group to develop guidance on liquidity management for Investment Funds, having also participated in an FSB working group developing the 2017 FSB Recommendations on Liquidity and Leverage of investment funds. He has also been a member of the Board of IOSCO and an alternate member of the board of ESMA. He holds postgraduate qualifications in philosophy, commercial law and economic policy as well as professional qualifications in banking and arbitration.

Luiz Awazu Pereira da Silva

Luiz Awazu Pereira da Silva became Deputy General Manager of the Bank for International Settlements on 1 October 2015.

Before joining the BIS, Mr Pereira da Silva, a Brazilian National, had been Deputy Governor of the Central Bank of Brazil since 2010. Prior to that, he worked in various positions for the World Bank in Washington DC, Tokyo, and southern Africa. He also served as Chief Economist for the Brazilian Ministry of Budget and Planning, and as Brazil's Deputy Finance Minister in charge of international affairs.

Lisa Quest

Lisa Quest is the Market Head for UK&I and European Head of the Public Sector Practice for Oliver Wyman.

Lisa has over 15 years of experience consulting in the UK, Continental Europe and North America. She has worked with top government officials, chief executives and other senior leaders of the world's leading organisations and governments on topics spanning digital transformation, governance, strategy, financial planning, risk management and public policy & regulatory response.

Lisa led Oliver Wyman's Anti-Financial Crime practice as well as our Public Sector Governance and Transformation platforms, representing each of these businesses on the firm's European Leadership Team.

Lisa has advised senior government leaders and policy makers on topics of industry competitiveness and stability and co-authored many articles and studies, including supporting the IBFed on BigTech entrance into Financial Services, Impact of Digitalisation of the economy on regulatory structures and future of supervision.

Lisa is a keen advocate of inclusion and a sponsor of diversity – she sits on the firm's inclusion council, is executive sponsor of Oliver Wyman's Women of Oliver Wyman and was shortlisted for Mentor of the Year by Management Today Magazine and names on of the Top 100 Female Executives on the HERos list.

Lisa is also a Visiting Academic Fellow at the London School of Economics, Centre for Risk and Regulation. She holds a First Class Honours degree in Business Administration from the Richard Ivey School of Business at the University of Western Ontario, Canada and a Masters degree in Public Administration in European Public and Economic Policy from the London School of Economics.

Cecilia Skingsley

Cecilia Skingsley became Head of the BIS Innovation Hub in September 2022. She is a member of the BIS's Executive Committee. Previously, she held the position of First Deputy Governor of the Riksbank since November 2019.

Most recently she chaired the BIS's Committee on Payments and Market Infrastructures Future of Payments Working Group, was the Governor of the Riksbank's alternate on the General Council of the ECB and member of the Advisory Technical Committee (ATC) of the European Systemic Risk Board (ESRB).

Prior to holding the position of Deputy Governor of the Riksbank from May 2013 to November 2019, Ms Skingsley held various roles including Head of FX and Fixed Income Research and Chief Economist at Swedbank (2007–2013); financial journalist and Head of Financial Market Section at Dagens Industri (2000–2007); Macro Analyst, ABN Amro Bank (1998–2000).

Ms Skingsley holds a degree in economics and political science from Stockholm University. She received a financial analyst degree from SSE Executive Education at Stockholm School of Economics (formerly IFL at Stockholm School of Economics) and studied journalism at Poppius School of Journalism in Stockholm.

Davide Taliente

Consigliere in the Draghi administration (Republic of Italy) on the execution of the country's Recovery & Resilience plan and attraction of foreign investment from investors & multi-nationals. With Oliver Wyman for >30 years, he is a Global Chair of the firm's Public Sector and Policy practice (formerly Managing Partner, EMEA). Davide specialises in Public Policy. Most of his work has been with national governments, international bodies (e.g. G20, WorldBank/IFC, IMF, Financial Stability Board, European Commission, European Central Bank), central banks and public/private development banks in Europe. His recent work has concentrated on innovation / economic development, "crowding in" foreign and private capital, national risk assessments, development finance, institutional reform, corporate governance enhancements and financial sector reform. Member of the Oliver Wyman Team that won the "Central Banking Awards".

Axel A. Weber
President, Center for Financial Studies, Goethe University Frankfurt, Chairman, Trilateral Commission Europe

Axel Weber serves as the President of the Center for Financial Studies at Goethe University Frankfurt since July 2023. He is the Chairman of the Trilateral Commission Europe and a member of the Group of Thirty.

From 2012 to 2022, Axel Weber served as the Chairman of the Board of Directors of UBS Group AG. Furthermore, he was a member and then Chairman of the Institute of International Finance.

Prof. Weber was President of the German Bundesbank between 2004 and 2011, during which time he also served as a Member of the Governing Council of the European Central Bank, a Member of the Board of Directors of the Bank for International Settlements, German Governor of the International Monetary Fund and as a member of the G7 and G20 Ministers and Governors.

He was a Member of the steering committees of the European Systemic Risk Board in 2011 and the Financial Stability Board from 2010 to 2011.

On leave from the University of Cologne from 2004 to 2012, he was a Visiting Professor at the University of Chicago Booth School of Business from 2011 to 2012.

From 2002 to 2004, Axel Weber served as a Member of the German Council of Economic Experts. He was a Professor of International Economics and Director of the Centre for Financial Research at the University of Cologne from 2001 to 2004, and a Professor of Monetary Economics and Director of the Center for Financial Studies at Goethe University in Frankfurt from 1998 to 2001. From 1994 to 1998, he was a Professor of Economic Theory at the University of Bonn.

Axel Weber holds a PhD in economics from the University of Siegen, where he also received his habilitation. He graduated with a master's degree in economics at the University of Konstanz and holds honorary doctorates from the universities of Duisburg-Essen and Konstanz.

Dominik Weh

Dominik is Co-Lead of Oliver Wyman's Public Sector & Policy practice in Europe. He has worked in-depth with major financial institutions, central banks, supervisors and regulators as well as multilateral and public sector institutions in Europe on a variety of topics, including strategy, organisation and governance (Target Operating Models), as well as transformation/ change management.

Since its inauguration in January 2019, Dominik serves on the Leadership Team of the OLIVER WYMAN FORUM where he supports the FORUM in achieving its strategic ambition: *"The Oliver Wyman Forum is committed to bringing together business, public policy, and social enterprise leaders to help solve the world's toughest problems"* (https://www.oliverwymanforum.com/).

Dominik holds a Master in Business and Economics from WHU Otto Beisheim School of Management. He studied in Germany, Australia and Canada. Dominik joined after his graduation in 2008.

Oliver Wuensch

Dr Oliver Wuensch is Partner of Oliver Wyman's Banking and Sovereign Practice, advising banks, governments and central banks on strategy, economic policy and transformation. Before turning to advisory, Oliver held positions at the International Monetary Fund, where he was co-responsible for the financial turnaround of several countries struck by the Euro crisis. During and after the Great Financial Crisis, he was the strategy chief of the Swiss Financial Supervisor FINMA and represented Switzerland to the Financial Stability Board and the Basel Committee on Banking Supervision. Oliver started his career with a global investment bank and also spent several years in academia as researcher and lecturer.

Klaas Knot

Daring to know in Times of Uncertainty and structural Shifts

© *DNB*

Hello everyone.

This beautiful wood engraving (Note 1) depicts a scene in 1794. You can see four well-dressed men, sitting in a flourishing garden in Jena – a city a few hours east from Frankfurt.

The four men are sitting around a table, filled with wine and grapes– and they appear to be engaged in a civilized discussion.

The four men on the drawing are the brothers Wilhelm and Alexander von Humboldt, respectively statesman and explorer, the poet Friedrich von Schiller and, of course, scientist, writer and poet, Johan Wolfgang von Goethe.

The four of them were the intellectual fab four of late 18th century Germany. They strongly believed in the powers of reason – as opposed to royal decrees or religious dogmas. They strongly believed that individuals were to be enlightened – through science, art, and literature. They strongly believed in "sapere aude" – in daring to know.

I was asked to talk about systemic risks today. More precisely, about where the next systemic financial crisis might come from. And truth be told – this is hard to say. We can't predict that with any reliability. One only needs to recall the way that the covid pandemic hit us to know that a crisis can emerge unexpectedly. This is exactly why predicting the next crisis is not what we aim to do at the Financial Stability Board (FSB).

Instead of predicting, our aim is to approach financial stability with a different way of thinking. Financial stability is the capacity of the global financial system to withstand shocks, by containing the risk of disruptions in the financial intermediation process that would be severe enough to adversely impact the real economy.

In short: our work is about enhancing the resilience of the global financial system. So that, when the next crisis materialises, the system as a whole can cope with it.

In order to increase that resilience, we try to know as much as possible about the vulnerabilities in our financial system. And we do this by relying on the powers of reason, logic, cooperation and data. In other words, by following the brothers von Humboldt, Friedrich von Schiller, and Johan Wolfgang von Goethe in sapere aude.

So how do we go about that?

To increase the resilience of the global financial system and to enhance financial stability, we rely on the FSB's financial stability surveillance framework. Let me

https://doi.org/10.1515/9783111340937-207

start by walking you through this framework, and then I will illustrate how we apply it.

The FSB's financial stability framework is based on four guiding principles.

First, we need to identify the vulnerabilities that may threaten global financial stability. I say 'vulnerabilities' instead of 'shocks' or 'risks'. That is intentional.

The pandemic is a shock. The war in Ukraine is a shock. A rapid shift in financial market conditions would be a shock. Shocks are by definition unpredictable – so they don't offer a solid starting point for financial stability policy. Risk – that is the risk of a shock large enough to have a financial stability impact – is similarly very difficult to assess.

Vulnerabilities, on the other hand, can usually be measured, at least to a certain extent. Think for instance about the build-up of imbalances, like a rise in leverage during a credit boom. And so, they do offer a starting point for financial stability policy – policy that is aimed at reducing these vulnerabilities. Through this approach we can mitigate potential systemic disruption, once a shock hits our global, highly interconnected financial system.

And so, in the spirit of Alexander von Humboldt, who measured and mapped large parts of the world, we, in turn, try to map and measure global vulnerabilities – rather than the shocks that may or may not materialise.

Second, once mapped and measured, we monitor these vulnerabilities, taking into account the potential interactions between them. We also deploy a forward-looking perspective, by considering emerging vulnerabilities in addition to current ones. It is better to prevent vulnerabilities from growing in the first place, rather than having to reduce them once they already pose a global threat.

Our third guiding principle is that we recognise the differences among countries. The FSB's membership reflects the diversity of our global financial system, with members from both emerging market and advanced economies. And these differences are reflected in our assessment of vulnerabilities. We fully recognise that some vulnerabilities may be more relevant for emerging market economies, and others for advanced economies, or for different sets of jurisdictions.

For example, the urgency policymakers ascribe to some of the risks relating to crypto-assets and crypto-markets differs across countries. In some economies, the most pressing concern is the potential loss of monetary sovereignty. In other economies, the risks of money laundering and fraud are perceived to be more urgent.

The fourth and final guiding principle, is that the FSB leverages on this diversity of its membership. There lies tremendous strength in that diversity. FSB members not only come from different kinds of economies, but they are also represented by different kinds of authorities: ministries of finance, central banks, and securities and market authorities. Our members also include global standard-setting bodies and international organisations. Many of those members carry out and publish financial stability assessments. The FSB's vulnerabilities assessment therefore builds on those analyses.

With these four guiding principles, I have given you a brief and mainly theoretical outline of the FSB's financial stability surveillance framework. I hope that this approach, this way of thinking about how to enhance the resilience of the global financial system, provides you with some stimulus for today's discussions.

But what does it look like when we actually apply this framework? To illustrate this, allow me to touch on several of the key FSB priorities that are also on your agenda today.

First, I will focus on the cyclical vulnerabilities that emerge from the current outlook. The combination of rising inflation, tightening financial conditions and the fallout from Russia's invasion of Ukraine has led to a synchronised slowdown in global economic activity. This is occurring against a backdrop of high levels of debt of households, non-financial corporates and sovereigns. The latter implies that some governments have limited fiscal space to provide additional targeted policy support. And given the increases in inflation, central banks also have less policy space to react to financial stability shocks.

Although this outlook is challenging, so far the global banking system has shown itself to be resilient. Global financial markets have largely coped in an orderly manner, with limited and temporary support when necessary. And systemic financial institutions have shown resilience to market strains – in large part due to the financial reforms, following the 2008 Global Financial Crisis, that were coordinated through the FSB.

However, there is no room for complacency. Financial institutions and market participants have not experienced sharply rising interest rates for a long time. Very low interest rates may have become embedded in business models, making the adjustment to a world of higher rates challenging. Companies and households that have borrowed money will also need to adjust to higher interest payments, and problems may materialise only with a lag.

So, we need to remain vigilant. A deterioration of banks' asset quality may still occur, and other vulnerabilities, like the ones on today's agenda, need to be monitored closely. Some of these vulnerabilities may have been previously prevented from materialising by authorities' COVID-19 support measures. But now these measures are being lifted. So it is important to address debt overhang issues of non-financial corporates, and to respond to potential issues of underinvestment due to excessive indebtedness or misallocation of resources to unviable companies.

All of these are what I would call cyclical vulnerabilities.

But, more fundamentally, we also need to be wary of vulnerabilities that stem from structural shifts in the global financial system.

So allow me to say a few words on three structural shifts that the FSB is currently focusing on, and the associated vulnerabilities. It is, of course, no coincidence that the topics of today's panels overlap with many of the FSB's priorities.

First – the structural shift in the provision of finance from banks to non-banks.

In our Global Monitoring Report on non-bank financial intermediation, from December 2022, we highlighted that the NBFI sector reached 239 trillion US dollars in 2021. If a number on that scale is hard to put into context, a more telling figure is perhaps that the NBFI sector increased its relative share of total global financial assets to 49 % in 2021, compared with 42 % in 2008. Almost half of all global financial assets are now being intermediated by non-banks.

While diversifying the sources of credit can make the global economy more resilient, the growth in NBFI has exposed important vulnerabilities in the non-bank sector. We have seen the problems that these vulnerabilities can cause several times in recent years: for instance, the 'dash for cash' episode during the onset of the pandemic, the strains in commodity markets last year, and more recently the challenges faced by UK pension funds. Thankfully, these strains have proved temporary, but only after massive official sector interventions were deployed. These examples therefore serve as a warning to remain vigilant on the recurring themes of leverage, including hidden leverage, liquidity mismatches, and data gaps.

The FSB's NBFI work programme and policy proposals aim to address these vulnerabilities. In 2023, we will continue to focus on some key vulnerabilities within the sector. Apart from monitoring systemic risk in NBFI, we will review the effectiveness of our money market funds policy proposals from 2021; revise our recommendations from 2017 on liquidity mismatches in open-ended funds; and conduct follow-up work on margining practices and hidden leverage in NBFI.

A second structural shift we have witnessed, is the digitalisation of finance. This comes in many shapes and forms, but I will focus on the rapidly developing crypto-asset ecosystem. Crypto-asset markets and activities bear a multitude of risks and vulnerabilities. While the technology behind crypto-assets is often being promoted as game-changing, the vulnerabilities associated with them are in fact quite similar to those we know from traditional finance.

Liquidity mismatches, hidden leverage, and counterparty credit risk are all examples of well-known financial risks that have also materialised in crypto-asset markets in the past year. National regulatory authorities have recognized that these activities are in essence financial activities and have begun regulating them. This is challenging for national authorities, however, because crypto-asset markets are inherently global in reach.

So, in the presence of structural vulnerabilities and in the absence of globally consistent regulation, the FSB is concerned crypto-asset markets may soon pose a challenge to global financial stability.

The FSB therefore concluded that crypto-asset activities and markets must be subject to effective regulation and oversight commensurate to the risks they pose, both at the domestic and international levels.

To this end, the FSB proposed a comprehensive global framework for the effective regulation of crypto-asset activities, including stablecoins, in October last year. This framework embeds the principle of 'same activity, same risk, same regulation'. Finalising these recommendations and monitoring their effective implementation across all jurisdictions will be a priority for the FSB in 2023.

Of course, the FSB does not operate alone. Just like in the traditional financial sector, there is a myriad of functions that the crypto asset ecosystem covers or otherwise touches. So it is key to have solid cooperation between the different standard setting bodies, all with their different mandates.

Third – it is impossible to talk about systemic risk without mentioning one of the most fundamental challenges of our time: climate change.

This third structural shift is not on the agenda today, but the events of the past year have again emphasised the importance of addressing these vulnerabilities. The volatility in energy markets, exposures to hard-to-predict physical risks and the challenges of the transition to net zero are all examples of vulnerabilities that have an impact on the financial sector.

So addressing the financial risks stemming from climate change is, and will remain, high on the FSB agenda. One way we are working on this, is with our roadmap. With that roadmap, we are coordinating the international efforts to address climate-related financial vulnerabilities. It consists of four key elements: disclosure, data, vulnerability analysis and supervisory and regulatory tools.

One of the main priorities is the reliability and consistency of data, because that is what good risk management starts with. A key priority for this year is the finalisation and implementation of a global climate-related disclosure standard. Other priorities are analysing the use of transition planning and the improvement of our framework for monitoring climate-related vulnerabilities.

Let me wrap up.

NBFI, crypto and climate-related financial risks – these are just three priorities for the FSB and the global financial system I wanted to touch on today.

But for every risk or vulnerability we focus on, be it cyclical or structural, the same principle applies: the FSB diligently maps, measures and monitors all threats to the stability of our global financial system.

We provide a global, cross-border, cross-sectoral and forward-looking perspective on the vulnerabilities we identify. And we do this by drawing on the collective perspective of the broad membership of the FSB.

And this way of working, fearless and in the spirit of "sapere aude", does not allow me to predict where the next systemic crisis might come from, but it does allow us to enhance the resilience of the global financial system, to whatever may come its way.

In that spirit, the FSB decides where coordinated action is required, monitors the effects of its actions, and assesses where further adjustments are needed. Or, as Goethe said: "Knowing is not enough; we must apply. Willing is not enough; we must do."

The four men in the wood engraving I talked about at the beginning continue to be an inspiration today. Each with their own merits – and together, as an example of how reason advances humankind.

After Friedrich von Schiller's death, and as an introduction to the correspondence between the two men, Wilhelm von Humboldt wrote an essay on his close association with the famous poet. And in that essay, he stresses the importance Schiller attached to conversation – to how conversation, expressing ideas, exchanging views, ultimately leads to deeper understanding.

To how conversation, you could say, embodies "sapere aude". Or in Schiller's words: "Erkühne dich, weise zu sein".

And this is just the kind of conversation I hope you will have today.

Thank you.

Fig. 1: "Schiller, Wilhelm and Alexander von Humboldt and Goethe in Jena" (Verwijst naar een externe site) (Event date: 1794, image date: 1860). Wood engraving after drawing by Andreas Müller (1831–1901). © iStock

I. Macroeconomic Factors

Claudio Borio
Macro-Financial Challenges

The big Picture

Policymakers worldwide are facing a constellation of challenges that is unprecedented, at least since World War II. They are confronted with recession risk in the context of a monetary policy tightening to quell inflation alongside widespread financial vulnerabilities. Most notably, debt levels, both private and public, are historically high, asset prices, especially for property prices, elevated and financial markets overstretched following an unusually long phase of unusually low interest rates.

Why unprecedented? Until the mid-1980s, downturns were caused largely by efforts to rein in inflation. As finance was repressed, so too was the scope for overt financial fragilities. Thereafter, with the exception of the one-of-a-kind Covid-19 recession, with inflation generally low and stable, downturns were caused by financial booms that turned into busts, as during the Great Financial Crisis (GFC). The current landscape combines elements of both these downturn typologies (Borio (2022)).

This configuration greatly complicates the calibration of monetary policy. The economy has surely become more sensitive to higher interest rates, but by how much? What might a tighter stance do to the economy and the financial system? One thing is for certain. Should financial stresses emerge, the need to bring inflation back to target and to stabilise the financial system would pull in opposite directions – towards tightening and easing, respectively. Central banks would no doubt rise to the challenge. We saw this recently with the Bank of England's interventions in the gilts market. But policymakers' room for manoeuvre would be curtailed, as if forced to fight with one hand tied behind their backs. This contrasts sharply with experience from the 1990s on.

The State of the financial System

Against this backdrop, one question looms large: how resilient is the financial system? This is, in fact, a tale of two subsystems.

Banks are in much better shape than they were in the run-up to the GFC, thanks in no small measure to regulatory reforms (Borio et al (2020)). During the Covid cri-

Note: The views expressed are my own and not necessarily those of the BIS.

https://doi.org/10.1515/9783111340937-001

sis, indeed, banks were part of the solution, not of the problem. Still, there are no grounds for complacency. Given high debt levels and rich valuations, losses on exposures to firms and households could be substantial, as illustrated by simulations in the latest BIS Annual Economic Report (2022). Among the larger known unknowns are the potential losses on banks' direct and indirect exposures to non-bank financial intermediaries (NBFIs), notably various kinds of asset management and trading firms. But they are not the only ones.

The NBFI sector is more vulnerable. Think of the surprising bank losses in the case of Archegos, or of the dash-for-cash in March 2020, or of the recent gilts market turmoil. The NBFI sector has grown in leaps and bounds since the GFC. This was, in part, an intended consequence of the reforms – shifting risk out of the banking sector to less leveraged NBFIs. That said, hidden leverage and liquidity mismatches are common. In addition, there was a lot of risk-taking during the unusually long phase of exceptionally low interest rates. And what was not intended at the time of the reforms was the subsequent disappointing progress in developing a systemic-oriented – macroprudential-type – regulatory framework for the NBFI sector. This gap needs to be filled with some urgency (Carstens (2021)).

It is not hard to identify specific vulnerabilities in the sector. But, just as with banks, they all share the same feature: they reflect business models and trading strategies designed for a world in which interest rates would stay low for long – for the foreseeable future – and are now facing one in which rates will be higher for longer.

Let me mention just a few examples. There are vulnerabilities in core government bond markets: quite apart from those linked to interest rate risk of specific structural features, they reflect the seismic shift to what has become a collateral-based financial system. There are vulnerabilities in commercial real estate markets, as cyclical and structural headwinds come together. There are vulnerabilities in private credit markets, where valuations are especially opaque. And there are vulnerabilities in the foreign exchange market.

Here, let me mention an underestimated segment: the FX swap/forwards market. As argued with colleagues recently, these instruments amount to a form of debt which is huge, growing and missing (Borio et al (2022)). Of particular importance is the US dollar portion of the market, since the US dollar is the dominant international currency, involved in close to 90 % of trades.

The market trades a *debt* instrument because, in contrast to other derivatives, FX swaps/forwards call for the exchange of principal. It is huge because, at some USD 85 trillion, the dollar portion exceeds the stocks of dollar Treasury bills, repo and commercial paper combined. It is *growing* because it has risen substantially in the space of just a few years. For example, for non-banks outside the United States – largely NBFIs – it went from around USD 17 trillion to about USD 26 trillion, roughly twice their on-balance sheet debt, between 2016 and 2022. Similarly, for non-US banks, which have direct access to the Fed's discount window only in the United States, the stock approached USD 40 trillion in 2022, which dwarfs the USD 15 trillion of dollar debt on their balance sheets. And it is *missing* because it is not in firms' disclosures and not directly captured by international financial statistics. Its distribution can be ferreted out, roughly, only by making joint use of the BIS derivatives and international banking statistics.

Let me be clear. I am not saying that the FX swap market will be at the origin of stress. The instrument is used largely to hedge foreign exchange risk, which is a good thing. But it can be a major amplifier of stress, as it repeatedly has been in the past. It is a source of potentially huge US dollar funding liquidity pressures. Indeed, much of this debt is very short-term.

Sovereign Debt

If private sector debt is an issue, the elephant in the room is public sector debt. After all, the sovereign is the ultimate backstop of the financial system: a weak sovereign means a vulnerable financial system.

The uniqueness of initial conditions, as inflation flared up, is sometimes not sufficiently appreciated (Borio and Disyatat (2021)). Globally, public sector debt was – and still is – at its historical peak, roughly where it stood after World War II. Interest rates were at historical lows, sometimes negative even in nominal terms. As a result, the debt service burden never appeared so light. Together with the expectation that interest rates would remain low as far as eye could see, this provided a powerful incentive to keep piling on debt.

Now, higher interest rates are poised to test the resilience of public finances. Back-of-the-envelope calculations indicate that, should rates go back to mid-1990s levels, the debt service burden would climb to its historical peak – again, the one prevailing after World War II.

In the background, central banks' large-scale purchases of sovereign debt heighten this sensitivity. From the perspective of the consolidated state sector balance sheet – government plus central bank – they amount to a large debt management operation. That is, long-term government debt is retired and replaced with debt indexed to the overnight rate, ie bank reserves. Again, back-of-the-envelope calculations suggest that, for the central banks that have used such purchases more actively, some 30–50 % of long-term debt is, de facto, overnight. This will show up as lower central bank remittances to the government and hence lower government revenues. And central bank losses will not just mean a weaker fiscal position, but they could also raise reputational and institutional challenges for central banks.

Conclusion

The picture that emerges from this analysis is a sobering one. Historically, it is not uncommon for financial stress to emerge after a monetary policy tightening – roughly a fifth of the time within three years of the first interest rate hike. And the incidence of distress is higher when debt is large or inflation surges (Boissay et al (2023)). Now, we have a combination of both. We have the tinder, and maybe also the spark.

References

Bank for International Settlements (2022): *BIS Annual Economic Report*, June.

Borio, C (2022): "Monetary policy: past, present and future", remarks at the Cato Institute's 40th Annual Monetary Conference, 8 September.

Borio, C, F Boissay, C Leonte and I Shim (2023): "Prudential policy and financial dominance: exploring the link", *BIS Quarterly Review*, March, pp 15–31.

Borio, C and P Disyatat (2021): "Monetary and fiscal policy: Privileged powers, entwined responsibilities", *SUERF Policy Note*, no 238, May.

Borio, C, M Farag and N Tarashev (2020): "Post-crisis international financial regulatory reforms: a primer", *BIS Working Papers*, no 859, April.

Borio, C, R McCauley and P McGuire (2022): "Dollar debt in FX swaps and forwards: huge, missing and growing", *BIS Quarterly Review*, December, pp 67–73.

Carstens, A (2021): "Non-bank financial sector: systemic regulation needed", *BIS Quarterly Review*, December, pp 1–6.

Sarah Breeden

Systemic Risks posed by the Non-Bank Sector, and the Need for Policy Action

This article will set out how leverage outside the banking sector can create risks to financial stability, drawing on the stress faced by UK Liability Driven Investment (LDI) funds in September 2022 as an illustrative example. That event showed how poorly managed leverage can result in a vicious, self-reinforcing spiral of collateral calls, forced gilt sales and market dysfunction, leading to an excessive tightening of financing conditions for households and businesses. The article will set out what needs to be done – by participants, by their regulators and by financial stability authorities – to ensure those risks to financial stability are reduced.

How did a small Corner of the UK Pensions Industry threaten financial Stability?

Many UK Defined Benefit (DB) pension schemes have been in deficit, meaning their liabilities – their commitments to pay out to pensioners in the future – exceed the assets they hold. DB pension schemes invest in long-term bonds to hedge the interest rate and inflation risk that arises from these long-term liabilities. But to close their deficit, DB pension schemes also need to invest in 'growth assets', such as equities, to get extra return to grow the value of their assets. An LDI strategy delivers this, using leveraged gilt funds to allow schemes both to maintain material hedges, and to invest in growth assets.

The rise in gilt yields in late September 2022 – 130 basis points in the 30-year nominal yield in just a few days – caused a significant fall in the net asset value of these leveraged LDI funds, meaning their leverage increased significantly. And that created an urgent need to delever to prevent insolvency and to meet increasing margin calls.

The funds held liquidity buffers for this purpose. But as those liquidity buffers were exhausted, the funds needed either to sell gilts into an illiquid market or to ask their DB pension scheme investors to provide additional cash to rebalance the fund. Since persistently higher interest rates would boost the funding position of DB pension schemes[1], they generally had the incentive to provide funds. But their resources took time to mobilise.

---

[1] As an illustration, the Pension Protection Fund's **PPF 7800** index suggests that, between end-2021 and end-September 2022 – a period in which interest rates rose substantially – the liabilities of UK

https://doi.org/10.1515/9783111340937-002

The issue was particularly acute for one small corner of the LDI industry – pooled funds. In these funds, which make up around 10–15 % of the LDI market, a pot of assets is managed for a large number of pension fund clients who have limited liability in the face of losses. The speed and scale of the moves in yields far outpaced the ability of the large number of pooled funds' smaller investors to provide new funds who were typically given a week, in some cases two, to rebalance their positions. Limited liability also meant that these pooled fund investors could choose not to provide support. As a result, pooled LDI funds became forced sellers of gilts at a rate that would not have been absorbed in normal gilt trading conditions. The stressed market conditions that prevailed in September 2022 exacerbated this.

Other LDI funds, with segregated mandates, were more easily able to raise funds from their individual pension scheme clients. However, given their scale, at 85–90 % of the market, some of these funds were also contributing to selling pressure, making the task at hand for pooled LDI funds even harder. And if the pooled funds had defaulted, the large quantity of gilts held as collateral by those that had lent to the funds would potentially be sold on the market too.

With the gilt market unable to absorb such forced sales, yields would have been pushed even higher, making the scale of selling that is needed even larger. This is the self-reinforcing spiral that the Bank of England intervened to prevent.

The Bank's 13 day and £19.3 billion intervention was made on financial stability grounds. It was the first example of the Bank acting to deliver our financial stability objective through a temporary and targeted intervention in the gilt market. The asset purchases were designed to create the right conditions in the right part of the gilt market for long enough to enable the LDI funds to build resilience to future volatility in the gilt market.

What does this Episode remind us about the Risks from Non-Bank Leverage?

Leverage is an integral part of the economy. It enables households to borrow to buy houses and smooth consumption. It enables companies to invest in projects or to smooth cashflows. It allows banks to finance these activities.

In the non-bank financial system (or system of market-based finance), leverage is used: to facilitate trading; to invest in companies and infrastructure; and to arbitrage price discrepencies, improving the efficiency of financial markets.

DB schemes fell by 36 % (from £1,689bn to £1,076bn), whereas their assets fell by only 20 % (from £1,818bn to £1,451bn), leaving their net assets nearly three times higher.

Leverage is created in different ways. Its most obvious form is to borrow money to buy assets – 'financial leverage'. But it arises also through 'synthetic leverage' using derivative instruments. This allows users to adjust risk profiles through a relatively small initial outlay, with future gains or losses contingent on changes in underlying market prices. Those future gains and losses create financial obligations – a form of contingent 'hidden' leverage.

It's clear that leverage is a key function provided by the financial system in support of a thriving and productive economy. But it comes with inherent risks that need to be managed.

A common factor across all the uses of leverage described above is that it can increase the exposure of the leverage taker to underlying risk factors – whether that be house prices, earnings, interest rates, currencies or asset prices. It follows therefore that leverage can amplify shocks to each of these risk factors. In a stress, that can lead both to sudden spikes in demand for liquidity – either to support the financing of leveraged positions or as de-leveraging leads to forced sales – and a corresponding contraction in liquidity supply, with potentially systemic consequences.

Leverage is of course not the only cause of systemic vulnerability in the non-bank system – as we have seen with liquidity mismatch driving run dynamics in money market funds (MMFs) and open-ended funds (OEFs) during the 'dash for cash' in March 2020. But leverage is important when it is core to a non-bank's business and trading strategy. What happened to LDI funds is just the latest example of poorly managed non-bank leverage posing risks to financial stability. From Long Term Capital Management in 1998; to the 2007 run on the repo market; to hedge fund behaviour in the 2020 dash for cash; and the failure of Archegos in 2021.

These episodes highlight the need to take into account the potential amplifying effect of poorly managed leverage, and to pay attention to non-banks' behaviours which, particularly when aggregated, could lead to the emergence of systemic risk.

Systemic risk from leverage in the non-bank system could arise through two different channels of contagion:
– to markets – both those in which non-banks invest and those from which they borrow; and
– to counterparties – who either provide cash, or take the other side of instruments that are used to provide synthetic leverage.

To the extent that these markets and counterparties are important for the functioning of the financial system and for the real economy, problems transmitted can have adverse consequences for economic growth and financial stability.

The Market Channel

First is the market channel – where excessive or poorly-managed leverage increases the potential for forced asset sales in the face of shocks, with adverse implications for market functioning and so the real economy.

Feedback loops and amplification mechanisms can arise in two ways: through unexpected liquidity strains (most obviously as a result of margin increases), or through large, concentrated positions.

Focussing on liquidity strains first – banks and CCPs typically require their counterparties to place collateral, in the form of margin or haircut, to protect against counterparty risk. Sharp changes in asset prices, high volatility, or correlated shocks affect the amount of counterparty risk to which they are exposed.

As market prices change and as risk rises, the bank or CCP can request more collateral (variation margin to reflect the change in market prices and higher initial margin to reflect greater risk in a given position). And meeting those collateral demands creates liquidity risk for the leveraged institution that needs to be managed.

This more widespread collateralisation of derivatives has been an essential part of the package of reforms to address the vulnerabilities exposed in the Global Financial Crisis. Initial margin requirements are vital to limit cascading counterparty credit risks – this will be covered later.

But more widespread collateralisation has increased the sensitivity of liquid-asset demand to market volatility. And, if market participants are not prepared for collateral calls, their actions to raise cash can squeeze liquidity in already stressed markets, further amplifying shocks.

So whilst greatly reducing counterparty credit risks, with important systemic benefits, collateralisation may also increase systemic liquidity risks.

This dynamic was at play in the 'dash for cash' in March 2020, where hedge funds with highly leveraged positions in US Treasury cash-futures basis trades were one source of the boost in demand for liquidity. When markets turned against them, these investors unwound their positions, selling US Treasuries at scale, which contributed to a short but extreme period of illiquidity in these usually safe and liquid markets. That added to dysfunction and necessitated unprecedented central bank intervention.

The behaviour of financial intermediaries can also matter when a stress hits too, since what can seem rational behaviour for an individual firm has the potential to cause negative second-round effects when aggregated across the market as a whole. For example, low initial margins and haircuts in normal times can result in significant margin increases when a stress hits. If these occur market-wide, it can lead to a reduction in market activity, damage market functioning, and potentially amplify market moves at a time of stress.

The second mechanism is via large, concentrated exposures, which can exacerbate the impact of liquidity strains and so amplify the impact of deleveraging on markets in the event of a shock. It can be seen in the events in the gilt market described earlier.

The concentrated and correlated nature of pooled LDI funds' exposures meant that their forced selling behaviour represented a sudden and profound shift in supply-demand dynamics. Indeed, the self-reinforcing spiral it led to meant that around £200 billion of pooled LDI funds[2] threatened the £1.4 trillion traded gilt market, which itself acts as the foundation of the UK financial system, underlying around £2 trillion of lending to the real economy through wider credit markets[3]. As such, it was a timely reminder that large concentrated exposures and correlated behaviours can strain market functioning so much that financial stability can be threatened.

The Counterparty Channel

Second is the counterparty channel – where leverage increases the risk of an entity's default and so brings losses for their counterparties, threatening the resilience of systemically important firms and so the real economy.

Collateral and margining are at the core of bank and CCP toolkits for managing these counterparty risks. They are essential to stop cascading counterparty losses around the system.

But margins will only be adequate if counterparty credit risks can themselves be adequately assessed. And assessing the risk of a leveraged institution can be challenging – perhaps because its exposures are in the form of synthetic or "hidden" leverage or because its exposures are more concentrated or correlated than the counterparty is able to understand.

In the case of Archegos, for example, individual counterparties were not sighted on the total size of the firms' sizeable and concentrated swap positions, meaning they had imperfect information on which to manage counterparty credit risk.

---

2 The Pensions Regulator has noted that as of end-2021, c. 15% of the roughly £1.4tn in UK LDI assets were in multi-investor pooled funds, which equates to roughly £200bn. Due to the volatility of gilt prices and yields, these estimates will not reflect the current position, and the rise in gilt yields in 2022 will have reduced the total amount of hedging.
3 The UK corporate bond and fixed rate mortgage markets are around £2 trillion, and gilt pricing also underlies a broader set of markets beyond these.

In fact, when margin was called as prices moved against Archegos in March 2021, the firm was forced to liquidate its concentrated positions, further amplifying adverse price movements through the market channel already described. The end result was that Archegos could not meet all of its margin calls, and its default left its bank-affiliated prime brokers sharing around $10 billion in counterparty credit losses.

Just as with LTCM in the late-1990s, the Archegos case highlights how financial strains on leveraged non-bank investors can transmit directly to the large banks at the core of the financial system. And it highlights again that if leveraged investors use several counterparties, overall leverage is hidden from each of them.

Banks and CCPs may therefore need to have access to more information on the risk positions and balance sheets of their leveraged counterparties if they are to understand fully concentrated and hidden exposures.

A second lesson for banks' and CCPs' counterparty credit risk management from recent extraordinary events is that the past is not always a good guide for the future. And so they need to be creative in identifying stress scenarios that best illustrate their counterparties' credit risk and so the conditions under which margin calls might not be met. As will be explained, that could relate to 'wrong-way' risk, market dynamics, the behaviour of other market players, or even operational details. Further progress on both these fronts is needed if we are to be confident the counterparty channel is fully managed.

Are these Risks unique to Non-Banks?

It's helpful at this stage to draw a very brief comparison to a market which has already been widely studied and embedded in the macroprudential toolkit: the mortgage market.

Banks manage their exposures to mortgagors, through affordability testing, leverage limits and collateral. And that's important from a financial stability perspective, given the feedback and amplification mechanisms that have been seen during stresses in the past. For example, stress test scenarios cover house prices falling and borrowers defaulting, and so can capture the potential for amplified price moves and a self-reinforcing price dynamic, as a result of forced sales by bank lenders into a falling housing market. Perhaps correlated falls in asset prices and leverage can create amplifying price dynamics in non-bank financial institutions as well as with households.

In addition, in financial stability analysis of the mortgage market it is recognised that reductions in spending by highly indebted mortgage borrowers, as they keep up with debt repayments, can create negative spillover effects to the rest of the economy.

And perhaps in the same way, forced asset sales into stressed financial markets might have negative spillovers for all other users of that market. In the case of the core government bond market that could be significant.

What is being done to address Risks from non-bank Leverage, and where is there further Progress to be made?

The onus for building resilience in the non-bank system sits first and foremost with the firms themselves. If firms use leverage, they must be able to manage the liquidity consequences of their risk exposures. As part of this, they need to learn from the decades of experience that show how leverage and liquidity risk create: rollover risks; volatility; operational challenges in accessing liquidity; and exposures to amplification mechanisms from the wider system.

Firm stress testing and resilience must be set with reference to the system and to market dynamics, not just a firm's own individualistic actions. That includes the systemic consequences of forced selling, concentrations and correlated strategies amongst market participants. It also needs to consider potential scenarios which go beyond historical experience, as is the case for bank stress testing. LDI funds have demonstrated what is possible here, by building resilience at speed when severe stress demonstrated the clear need for it.

Regulators worked with LDI funds during the Bank of England's operation in September 2022 to ensure greater resilience to future stresses. In aggregate, intelligence suggests that LDI funds raised over £40 billion in funds and made over £30 billion of gilt sales during our operations, both of which have contributed to significantly lower leverage.

As a result, LDI funds report that their liquidity buffers can withstand very much larger increases in yields than before, well in excess of the previously unprecedented move in gilt yields. And so the risk of LDI fund behaviour triggering 'fire sale' dynamics in the gilt market and self-reinforcing falls in gilt prices has been reduced.

It is of course critical that such resilience is maintained. In support of this, the Financial Policy Committee (FPC) of the Bank of England recommended in December 2022 that The Pensions Regulator (TPR), in co-ordination with the Financial Conduct Authority (FCA)[4] and overseas regulators, put in place arrangements to ensure that LDI funds maintain the levels of resilience they had built up, and that appropri-

---

4 In the UK, TPR regulates pension schemes, the FCA regulates LDI managers.

ate steady-state minimum levels of resilience for LDI funds be put into place (as described below).

Others need to act too. Banks have an important role to play in reducing risks, both to themselves and to the wider system from non-bank leverage.

That starts with information. As seen with Archegos, imperfect information on overall positions leads to inadequate risk management. So a first step is for lenders to require greater transparency of hidden leverage taken by their counterparties. Prime brokers should have access to data on a fund's overall leverage, not just the portion to which they have contributed, just as banks ask household borrowers about their student loan repayments and credit card debts when issuing a mortgage.

Banks, like their non-bank clients, need also to improve their stress testing to better capture market dynamics and structural shifts that might change correlations and norms.

Banks need to develop a laser-like focus on 'wrong-way' risk, where the value of collateral held as security falls in the very situation where the counterparty defaults. They also need to consider if attempts to realise collateral might further add to negative price dynamics.

Stress testing is also needed across sectors to understand how correlations in risk exposure can lead to correlated behaviours in stress. And stress tests need to account for institutional structures, governance and processes for liquidity management, to capture examples like the LDI event above where DB schemes had assets available but were simply unable to get them to where they needed to be quickly enough.

Regulators – as well as market participants – have a role to play in developing these stress testing frameworks. In support of this, the Bank of England will run a system-wide exploratory scenario exercise to consider both what drives banks' and NBFIs' behaviours in a severe but plausible market stress and the potential consequences. It will focus on the potential for these actions to interact and to amplify shocks in ways that might cause adverse outcomes in UK financial markets core to UK financial stability. This exploratory exercise will be focused on market resilience and its importance for financial stability; it will not be a test of individual firms' resilience.

Bank supervisors can also play a role in limiting the risks from leverage in the non-bank system to the core financial system by strengthening dealer bank and prime broker risk management practices.

The Challenges facing Policymakers

Unfortunately for the policy community, the challenges are complex. That reflects the large number and variety of institutions involved. And as the system of market-based finance is global, effective reform needs to be co-ordinated across jurisdictions.

The FPC has put vulnerabilities in the non-bank financial system at the core of its work in recent years. That included work on the specific issues of leverage and liquidity of LDI strategies, which was assessed with a stress simulation in 2018. This led to further close collaboration with the Pensions Regulator and the FCA to enhance understanding of financial stability risks, enhance monitoring and inform further work.

The vulnerabilities in market-based finance that the FPC had articulated were exposed in dramatic fashion in the 'dash for cash' in the early stages of the Covid pandemic. That gave additional momentum to this work. And there has been some progress in recent years, on the regulation and monitoring of the non-bank sector[5], particularly relating to liquidity mismatches in MMFs and OEFs.

But the international community has made less progress in addressing the risks from non-bank leverage, and urgently needs to develop and implement appropriate policy reforms to address the risks from MBF, and to reduce the likelihood and impact of future stresses. Until this policy work is complete – and the policy responses are agreed and implemented across different jurisdictions – the underlying risks remain significant and could resurface. The UK's experience in September 2022 is a timely reminder of the risks here.

That starts with transparency. It is vital that regulatory authorities have sight of leverage building up in the system, and what that means for resilience. For this, there is a need for better regulatory disclosures for non-banks and investment in monitoring capabilities.

But the data available currently provide only a partial view of portfolio leverage, either because they do not provide a link between borrowing and investment activities, or because they only show part of the portfolio due to non-banks' multi-jurisdictional presence, or because the data are simply not sufficient to assess the risk of leverage[6].

Given the global nature of non-bank business models, it is essential that transparency and data availability are enhanced through international efforts, and that

---

5 This progress has been led by the FSB, with the involvement of international standard setting bodies.
6 To assess the risk of leverage we need balance sheet metrics (e.g. notional) as well as risk and liquidity measures. (see NBFI leverage deep dive, November 2018 FSR)

authorities have the right metrics to assess the risks of leverage[7]. It is encouraging to see progress being made, for example by the Securities and Exchange Commission (SEC), who have proposed to enhance private fund reporting in the US.

Beyond improving transparency, regulators will need to consider how best to ensure leverage is well managed. These could, for example, include broad market-wide measures such as market regulations to ensure excessive leverage is better controlled by market pricing and margins.

Targeted interventions may be appropriate too. Domestically in the UK, for example, as part of its response to the autumn 2022 stress, the FPC has put in place a recommendation that TPR takes action to specify the steady state minimum levels of resilience for LDI funds.

Indeed in March 2023, the FPC recommended that the severe but plausible stresses to which LDI funds should be resilient should account for both historic volatility in gilt yields and the potential for forced sales to amplify market stress and disrupt gilt market functioning. Such an approach explicitly recognises that resilience needs to be set with reference to the system and to market dynamics – and that if LDI funds were not resilient to such a shock, their defensive actions could transmit stress to financial markets or institutions, and so businesses and households. And recognising the global nature of this market, the FPC noted that TPR should continue its effective collaboration with other domestic and overseas regulators.

Some broader international work is underway. An internationally led group[8] has published its final report on margin practices. The report recommends policy work in six areas – including increasing the transparency and predictability of margin calls, evaluating their responsiveness to stress, and enhancing liquidity preparedness by clearing members and non-banks. As part of the 'next steps', there is already work underway evaluating the responsiveness of cleared and uncleared margin models.

Finally, there are important questions about the role of central bank balance sheets. During a number of recent episodes, central banks have had to intervene in size, using public money, to remove the threats to financial stability. Providing backstop liquidity insurance when tail risks to financial stability crystallise is a core part of central banks' job. And the FPC has discussed the importance of examining whether central banks should have facilities to provide liquidity to a wider set of financial market participants in stress.

---

7 The Bank highlighted the need for developing consistent leverage metrics in its public **response** to **IOSCO report** on leverage.
8 The BCBS-CPMI-IOSCO margin group.

But central banks cannot be a substitute for the primary obligation of market participants to manage their own risk, or for internationally co-ordinated reforms that enhance the resilience of the non-bank financial sector.

For that reason, such facilities must be carefully targeted on the financial stability vulnerability at hand, and designed in ways that incentivise the right private sector behaviours, including reducing incentives for excessive risk taking in the future. A number of these principles were implemented in the Bank of England's LDI interventions.

Conclusion

Events of recent years have once again reminded us of the systemic risks posed by poorly-managed leverage in the non-bank financial system.

All too often, excessive risk taking alongside improper liquidity risk management has threatened conditions in the real economy – an issue that feels especially pertinent in the current environment of high volatility and tightening financial conditions.

Lessons must be learned from these episodes, most importantly by non-banks themselves. But there are also lessons for their counterparties and regulators, central banks, bank supervisors, market infrastructures, and for the global regulatory community more generally, as we continue our global efforts to ensure the resilience of the system of market-based finance.

Transparency is an important first step. That enables the necessary next step of ensuring that non-banks' positions and interlinkages with the rest of the financial system can be comprehensively stress tested and understood in a system-wide manner.

Non-banks themselves can use that understanding to increase their resilience and liquidity preparedness. Dealer banks and prime brokers equipped with better data on clients' overall leverage and positions can strengthen their risk management. Given the need for a macroprudential perspective, our journey to better resilience of market-based finance must not end there.

Alice Carr

(Credible, Comparable, Comprehensive) Transition Planning beats no Transition Planning

This short paper builds on remarks made at the 11th annual Future of the Financial Sector conference at the Institute for Law and Finance, Goethe University, Frankfurt am Main.

Where to focus during an Era of Polycrisis?

It can be hard for financial stability policymakers to determine where to focus when one shock to the system seems to come hot on the heels of another. A recent conference at the Institute for Law and Finance, Goethe University, considered how the early 2020s appears to be an era of "polycrisis" and the challenges that this can pose. Despite the challenges, it is well understood that the science and art of financial stability policy making is being able to identify a short list of material vulnerabilities and to take timely preventative action such that the financial system can absorb – rather than amplify – the shocks that do materialise.

The financial stability risks posed by climate change firmly merit being on this shortlist. Indeed, in the World Economic Forum's annual Global Risks Report, six of the top ten risks most likely to negatively impact Global GDP over the next 10 years were climate-related and three of the remaining four would be exacerbated by the effects of climate change: large scale involuntary migration, erosion of social cohesion and geo-economic confrontation.[1] Time is running out when it comes to mitigating climate change threats, which manifest via physical effects associated with temperature rises and the risks of not transitioning effectively. These risks are not cyclical but building. Indeed, climate change will likely come to dominate this decade in terms of the materiality of the risks posed to financial stability. So while financial policymakers face some ongoing uncertainties – in terms of knowing which transition path we are on, and precisely how material the related economic and financial stability impacts will be – it is important to move quickly to secure system-wide resilience while we still can.

Helpfully there is scope to draw from some of the techniques that the private financial sector is already using to seize the opportunities and mitigate the risks associated with transition. For everyone, from governments to companies and financial

---

1 World Economic Forum, *Global Risks Report 2023*.

https://doi.org/10.1515/9783111340937-003

institutions, 2023 needs to be the year of the transition plan. Indeed, transition planning firmly beats no transition planning.

State of Play

It is important to be clear on what we know, and don't know, about the scale and nature of climate-related financial risks, and what that means for the economy and financial stability.

That we face a highly constrained carbon budget is clear. To keep the 1.5 degree warming goal alive, we need to reduce emissions by 45 % between now and 2030 and continue reducing them rapidly thereafter.[2] That implies a fundamental transformation of our economies — with significant implications for the financial system — in well under a decade. This is a small window.

We know too that despite the commitments nearly all countries have made to achieving net zero greenhouse gas emissions, the policy that has been made to implement these has so far been inadequate. Climate Action Tracker suggests that the current set of global policy *commitments* would put us on track for 2 degrees C of warming by 2100. Policy actually *implemented* leaves us on track for 2.7 degrees C of warming by 2050 compared to pre-industrial levels – far in excess of the 1.5 degrees C most climate scientists agree is necessary to avoid the catastrophic effects of climate change.[3] How far off track we are will be formally considered by the UNFCCC's global stocktake during 2023.[4]

The macro-economic Impact of Failing to act

If we fail to deliver an orderly transition, and instead face a "hot house" world, the impacts will be severe, even if they are hard to model.[5]

The precise scale of the effects globally, regionally and nationally – and the nature of the way in which these may unfold and affect key economic variables – is hard to be precise about. This is in part because it is genuinely difficult to model how changes to the climate, and resulting physical effects, will feed through to the

---

2 UN, *Net Zero Coalition* (2022).
3 CAT, *Temperatures* (2022).
4 UNFCCC, *Global stocktake* (2022).
5 GFANZ uses the term "orderly transition" as defined by the *Network for Greening the Financial System* (2022).

economy, including factoring in non-linearities, feedback loops and any available policy response.

We also haven't done enough to develop our economic capabilities. As recently as 2019, Lord Stern felt moved to write that "We are sorry to say that we think academic economists are letting down the world" and provided supporting evidence such as that "the Quarterly Journal of Economics, the most-cited journal in economics, has never published an article on climate change."[6] Lord Stern has helped to address this gap by setting out, in the Journal in 2022, how policy and economics need to change.[7]

Since then, a growing but still small number of economists are seeking to model the macroeconomic impacts of climate change. They find that these will be severe and rise with the amount by which we overshoot 1.5 degrees C. Ahead of COP26, Swiss Re analysis found that with implementation of the climate mitigation pledges made as of early 2021, the world would be on track for 2.0–2.6 degrees C of warming by mid-century, and GDP would be 10–14 % lower than absent climate change, with bigger impacts still in vulnerable regions such as Asia Pacific.[8] A UCL study also published, ahead of COP26, suggested that global GDP by 2100 could be up to 37 % lower than it would be absent the impacts of climate change, using the IPCC's SSP2-4.5 scenario. This figure is based on a recently updated PAGE-ICE integrated assessment model and is, notably, roughly six times higher than previous estimates.[9] The modelling also suggests significant impacts do not just lie off in the future. AfDB estimates that the African continent, which is on the front line of the physical effects of climate change, is already losing up to 5 % of GDP to the impacts of climate change against a 2005 baseline, and that this could increase to 13 % by 2050.[10] A more recent paper by BIS economists starts to get granular by exploring the macroeconomic effects of energy transition for countries that are variously currently fossil fuel energy importers who benefit from a switch to renewables, and fossil fuel energy exporters who are negatively impacted, while noting that precisely how these transitions occur makes a significant difference.[11]

There is much need to invest further not just in sizing these potential impacts, but in better understanding how they may differ across regions, countries, and sec-

---

6 Stern, *The economics of climate change* (2006), Stern and Oswald, *Why economists are letting down the world on climate change* (2019).

7 Stern, *A time for action and a time for change* (2021).

8 Swiss Re Institute, *The economics of climate change* (2021), p. 2.

9 Kikstra et. al, *The social cost of carbon under climate-economy feedbacks and temperature variability* (2021).

10 AfDB, *Climate impacts on Africa's Growth* (2020), pp. 13–19.

11 Americo et al., *The energy transition and its macroeconomic effects* (2023).

tors, including in a dynamic way that considers changing science, policy, and mitigation efforts. Further investing in such modelling is urgently needed because it helps motivate and inform the policy response globally and nationally, but it cannot be something we seek to get completely right ahead of policy action. The pathway to 1.5 degrees C is rapidly narrowing.

Financial Stability Impact of Failing to act

If it is hard to model the macroeconomic effects of climate change, modelling the financial stability effects with precision is also difficult. It has become increasingly common for financial policymakers to use scenario analysis to explore the risks to individual financial institutions and the system as a whole. This scenario analysis typically considers both a "hot house world", and then a range of scenarios where policy action helps mitigate the risk to differing degrees.

As set out in a recent FSB paper, many financial policymakers are deploying Network for Greening the Financial System (NGFS) scenarios, first launched in late 2017, where integrated assessment models (IAMs) and a damage function are used to translate climate variables into a core set of macroeconomic variables, such as GDP, energy, or carbon prices.[12] An economic model then translates these outputs into a large set of macroeconomic and financial variables. This modelling helps to develop understanding of transition dynamics, and to some degree to size the impacts, confirming that severe impacts are avoided through orderly transition, with more significant GDP and financial losses for disorderly transition scenarios, and with the most material impacts being experienced in the case of a "hot house" outcome. These are very valuable insights. It is well recognised that the scenarios likely understate impacts however, for a variety of reasons including data inadequacies and the challenges of modelling non-linearities, second-round effects and policy and private sector reaction functions. At this stage such exercises are not comparable to traditional stress tests that assess resilience to tail risks.

Further necessary work is planned by the NGFS to improve its scenarios and many central banks and regulators will further invest in their own scenario analysis capabilities. This is important work to pursue, again because it helps motivate and inform policy. But work to develop scenarios and scenario analysis capabilities – which is already some six years old – will need to proceed in parallel to work on risk mitigation given the closing window to 2030.

---

12 FSB, *Climate scenario analysis by jurisdictions* (2022).

How should financial Policymakers proceed given all this Uncertainty?

Despite this uncertainty, there is much we don't know about transition – how to secure it, how to measure progress against it, and so on. As outlined above, we know that macroeconomic and financial stability outcomes will be better if we secure an orderly transition, and so policy that helps support such a transition and helps monitor progress being made across the economy and financial system is hugely important.

At this stage, the risks are not primarily about a leap into the unknown, but about how effectively the transition can be delivered for the energy and highest emitting sectors, and whether the financial system is facilitating this such that it can seize the opportunities and mitigate the associated risks. Roughly 75 % of the emissions reductions needed will come from transitioning away from fossil fuel energy sources.[13] We have seen over the last year or so how a shock to these markets can affect the macroeconomic outlook and raise financial stability concerns, and know we need to focus on delivering an orderly transition. It's a given that this must be done in a way that secures affordable, accessible, and resilient energy supply, across all economies.

The good news is that we have a good sense of what is needed to bring about decarbonisation of the energy sector. While energy transition undoubtedly presents complexities which vary across countries, the core low carbon energy sources we must transition to are tried and tested technologies. These are – in most countries in the world – significantly cheaper to run than high carbon alternatives. In the IEA Net-Zero Emissions Scenario, the combined share of global power capacity from wind and solar is projected to increase from roughly 10 % globally in 2020 to 70 % in 2050.[14] The levelized cost of these renewables has been steadily declining in most countries since at least 2010.[15] Clearly, this is good news for those worried about inflationary and related effects.

Still, we need government policy to create the right incentives and enabling environment for transition in the energy and other high emitting sectors, to secure the necessary financing, and to track progress being made. There is still much to do: renewables have become a much more attractive investment, and in 2021, Bloomberg reported that investments in renewables outperformed fossil fuels threefold during

---

13 IEA, *Net-zero by 2050* (2021).
14 IEA, *Net-zero by 2050* (2021).
15 IRENA, *Majority of new renewables undercut fossil fuels on cost* (2021). The levelized cost of electricity (LCOE) is a measure of the average net present cost of electricity generationover a generators lifetime.

the prior decade.[16] That said, the ratio of financing of current high carbon to low carbon energy systems is currently around 1:1 and needs to average 1:4 between 2021 and 2030.[17]

Transition Planning beats no Transition Planning

Financial institutions are engaging with this transition challenge, motivated by government policy and their individual drive to seize opportunities and mitigate risks. All financial sector policymakers, including but not limited to the guardians of financial stability, will benefit from the fact that major financial institutions are increasingly undertaking transition planning, because it will provide valuable forward-looking information on progress being made, as well as because of the real-world risk mitigation it delivers.

Founded in 2021, the Glasgow Financial Alliance for Net Zero (GFANZ) brings together more than 550 financial institutions across 50 countries, each of whom have individually committed to supporting real economy decarbonisation in line with science-based pathways to 1.5 degrees C with low or no overshoot.

Ahead of COP27, GFANZ-convened workstreams delivered definitions of transition finance that extend well beyond the around 10 % of economic activity that is unambiguously green, to address the majority that needs to transition or be managed out in an orderly manner if we are to meet our climate and wider objectives. Four transition finance strategies are important to reducing real economy emissions, namely:

- **Climate solutions**: technologies and services, including nature-based solutions, to replace high-emitting activities, remove GHG from the atmosphere, or otherwise accelerate the net-zero transition in a just manner.
- **Aligned**: investments in companies with credible net-zero transition plans, who have made demonstrable progress against those plans and are aligned with relevant science-based pathways.
- **Aligning**: investments in both high-emitting and low-emitting firms with robust net-zero transition plans, who have targets aligned to sectoral pathways and are implementing changes in their business and showing progress in converging on relevant science-based pathways.

---

16 Bloomberg, *Renewable Returns Tripled Versus Fossil Fuels in Last Decade* (2021).
17 BNEF, *Investment requirements of a low carbon world* (2022).

 – **Managed phaseou**t: a net-zero aligned strategy that delivers credible, finan-
   cially viable and just financing to accelerate the early retirement of high-emitting assets.

All these strategies – see Figure below – need to be significantly scaled up for the
net-zero transition to be feasible, and ideally would inform much needed global frameworks for transition finance.

Four key financing strategies to enable the net-zero transition

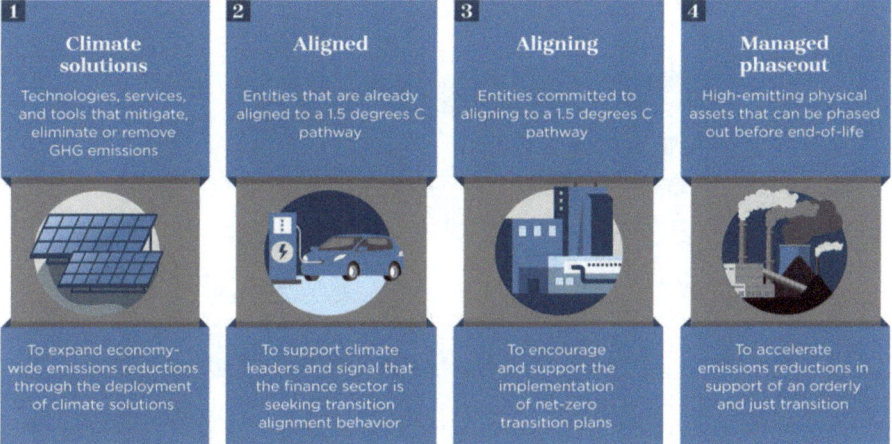

Fig. 1: Net-zero aligned financing strategies.

GFANZ workstreams also delivered a common framework for financial institutions
to support the credible, comprehensive, and comparable net zero transition plans
that will play a central role in translating net zero commitments into specific actions. Governments, businesses and financial institutions, need a strategy to navigate the risks of climate change and seize the economic opportunities from the
net-zero transition.

   The GFANZ Transition Plan framework can help financial institutions across all
sectors, as well as the companies to whom they lend, invest in, or underwrite, to implement their own transition plans and measure progress in a consistent way. The
GFANZ framework identifies ten components of a transition plan grouped into five
themes (for more detail see Figure 2):

 – **Foundations:** defining organisation-wide objectives and priorities to reach net-
   zero by 2050 or sooner, in line with science-based pathways, and clearly stating
   measurable interim and final targets;

- **Implementation strategy:** how you work across the business to align products and services, decision-making processes and organisational policies with transition objectives;
- **Engagement strategy**: how you align your engagement with the public sector, industry peers, and your clients and portfolio companies with transition objectives;
- **Metrics and targets**: how you measure and report against progress; and finally
- **Governance:** how you ensure that there is accountability, incentives, and proper training for meeting the transition plan objectives at all levels of the organisation.

Fig. 2: Core components of a Net Zero Transition Plan.

2023 is the Year of the Transition Plan

Converging around a practitioner-led common global framework for net zero transition plans – and specifically the framework developed by the global financial system through GFANZ-convened work – is essential to delivering the forward-looking information policymakers need on transition risks, alongside meaningful risk mitigation by financial institutions. It is encouraging then, that so many major financial institutions are voluntarily undertaking and disclosing transition planning aligned with the GFANZ framework in 2023.

Building out from these private sector efforts, governments and companies can step up their own transition planning. By engaging with and hastening these private sector efforts – including by moving towards common baseline disclosure standards building on the recently issued ISSB standards – financial policymakers can secure both forward looking information on risks and ensure those risks are reduced through real world mitigation.

2023 is the year of the transition plan. This is good news given that to seize transition opportunities and mitigate risks, it is also the case that a plan beats no plan.

Credible, comprehensive, and comparable transition plans for the global financial sector would be better still and so work planned by global financial policymakers on transition planning in 2023 comes not a moment too soon. Indeed, it is essential for all our efforts – governments, companies, and the financial sector – that it helps to normalise transition planning as the principal way to mitigate risks and assess progress.

Acknowledgement: With thanks to Raphael Chaskalson, GFANZ Policy Technical Lead, and the Oliver Wyman team.

Axel A. Weber

Financial Markets and monetary Policy in the Eurozone Economy – Outlook and Risks ahead

Let me start with some key economic facts about the European economy today and then provide some more details, colour, and background thereafter:

The war in Ukraine and rising energy, food, and raw material prices are taking their toll on the Eurozone economy. Nevertheless, the economy is proving more resilient than feared. Sentiment indicators point to a sharp slowdown in manufacturing, the recovery in services has also stalled. I therefore expect the region to experience a short, mild recession next year. Inflation concerns are driving policymakers at the ECB and will force the ECB to continue its monetary tightening.

The more detailed picture of the Eurozone economy can be described as follows:

The Eurozone economy is slowing, with both consumer and business confidence falling. However, hard data is showing that the economy is proving more resilient than feared. Fiscal support is increasing aimed at cushioning the economic shock, a mild winter so far, and easing back of prices, all explain this outcome. Europe continues to reduce its dependence on Russian hydrocarbons, with plans to reduce consumption across the bloc. Reduced consumption means that, despite disruptions to supply, gas storage is ahead of expectations. The threat of supply disruptions from Russia remains, but I expect rationing of supplies this winter will be avoided.

I think inflation will continue to trump growth concerns for the ECB, with 50bps of hikes likely at its December meeting, taking the deposit rate to 2%. I expect the deposit rate after a 50bp rate hike in December to be further increased with more rate hikes of 50bp in February and March, followed by two 25bp hikes thereafter. I then expect an end of the rate hikes in summer 2023.

The ECB also recently announced a Transmission Protection Instrument (TPI) aimed at easing concerns about peripheral spreads in the short term. Its effectiveness will only be known if it ever needs to be used. The ECB will also at the next meetings provide some information about its approach to QT and the balance sheet reduction, with LTROs (outright operations) unwinding relatively fast and excess liquidity falling sizeably in the next few quarters if LTROs are not prolonged.

Wage negotiations in the bloc are key to watch. Although wages are rising, settlements for the most part are still resulting in negative real wage gains. This suggests that the bargaining position of workers is not high, despite falling unemployment. The threat of a wage price spiral cannot be ruled out but remains contained.

https://doi.org/10.1515/9783111340937-004

Inflation is set to fall through 2023 as base effects from energy prices fades, and demand falls. The key geopolitical and economic risk in Europe next year will continue to be the war in Ukraine. I expect the war to continue well into next year without a negotiated settlement. Within the range of upside and downside risk scenarios, I see the balance of risks skewed severely to the downside, uncertainty remaining elevated and volatility remaining high. I expect Europe to manage the 2023 refilling season without government mandated gas rationing. Europe will most likely continue to depend on suppliers like Norway, the US, and LNG spot cargoes for its gas consumption in the year ahead. This will likely come with a sizable price tag: Natural gas prices in the Eurozone are likely to remain much higher than pre-invasion levels in 2023 and higher than prices in the United States. With higher prices and ongoing uncertainty, I expect the Eurozone economy to grow at a below-trend rate next year and I expect Germany to encounter a mild technical recession.

Given this general economic outlook and the big picture for the monetary and fiscal policy in the euro zone, let's take a closer look at financial markets, their likely evolution in the year ahead and their links with fiscal and monetary policy.

The most important driver of financial markets today is again monetary policy. The surge of inflation to levels unprecedented in recent history after a period of too-low-for-too-long interest rates has forced central banks to reverse course. But the too-late and behind-the-curve tightening of monetary policy has necessitated an unprecedented speed and size of interest rate adjustments to get ahead of the curve. The tailwinds for asset prices and financial markets from low interest rates and expanded central bank balance sheets has turned into headwinds as central banks normalizing monetary policy by increasing interest rates at high speed and with large steps. At the same time, risks of renewed financial instability in markets and in the global banking sector cannot be ignored.

One reason for the strong link between monetary policy and asset prices is the zero-interest-rate environment. Monetary policy traditionally works through four channels – the so-called transmission channels of monetary policy: (1) the interest rate channel, (2) the credit channel, (3) the exchange rate channel, and (4) the wealth channel.

In large open economies, such as the US and the Eurozone, the interest rate channel is the most powerful channel of monetary policy transmission. However, in the past zero interest rate environment, the interest rate channel was largely ineffective. Rates can't go much lower than zero or slightly negative. The credit channel was also congested because it depended on rates expected to go even lower. Monetary policy in a zero-rate environment was confined to the exchange rate channel and the wealth channel. That's why we have seen these strong reactions of exchange rates and asset prices on recent monetary policy decisions.

Policymakers are today again facing huge structural and cyclical challenges. Out of the three main policy instruments (fiscal, monetary, and structural policy), policymakers are limited to just one instrument – monetary policy. And out of the four transmission channels of monetary policy, the two most powerful channels (the interest rate channel and – partly – the credit channel) have become relatively ineffective.

Policymakers are thus trying to solve the world's huge structural and cyclical economic problems by tampering with exchange rates and stocks and bonds prices.

Also note that, in large, closed economies, the exchange rate channel does not work very well. And inflating asset prices works just once – on the way up. And when the easing stops, or is even reversed, the wealth effect is undone. Furthermore, both remaining channels (exchange rate channel, wealth channel) are "win-lose" channels: on a global level, a weakening of the currency of one country always implies a strengthening of the currencies of other countries, which cancels out on a global level. And the wealth effect does not create real wealth, it redistributes wealth. In contrast, the interest rate channel is a "win-win" channel: a boost to domestic demand also increases demand for imports and thus benefits other countries as well.

Personally, I don't believe that we can solve our problems by distorting exchange rates and asset prices. On the contrary. Our problems are not being solved, but postponed and they are growing with time. The room for manoeuvre for fiscal policy is decreasing by the year, and the willingness to undertake structural reforms is still mostly absent. Monetary policy will therefore remain the main determinant of financial markets, and financial market volatility will remain elevated.

What does this all mean for monetary policy in the Eurozone economy?

The ECB is counting on the fact that the increase in inflation since 2021 will only be temporary and that inflationary pressure will decrease in the coming months. However, the ECB is playing a dangerous game by betting everything on this card. Economic forecasts have always been subject to a high degree of uncertainty, but they have become even more unreliable since the Covid pandemic and the war in Ukraine. The impact of lockdowns, the unprecedented expansion of monetary and fiscal policies during the pandemic and the sweeping economic sanctions against Russia are virtually impossible to model and predict. The fact that inflation forecasts are all pointing downwards does not mean that inflation will fall or that uncertainties about future inflation developments have diminished. In fact, the ECB's inflation forecast have turned out to be grossly wrong quarter after quarter after quarter.

In the medium term, model-based inflation forecasts always tend towards the historical mean and are often restricted to in the long run coincide with the central bank's inflation objective, and this is again the case here. Over the past two years, model-based inflation forecasts have been proven dead wrong. The increase in the inflation rate in the euro area since 2021, which peaked at 10.6 % in October 2022, was not foreseen. As late as December 2021, the ECB forecast a declining inflation rate in 2022 and an average inflation rate of 3.2 % for the year 2022. In fact, inflation currently runs at three times that rate – a huge forecast error. This illustrates the high degree of uncertainty in inflation forecasts.

The forecast uncertainty today is not lower than before the war in Ukraine, it is greater. It is very easy to imagine an escalation scenario could lead to a renewed surge in energy prices. The ECB is therefore counting on a fall in inflation despite forecast uncertainty remaining high.

The long and variable lags of monetary policy transmission combined with the too-late reaction of monetary policy to the rise in inflation poses major challenges for the ECB and its anti-inflation credibility. To be successful, monetary policy must act with foresight and thus be based on forecasts. But the more unreliable these forecasts are, the more important risk management becomes. In an environment of high uncertainty, monetary policy must above all avoid making major mistakes.

In principle, two mistakes are now possible: the ECB can be too restrictive or too expansionary.

In the first case of a too restrictive monetary policy stance, the ECB causes an unnecessarily deep recession, accompanied by stronger disinflation and a possible renewed pockets of weakness and crisis in the financial or real estate markets. This is undoubtedly an unpleasant scenario, but not an existential risk for the monetary union. The tools for fighting such a deflation scenario, should it again emerge, are well known by now. In the past, the ECB has gained ample experience with pursuing ultra-loose monetary policy should it again be needed to fight deflation risks. In principle, there are few limits to loosening monetary policy, especially when considering the expansion of the central bank's balance sheet. Monetary policy can always fight deflation and create inflation if it pursues this goal with enough determination.

Furthermore, central banks should have been more mindful of the long-run consequences of a period of too-low for too-long interest rates. In addition, the current too-late and behind-the-curve tightening of monetary policy has made it necessary for central banks to tighten at an unprecedented speed and with mega-sized interest steps to get ahead of the curve. A decade of tailwinds for asset prices and financial markets from ultra-low or even negative interest rates combined with ample liquidity from massively expanded central bank balance sheets has now turned into headwinds. The eruption of renewed instability in financial markets and in banking are now seen by markets not just as a reason for central banks to pause, markets even bet on a quick reversal of the entire monetary policy tightening of recent quarters. This would be a grave policy mistake. The long-run costs of a prolonged period of ultra-loose monetary policy would be huge. 'Mission aborted' instead of 'mission accomplished' would undermine central bank credibility even further. Central banks should not allow themselves to be held hostage by markets.

In the second case of keeping monetary policy too expansionary, inflation continues to be high and may even rise further. The ECB would then be forced to raise interest rates significantly further, possibly to a level above the rate of inflation. This scenario would pose an existential risk for the euro area, because many highly indebted member countries would face the risk of unsustainable debt dynamics and may be confronted with bond markets again betting against some governments' ability to service their debt. If central banks act too hesitantly on inflation due to concerns about the impact of its monetary policy tightening on public finances, they could risk being held hostage by governments and being subjected to fiscal dominance.

A persistent inflation scenario in my view is undoubtedly today the more dangerous scenario and the best choice currently is to maintain a restrictive monetary policy stance in the face of high uncertainty amidst emerging signs of second round effects in wage-price dynamics. It remains to be seen whether the ECB's bet on falling inflation rates will work. From today's perspective, however, a too-early ECB's policy shift to a neutral policy stance would be poor risk management. It would not take sufficiently into account the risk of inflation. If inflation surprises on the upside again in the future, which I do not think is unlikely, the ECB pausing too early could in the long run turn out to be a bigger challenge for the cohesion of the euro zone than further removing monetary stimulus and exiting its still very loose monetary policy stance. Not doing so is playing with fire.

Dominik Weh and Lisa Quest

The Solution for a polycrisis World: bold Action and bold Actors

We are truly living in a polycrisis world. We now face multiple crises, from the financial to the geopolitical to the environmental, all at the same time. These crises compound on themselves, and the impact is greater than the sum of the individual crises operating alone. Working to solve one crisis at a time or separate from the other will not be sufficient. Instead, policy makers and other actors must approach this polycrisis world through bold, cross-cutting solutions that can appropriately respond to the complexity of the times.

The Institute for Law and Finance at the Goethe University Frankfurt am Main hosted its annual Future of the Financial Sector conference in January 2023, bringing together a cross-section of business leaders, policymakers, and others to explore trends and assess the current state of our global economy. This event occurred as we approached the one-year anniversary of the Russian invasion of Ukraine, with inflation levels stubbornly high, and (unknown to us at the time) the collapse of major US-based banks just a few weeks in the future. The discussions of the day encapsulated the unique challenges of our current economy and made it clear that the question of the next financial crisis is not "if" but "when."

Before we explore the specifics, we must pull back and consider the unique time we are in and the nature of our polycrisis world. How did we get here? Where will the next major crisis come from? And what can we do about it?

How did we get here?

Typically, we discuss 2008 as the last major financial crisis, with the collapse of Lehman Brothers and the financial panic that it set off. While that was a major global event, one can go back to the dot com bubble and the 9/11 attacks as the start of our polycrisis world. The stock decline that began in early 2000 continued through the 9/11 attacks, which caused its own market collapse. That terrorist attack had massive effects across the globe, with the invasion of Afghanistan and Iraq by the major western powers leading to further instability. The 2008 crisis directly influenced the European debt crisis, creating more instability in the markets. Austerity measures and the reaction to the fall-out of the financial crisis and debt crisis led to more geopolitical risk and supported, in part, the rise of a global right-wing authoritarian movement. The Brexit vote created a huge level of uncertainty within the financial sector and our global commerce system. As the climate crisis worsened, humanitar-

https://doi.org/10.1515/9783111340937-005

ian needs grew and refugees began moving across borders, adding further stress to our global system.

Then, in 2020, we faced a global crisis unlike anything in our lifetime. The COVID-19 pandemic completely upended our way of life and stressed our modern economy in a way we have never seen. The entire world was unified by this unknown risk, which presented us with many novel challenges. Parts of our economy were shut off and others were dramatically expanded in ways with little precedent. While we are getting "back to normal" post-pandemic, the road to normalcy has been slow and winding.

Since the pandemic, the crises have multiplied and compounded. Our global economic and political system was stressed in unexpected ways and the results continue to produce unexpected outcomes. Our global supply chain broke down in many places, and is only beginning to heal. Inflation remains stubbornly high, despite predictions, and the effects of higher prices are filtering throughout the economy. The first ground war in Europe since World War II illustrates the uncertain geopolitical situation. Climate change continues to worsen with greater natural disasters, further stressing humanitarian crises and creating more instability.

While we will never go back to the way things were pre-pandemic, the same could be said of any previous crises. The challenges of pre-2020 may have seemed more manageable and linear, but we have always faced compounding events that lead to unexpected outcomes. The only difference is, post-COVID, we are aware of what is possible when the systems we assumed would always function completely break down.

The next Crisis: where will it come from?

There will be another financial crisis. There is no doubt about that. As we are writing this, the US is dealing with its biggest bank collapse since 2008. We could be at the beginning of this next crisis right now without knowing it. The collapse of Silicon Valley Bank, Signature Bank, and Credit Suisse could be the start of another broad-based systemic failure. These events are of course urgent and require action. But we should not ignore the important because of the urgent. If we continue to only react to the many crises of our time, we can never plan and prevent the next one.

We hope that the next crisis will come from an unknown unknown–something we did not see coming. We should not expect another financial collapse like 2008, or another debt crisis like in the Eurozone. We have adapted and responded to what has come before. Facing unexpected crises means we are doing our jobs preparing for what we know. Any predictable crisis can be prevented. We should explore, plan, and prepare for anything we expect may be coming. We should invest in resiliency, risk management, and preparedness tools. That way, we can capture all of the unknown knowns, and translate some of the unknown things into things we can better prepare for and control.

What are the biggest potential risks in the coming years? The Global Risks Report, published by the World Economic Forum in collaboration with Marsh McLennan, examines how widening geopolitical, economic, and societal fissures will trigger and exacerbate crises to come. The 2023 version highlighted key potential risks in the next two years and then next 10 years:

Fig. 1: Global risks ranked by severity over the short and long term (Source: World Economic Forum Global Risks Perception Survey 2022–2023).

This research, conducted from surveying over 1,200 experts across academia, business, government, the international community, and civil society, shows that the cost of living is the expected major risk over the next two years, followed by natural disasters, and geopolitical confrontation. That should be no surprise–inflation remains persistently high and the "100 year disasters" seem to happen with greater regularity. No one now expects the Ukraine-Russian conflict to end anytime soon, and will only further upend geopolitical relationships.

However, as we expand our time horizon to 10 years out, we see that environmental risks grow in prominence. The top four risks are all environmental in nature, either as a failing to combat climate change, or a direct result of it, such as biodiversity loss or extreme weather events. In fact, if you consider the fifth-ranked risk, large-scale involuntary migration, as a symptom of climate change, as many existing refugees are climate refugees, the top six risks are all climate-related.

We should be preparing for this risk by investing in solutions to mitigate climate change. Not only stemming from a desire to limit warming, but also creating infrastructure that protects our existing way of life. The Paris Climate Accord has set us up with a framework to undertake these bold strategies, but more must be done as we continue to exist in a polycrisis world.

Bold Actions, bold Actors

To mitigate the risk of the collective impact from the threat of on-going polycrises, we must take bold action. We cannot address the situation with incremental change. Instead, we need to make bold statements and take bold moves to fundamentally mitigate the direction our society is heading. We should take global action that contains global solutions, incentivizing the right behaviours and the right culture we need to respond to the current landscape.

What does this response look like? We need to make bold investments in innovation and technology that can help us sufficiently mitigate risks. We need bold actors to stand up and make the case for these investments. We need an ecosystem of people across the planet to support these as a global solution.

How can we build this ecosystem? Consider the following recommendations:
- *Do not be afraid to disrupt and think the unthinkable.* Our polycrisis world demands all ideas to be put on the table. Conventional wisdom is how we got to where we are, and we need to be able to re-analyse everything that we assume to be true. An assumption that interest rates would remain low was one of the factors in leading to the collapse of Silicon Valley Bank. There should be no taboo in revisiting any commonly held assumption, because it is those forward-thinking analyses that will help us better mitigate future risk.
- *We need non-partisan action with global reach.* Only brave actions will be rewarded. Incremental changes will most likely not have an impact. The responses to COVID-19 illustrate that our current structures for responding to crises can be limited by our political and social constructs. We must not be lim-

ited by our borders and instead think about what we as a global society needs to
not only survive but thrive.

- *Do not let perfect be the enemy of good.* None of our crisis response or preparation will be perfect, but that does not excuse us to do nothing. Imperfect solutions will get us a step forward, allow us to learn and revisit. We should also not
be afraid of sunk costs or "being wrong" – it will be the only way to learn. We
should give ourselves the space to correct our decisions as needed.
- *Involve the young.* Decisions about our current socio-political context are frequently made by one generation only, and this generation will not be around
long enough to see the full scope of their impact. Given the long-term impact of
decisions, we should consciously incorporate cross-generational leaders to support the design of solutions. Much of this power sharing will be uncomfortable,
but the massive generational shift on our horizon gives us no other choice.

The future Generational Shift

The last recommendation to "involve the young" underscores the need for bold action. While the Global Risk Report highlights our best guess at what we expect to
happen in the next 10 years, it is based on the current state of our economy. But we
are about to undergo a massive transfer of power from one generation to the next,
which could upend things even further.

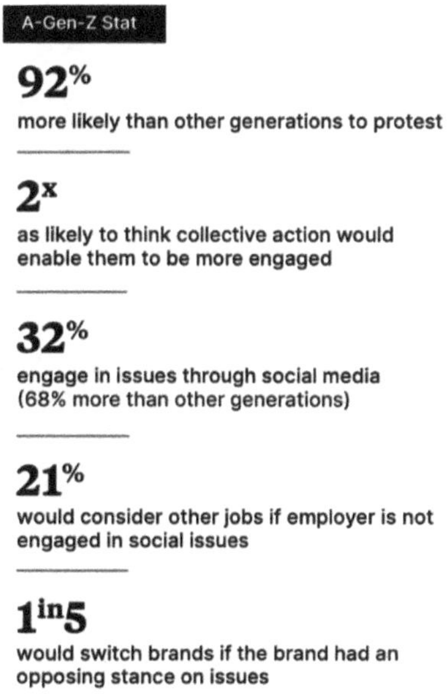

A-Gen-Z Stat

92%
more likely than other generations to protest

2ˣ
as likely to think collective action would
enable them to be more engaged

32%
engage in issues through social media
(68% more than other generations)

21%
would consider other jobs if employer is not
engaged in social issues

1ⁱⁿ5
would switch brands if the brand had an
opposing stance on issues

Fig. 2: The Change Generation: Small collective steps
for Gen Z can lead to one giant leap for humankind.
Source: A Gen-Z Report by Oliver Wyman Forum

As baby boomers retire, Millennials and Gen Z will take their place. These generations are different from generations before, having been raised during our technological explosion. They have different expectations and different considerations for how the world works. These younger generations will redefine our politics, our leadership, and our economy.

In research on Gen Z, Oliver Wyman found that this generation has been greatly affected by the crises they have lived through. The pandemic, opioid crisis, war on terrorism, lockdown drills, devastating natural disasters, and more have forced this generation into a greater maturity. They know they are fighting for their lives.

This has created a generation more resilient than previous. They understand the world they are inheriting and want to do something about it. Gen Z members are 92 % more likely to protest than other generations and twice as likely to consider collective action as a way to engage on social and environmental issues.

The resiliency and determination of Gen Z has implications for the workforce as well as consumer behaviour. Around 20 % of Gen Z would consider other jobs if their employer is not engaged in social issues, and 75 % more likely to look for employment that better aligns with their values. If an employer does not align with their values, they are 80 % more likely to not be as engaged in their work, creating lost productivity for their employer. This behaviour extends to purchasing decisions as well: around 20 % of Gen Z will switch brands if the brand has the opposite stance on an issue.

The Change Generation extends activism to the workplace

If their employers are not engaged in social issues **Gen Zers** are....

more likely to
**consider other jobs that better
align with their values**

more likely to be
**less engaged at work in
day-to-day activities**

more likely **to go to
fewer work events**

Employers need to change their activism playbook, or risk losing Gen Z talent and engagement

Source: Oliver Wyman Forum Global Consumer Sentiment Survey, September 2020–present, N = 4,042

Fig. 3: The Change Generation extends activism to the workplace.
Source: A Gen-Z Report by Oliver Wyman Forum

This focus on activism in response to the uncertain future has major implications for how businesses and policymakers respond to Gen Z as they grow in power in the workplace and as consumers. (These motivations for change are similar, if not less pronounced, with Millennials as well.) We must begin to focus more on environmental challenges and social issues, and the business community should begin to recognize that social and environmental issues are business imperatives as well. Ignoring them ignores the demands of future employees and customers.

The boldness of Gen Z will help tackle some of the major crises coming our way, but we should not have to wait for them to take charge. We can start to lead now.

Conclusion

Many people expect we will eventually get back to a simpler, quieter time. But we cannot, at least not in the short to medium term. We can only plan for the crises we face and take the bold actions required to successfully mitigate what is coming. Instead, we must not be afraid to disrupt and work towards nonpartisan action with a global reach. We should intentionally involve the future generations in our work and allow them to push us forward, even if those first steps are not perfect. Only by becoming bold actors taking these bold steps can we find the solution for our polycrisis world.

II. Crypto Assets and Cybersecurity

Michael J. Hsu

Tokenization and AI in Banking: how Risk and Compliance can facilitate responsible Innovation

In this article, I explore the topic of rapid innovation. In particular, I would like to focus on two innovations that are evolving quickly and have the potential to be highly impactful on financial services: tokenization and artificial intelligence (AI). The benefits of each are potentially quite significant, as are the risks—to consumers, to safety and soundness, and to financial stability.

There is a saying: The better a car's brakes, the faster you can drive it safely. In other words, strong controls *enable* sustained high performance. Too often risk and compliance are seen as nettlesome hindrances, roadblocks to getting to market, or drags on innovation and profitability. Some would say it is better to "move fast and break things," create "minimally viable products," "fail fast," and "rapid prototype" one's way to a market leading position.

In some domains, that approach can work. In banking and finance, however, it tends to end badly, as shown by the experience of the 2008 financial crisis with derivatives and last year's crypto winter.[1]

In banking, the *responsible* approach to innovation is the better way: by progressing in tightly controlled stages where the risks can be identified, measured, and managed at each stage, by building the brakes and the engine at the same time, and by working with regulators, instead of around them. This takes discipline and time. It requires engagement by, and trust in, risk managers and compliance professionals from the get-go through every step of the process. While this may slow things down initially, it helps to ensure that innovations *can be trusted* by the public and regulators to be safe, sound, and fair. In short, responsible innovation plays the long game.

Before addressing how that approach can be adapted to today's fast-paced environment, I want to spend some time considering the promise and perils of tokenization and AI—two areas where the pace and scope of innovation present special challenges.

---

[1] Regarding derivatives, refer to Gillian Tett, *Fool's Gold: The Inside Story of J.P. Morgan and How Wall Street Greed Corrupted Its Bold Dream and Created a Financial Catastrophe* (2010). Regarding crypto, refer to Mark, Julian and Gerrit De Vynck, "'Crypto winter' has come. And it's looking more like an ice age.," *Washington Post* (December 18, 2022). Refer also to remarks by Acting Comptroller Michael J. Hsu at the Blockchain Association, "Cryptocurrencies, Decentralized Finance, and Key Lessons from the 2008 Financial Crisis" (September 21, 2021).

https://doi.org/10.1515/9783111340937-006

Tokenization

In order to address tokenization, I have to address crypto, as the underlying block-chain technology is where most tokenization efforts are currently focused.

I have long been a crypto skeptic.[2] The crypto industry remains immature and rife with risks, despite several years in the mainstream spotlight, billions of dollars of venture capital investment, and millions of hours of code commits. In 2022, losses from fraud exceeded $1 billion, losses from scams exceeded $2.5 billion, and losses from hacks exceeded $3.8 billion;[3] one of the largest stablecoins imploded; and multiple crypto platforms failed due to outright fraud, poor risk management, or both. In light of these risks, the OCC, Federal Reserve, and FDIC issued two interagency statements reminding banks of supervisory risk management expectations regarding crypto activities and exposures.[4]

Public blockchains, which support the vast majority of cryptocurrencies circulating today, appear to suffer from a key design flaw: "trustlessness."[5] The goal of having a "trustless" or "trust-minimized" blockchain requires a decentralized consensus mechanism, such as proof of work or proof of stake. These mechanisms are inefficient and create a trilemma between decentralization, security, and scale—achieving all three simultaneously is not possible with a public blockchain.[6] To grow and manage the trilemma requires either ponzi-prone "toke-

---

2 Refer to remarks by Acting Comptroller of the Currency Michael J. Hsu to the Harvard Law School and Program on International Financial Systems Roundtable on Institutional Investors and Crypto Assets, "Don't Chase" (October 11, 2022).

3 Refer to Federal Trade Commission, "New Analysis Finds Consumers Reported Losing More than $1 Billion in Cryptocurrency to Scams since 2021" (June 3, 2022); Department of Justice, Office of Public Affairs, "Justice Department Seizes Over $112M in Funds Linked to Cryptocurrency Investment Schemes" (April 3, 2023); and Chainalysis, "2022 Biggest Year Ever for Crypto Hacking with $3.8 Billion Stolen, Primarily from DeFi Protocols and by North Korea-linked Attackers" (February 1, 2023).

4 OCC News Release 2023-18, "Agencies Issue Joint Statement on Liquidity Risks Resulting from Crypto-Asset Market Vulnerabilities" (February 23, 2023); OCC News Release 2023-1, "Agencies Issue Joint Statement on Crypto-Asset Risks to Banking Organizations" (January 3, 2023). Notably, cross contagion from crypto to the traditional banking system has been limited. The only bank failure attributable to the crypto winter has been that of Silvergate, a state-chartered bank, which self-liquidated in March 2023.

5 Refer to Vitalik Buterin, "Trust Models" (August 20, 2020), in which he states that "[o]ne of the most valuable properties of many blockchain applications is *trustlessness*: the ability of the application to continue operating in an expected way without needing to rely on a specific actor to behave in a specific way even when their interests might change and push them to act in some different unexpected way in the future."

6 Vitalik Buterin, *Proof of Stake: The Making of Ethereum and the Philosophy of Blockchains* (2022).

nomics,"[7] highly technical workarounds,[8] or both. As a result, the crypto industry remains largely self-referential and disconnected from the real world. Moreover, the non-permissioned nature of public blockchains makes them attractive to criminals and others engaged in illicit finance,[9] and full compliance with anti-money laundering rules is extremely difficult for crypto intermediaries to achieve.[10]

By contrast, centrally operated, *trusted* blockchains have the potential to deliver security and achieve scale efficiently. Embracing the need to trust a blockchain operator—and forgoing trustlessness—eliminates the need for decentralized consensus mechanisms and the associated tokenomics. It enables the technology to solve settlement problems more efficiently and securely at scale, without the need for hype. Such "trusted blockchains" are also easily permissioned, making full compliance with AML rules achievable.

The greatest promise for blockchain technology today may lie in its potential to improve settlement efficiency through tokenization of real-world assets and liabilities on trusted blockchains. Settlement occurs when a transaction is deemed final. Typically, there is a lag between when the terms of a transaction, such as price and quantity, are agreed upon and when all of the transaction components are performed, and obligations are fully discharged. That lag is due to the multiple entities and multiple steps that are typically needed for reconciliation and verification.

Tokenization of real-world assets and liabilities has the potential to improve settlement efficiency by minimizing those lags and thereby reducing the associated frictions, costs, and risks. For instance, if you want to sell shares of stock with today's technology, you have to send an instruction to a broker and then a whole host of other steps have to occur across multiple entities before that transaction is deemed final, usually two days later.[11] Each of those steps takes time and carries risk. With tokenization, the instruction, transaction, and settlement can theoretically be collapsed into a single step, removing those frictions—provided, of course, that the technology is interoperable with central bank money and real-world settlement systems.[12]

---

7 Vitalik Buterin, "The Revenue-Evil Curve: a different way to think about prioritizing public goods funding" (October 28, 2022).

8 Bank for International Settlements (BIS), "Annual Economic Report" (June 2022). Refer to Vitalik Buterin, "Why sharding is great: demystifying the technical properties" (April 7, 2021).

9 U.S Department of the Treasury, "Illicit Finance Risk Assessment of Decentralized Finance" (April 2023).

10 Refer to OCC News Release 2022-41, "OCC Issues Consent Order Against Anchorage Digital Bank" (April 21, 2022); New York State Department of Financial Services, "Notice Regarding Paxos-Issued BUSD" (February 13, 2023).

11 Refer to Depository Trust & Clearing Corporation, "Guide to Clearance & Settlement."

12 Organisation for Economic Co-operation and Development, "The Tokenisation of Assets and Potential Implications for Financial Markets" (January 17, 2020); Securities and Exchange Commission,

Some have estimated that tokenization of real-world assets could save 35 to 65 percent across the settlement value chain, including, for instance, cost savings of up to $5 billion for equity-post trading.[13] Tokenization of fiat currencies for cross-border payments also holds the promise of reducing frictions, costs, and delays.[14] Importantly, tokenization does not require decentralization and trustlessness. In fact, decentralization leads to fragmentation and imposes severe limitations on scalability. The Federal Reserve's Hamilton Project noted this in its Phase 1 detailed report[15]—a finding that has been reinforced by national bank pilot projects that the OCC has reviewed as part of our supervisory process.[16]

Importantly, the legal frameworks—and risk and compliance capabilities—for tokenizing real-world assets and liabilities at scale need further development. Specifically, ownership and other property rights are not clear, especially in bankruptcy and in cross-jurisdictional situations.[17] Are tokens simply representations of real-world things, like a bank statement, or are they a distinct bundle of legal rights and obligations, like a deed? If the latter, how is ownership of a token established, recorded, transferred, perfected, contested, and resolved *in real-world legal systems*?

Final Rule, "Shortening the Securities Transaction Settlement Cycle," 88 Fed. Reg. 13872 (March 6, 2023); BIS Bulletin 72, "The tokenization continuum" (April 11, 2023).

13 Finoa, "Cost disruption in the issuance market: The case for tokenization" (October 2, 2020); Frederick Van Gysegem, "Tokenization: The future of financial markets?" (December 13, 2021).

14 Refer to BIS, "Nexus: enabling instant cross-border payments" (March 23, 2023); Joint report by the BIS Committee on Payments and Market Infrastructures (CPMI), the BIS Innovation Hub, the International Monetary Fund (IMF), and the World Bank, "Exploring multilateral platforms for cross-border payments" (January 18, 2023); Federal Reserve Bank of New York, "Facilitating Wholesale Digital Asset Settlement" (discussing the Regulated Liability Network U.S. Proof of Concept); Hugh Son, "JP Morgan is rolling out the first US bank-backed cryptocurrency to transform payments business" (February 14, 2019).

15 Refer to Federal Reserve Bank of Boston, "Project Hamilton Phase 1 Executive Summary" (February 3, 2022).

16 OCC Interpretive Letter No. 1179 (November 18, 2021) clarifies and elaborates on aspects of prior interpretive letters addressing cryptocurrency and trust activities and discusses that those activities are legally permissible provided the bank can demonstrate, to the satisfaction of its supervisory office, that it has controls in place to conduct the activity in a safe and sound manner. Specifically, a bank should notify its supervisory office, in writing, of its intention to engage in any of the cryptocurrency activities addressed in prior interpretive letters and should not engage in the activity until it receives written non-objection from its supervisory office. The supervisory office will evaluate the adequacy of a bank's risk management systems and controls, and risk measurement systems, to enable the bank to engage in the proposed activities in a safe and sound manner and in compliance with all applicable law.

17 Refer to Uniform Law Commission, "2022 Amendments to the Uniform Commercial Code"; Juliet M. Moringiello and Christopher K. Odinet, "The Property Law of Tokens," 74 Florida Law Review 607 (2002); Law Commission, "Digital Assets."

What is the legal relationship between a owning a token and owning the underlying real-world asset or liability? How is that legal relationship enforced and how does it operate in bankruptcy? What is the process for un-tokenizing an asset or liability?

Clarifying the ownership and other property rights of tokenized real-world assets and liabilities is foundational. It will inform the broader risks and associated risk management and controls needed to transact with tokens in a safe, sound, and fair manner.[18]

Programmability is an amplifier, further expanding the range of potential benefits and risks of tokenization. In theory, programmability could further reduce settlement frictions by making certain payments automatic when specific conditions are met. In the crypto space, these are referred to as "smart contracts." While the concept of smart contracts is fairly straightforward, there have been practical challenges with implementation, including with so-called oracles and coding vulnerabilities.[19]

In sum, to the extent settlement efficiencies can create real value for businesses, households, and financial institutions, demand to tokenize real world assets and liabilities is likely to grow over time. Today, trusted blockchains are better positioned than public blockchains to facilitate that growth at scale securely and in a safe, sound, and fair manner. In time, future innovations may reveal that non-blockchain-based systems may prove even better suited to the task. Regardless, the legal foundations for tokenization need to be developed. That will inform the controls and risk management capabilities required to support innovation in that space. Being attuned to the risks and building the brakes along with the engine will help ensure that tokenization innovations can be sustained and trusted over time. I will come back to this after touching on AI.

Artificial Intelligence

To date, banks have generally approached machine learning and AI adoption cautiously. Use cases have ranged widely from customer chatbots to fraud detection to

---

18 The American Law Institution and the Uniform Law Commission approved amendments to the Uniform Commercial Code (UCC) in 2022 to provide rules for the transfer of and security interests in certain digital assets. States have begun to adopt these changes. The UCC does not address ordinary ownership interests in digital assets, and many digital asset structures remain subject to significant legal uncertainty, including ownership interests. Refer to Uniform Law Commission, "2022 Amendments to the Uniform Commercial Code."

19 Dylan Yaga, Peter Mell, Nik Roby, and Karen Scarfone, "Blockchain Technology Overview," National Institute of Standards and Technology Internal Report 8202 (October 2018).

credit screening. Banks broadly have been attentive to the need for controls when using machine learning, including with regard to fair lending, compliance and adhering to model risk management practices.[20]

But the fear of missing out, especially regarding generative AI, may gain traction given the hype and breakneck pace of change. The buzz from OpenAI's release of ChatGPT last November went parabolic this spring with the leak of Meta's large language model, Google's release of Bard, and DIY releases like AutoGPT.[21] The market has taken notice, with "AI" mentions during second quarter earnings calls with investors nearly double the five-year average.[22] My own observation is that, for now at least, recent press reports of generative AI adoption by banks have been based more on speculative inference and, perhaps, attracting clicks than on reality.

For banking, the potential benefits of more widespread adoption of AI are significant, but so are the risks. The use of AI has the potential to reduce costs and increase efficiencies; improve products, services and performance; strengthen risk management and controls; and expand access to credit and other bank services. But AI also presents significant challenges.

Alignment is the core challenge. AI systems, which are generally based on neural networks, are not programmed explicitly like most software. They require training, and their outputs are not predictable.[23] While this is part of their magic, it also creates a fundamental problem: since AI systems are built to "learn," they may or may not do what we want or behave consistent with our values.[24] This alignment problem is inherent to all AI systems and is the focus of intense research.[25]

---

20 See OCC Comptroller's Handbook booklet "Model Risk Management" (August 2021); OCC Bulletin 2011–12, "Sound Practices for Model Risk Management: Supervisory Guidance on Model Risk Management" (April 4, 2011).
21 Refer to Sawdah Bhaimiya, "ChatGPT may be the fastest-growing consumer app in internet history, reaching 100 million users in just over 2 months, UBS report says" (February 2, 2023); GPT-4 Technical Report, "OpenAI" (March 27, 2023); Dylan Patel and Afzal Ahmad, "Google 'We Have No Moat, And Neither Does OpenAI'" (May 4, 2023); Bernard Marr, "Auto-GPT May Be The Strong AI Tool That Surpasses ChatGPT" (April 24, 2023).
22 John Butters, "Highest Number of S&P 500 Companies Citing 'AI' on Q1 Earnings Calls in Over 10 Years" (May 26, 2023). Nearly one in five S&P 500 financial companies cited "AI."
23 OpenAI, "How should AI systems behave, and who should decide?" (February 16, 2023), notes that "the process is more similar to training a dog than to ordinary programming."
24 Refer to Richard Ngo, Lawrence Chan, and Sören Mindermann, "The Alignment Problem from a Deep Learning Perspective" (February 22, 2023).
25 Brian Christian, *The Alignment Problem: Machine Learning and Human Values* (2020); Jan Leike, John Schulman, and Jeffrey Wu, "Our approach to alignment research" (August 24, 2022); DeepMind, "Safety and Ethics." Refer to Defense Advanced Research Projects Agency, "In The Moment (ITM)" (March 14, 2022) (seeking proposals to enable trust in defense-related AI decision-making).

This alignment problem, in turn, creates a significant governance and account-ability challenge. The more an AI system learns, the further it gets from its initial programming. This creates "opportunities for plausible deniability" should things go wrong.[26] In addition, like most companies, banks generally must rely on third parties to develop and support their AI capabilities. Within a bank and among its AI vendors, who is responsible for an AI system's performance and results? Who can and should be held accountable for misaligned, unexpected, and harmful outcomes? To govern AI adoption and use AI prudently, banks need to be able to answer these questions clearly as the scope and complexity of their AI initiatives grow.

AI systems also present unique bias and discrimination challenges. The issue of biased training data is well known. (Google's early experience with automated photo captions unknowingly labeling pictures in highly inappropriate and racist ways in the early days of image recognition is a good reminder.) Bias challenges with supervised and reinforcement learning in the consumer lending context have also been flagged and are being discussed.[27]

Stepping back, though, a deeper fairness issue lurks. Even if an AI system could achieve complete color-blindness in decision-making at the individual level, it would still yield unfair outcomes at the group level if baselines across groups differ. The AI community has been grappling with this "impossibility theorem" for some time in the criminal justice context.[28] Banks and regulators should prepare for simi-lar discussions as AI adoption among banks expands. The compounding nature of money, wealth, and financial health—and the impacts on mobility and persistent inequality—adds further complexity to this debate.[29]

Banks and regulators must also grapple with generative AI's capacity for en-abling fraud and the spread of misinformation. Fraud has been increasing across all forms, from traditional check fraud[30] to sophisticated synthetic identity[31] and syn-

---

26 Robin Feldman and Kara Stein, "AI Governance in the Financial Industry," Stanford Journal of Law, Business, and Finance Vol 27, No. 1 (posted October 10, 2022).

27 Refer to Emily Flitter, *The White Wall: How Big Finance Bankrupts Black America* (2022).

28 Jon Kleinberg, Sendhil Mullainathan, and Manish Raghavan, "Inherent Trade-Offs in the Fair De-termination of Risk Scores" (November 17, 2016); Kailash Karthik Saravanakumar, "The impossibility theorem of machine fairness: a causal perspective" (January 29, 2021); Moritz Hardt, Eric Price, and Nathan Srebro, "Equality of Opportunity in Supervised Learning" (2016); Machines Gone Wrong, "Getting Started."

29 Some AI researchers have begun to look to philosophy as a potential guide. See Laura Weidinger, Kevin R. McKee, Richard Everett, and Jason Gabriel, "Using the Veil of Ignorance to align AI systems with principles of justice" (April 24, 2023); DeepMind, "How can we build human values into AI?" (April 24, 2023).

30 Amy Besci, "Check Fraud Running Rampant" (March 2023).

31 Tad Simons, "Trends in synthetic identify fraud" (April 21, 2023).

thetic media[32] fraud. The ability of AI agents to mimic human communication and the low cost of scaling AI agents increase opportunities for fraud. The speed and sophistication of such developments warrant close monitoring and coordination.[33]

In addition, the potential for AI and social media to facilitate the creation and dissemination of harmful misinformation is also concerning.[34] For instance, last month a fake Bloomberg Twitter account posted a fake picture of black smoke near the Pentagon, which was then shared by verified Twitter accounts, triggering a brief sell-off in equity markets.[35] Banks and regulators will need to update playbooks and strengthen defenses against such actions in the near future.

The Value of a Risk and Compliance Approach to Rapid Innovation

How should banks and regulators approach rapid, potentially transformative innovations like tokenization and AI prudently?

It helps to bear in mind three principles: (1) innovate in stages, (2) build the brakes while building the engine, and (3) engage regulators early and often.

Innovating in stages requires discipline. The concept is simple: start with what can be controlled, expand only when ready, monitor carefully, adjust, and repeat. Fortunately, banks with robust new product approval processes are familiar with this approach. It is captured at a high level in the OCC's 2017 New, Modified, or Expanded Bank Products and Services guidance, which starts with adequate due diligence and approvals before commencing a new activity, and then touches on policies and procedures regarding risk identification and monitoring, effective change management, and ongoing performance monitoring and review systems.[36] Putting these principles into practice provides space for innovation to occur, but with guardrails and gates to prevent things from getting out of control.

---

32 Department of Homeland Security, "Increasing Threat of DeepFake Identities."

33 William Dixon, "What is adversarial artificial intelligence and why does it matter?" (November 21, 2018); Marian Radu and Joel Spurlock, "CrowdStrike Advances the Use of AI to Predict Adversary Behavior and Significantly Improve Protection" (May 23, 2023); Consumer Financial Protection Bureau, "Chatbots in consumer finance" (June 6, 2023).

34 Bradley Honigberg, "The Existential Threat of AI-Enhanced Disinformation Operations" (July 8, 2022); Karen Hao, "How Facebook and Google fund global misinformation" (November 20, 2021).

35 Donie O'Sullivan and Jon Passantino, "'Verified' Twitter accounts share fake image of 'explosion' near Pentagon, causing confusion" (May 23, 2023).

36 OCC Bulletin 2017-43, "New, Modified, or Expanded Bank Products and Services: Risk Management Principles" (October 20, 2017).

To the extent a bank's innovation program involves algorithms or third-party vendors, the OCC's guidance on Model Risk Management and the recent interagency guidance on Third-Party Risk Management provide additional clarity on supervisory expectations, which should also help with promoting discipline and consistency in the face of rapid innovation.[37]

To build the brakes while building the engine, risk and compliance professionals need to be at the innovation table and have their voices heard. In the technology space, speed to market is an important factor in innovation. Slowing things down is seen as anti-innovative. Structurally and culturally, this casts the risk and compliance functions as barriers to innovation. In less regulated institutions, they tend to be ignored or pushed aside.

Those with experience know how this movie plot plays out in the banking space. A new product or service gets developed without any risk or compliance input. It launches and gains popularity. The bank becomes a leader. Problems appear. Financial, legal, and reputational costs mount. Finally, risk, compliance, and operations professionals are brought in to clean up the mess.

There is a better way: by giving risk and compliance professionals a seat at the innovation table from the get-go and heeding their input. Empowering them to identify risks and risk mitigants will help ensure that the products and services that result will be safe, sound, fair, *and trusted.* This is what supervisors and the public expect, and it makes good long-term business sense.

Asking for permission, not forgiveness, from regulators will help ensure the longevity of rapid and transformational innovations. The pressure to be a first mover and take advantage of network effects can incentivize firms to release first and engage with regulators later. This "ask for forgiveness" approach may work in certain technology contexts. But it doesn't work in banking and finance, where public trust is critical to long-term product success, and regulatory approval is a proxy for that trust.[38]

Regulators, of course, must be responsive, knowledgeable, and agile. This is why we recently expanded and upgraded our Office of Innovation to the Office of Financial Technology. Building a bigger and stronger team fluent in both financial technology and bank supervision will allow us to keep up with developments more

---

37 OCC Bulletin 2011–12, "Sound Practices for Model Risk Management: Supervisory Guidance on Model Risk Management" (April 4, 2011); OCC News Release 2023-53, "Agencies Issue Final Guidance on Third Party Risk Management" (June 6, 2023). Refer to OCC Comptroller's Handbook booklet "Model Risk Management" (August 2021).
38 Refer to Bent Flyvbjerg and Dan Gardner, *How Big Things Get Done: The Surprising Factors That Determine the Fate of Every Project, from Home Renovations to Space Exploration and Everything In Between* (2023). The first product to hit the market is often not the one with staying power.

easily, to engage banks and fintechs more actively, to educate examiners and policy staff more effectively, and to collaborate with peer agencies more regularly.

Conclusion

Rapid innovations like tokenization and AI present special opportunities, risks, and challenges for banks and regulators. While banks need to be adaptive and dynamic to thrive, they also need to safeguard trust by approaching innovation responsibly and purposefully. The risk and compliance professionals at banks play an invaluable role in making that a reality. They do so not by simply saying yes or no to a new product or service but by developing the necessary expertise and bringing their experiences and perspectives to bear in rapidly changing environments.

The OCC recognizes that rapid innovations also require a more responsive approach by regulators. We are committed to being agile and credible on financial technology developments so that we can balance prudence with innovation and growth. Freezing the banking system in place is not an option, nor is blindly embracing all innovation for innovation's sake. We must be able to navigate a more nuanced path, where responsible and purposeful innovations can be brought to market and a combination of controls, culture, and common sense can prevent irresponsible innovations from emerging.

Edward Bowles
The giddy Pace of Change

Since we met in Frankfurt in January 2023, the world has become fascinated and terrified – in almost equal measure – by 'Artificial Intelligence' (AI). It is just the latest, but perhaps most significant, recent tech-driven distraction for industry, policy makers and the public at large. The risk with this newest of shiny baubles is that it crowds out focus on some of the other areas of innovation – but that may not be a bad thing.

We have been through a phase where knee-jerk reactions to some of the other activities has been the defining characteristic, in some cases understandably – eg in the case of the fallout from FTX. What this event showed is that some more hasty prior policy responses, such as the EU's Markets in Crypto Assets (MiCA) Regulation, was inevitably focused on a few areas that inspired it, eg Asset Referenced Tokens (ARTs), but did not cover important aspects of the broader crypto ecosystem, which FTX exemplified, ie governance of crypto exchanges. As events have come to show, ARTs are largely non-existent as a feature in the industry, and that was true even as early as the Council meetings on MiCA – but it did not stop the European Council's Working Group from spending two-thirds of their time discussing them. This is not to criticize MiCA, but to illustrate the point that sometimes, moving too fast means you create a policy or piece of regulation that is, in some material aspects, out of date by the time it is implemented. This is the dilemma that regulators face with tech – it can move so fast that they can't keep up, but at the same time, some things just turn out to be hype and fizzle out. Therefore, the 'wait and see' approach has its merits.

For those jurisdictions that do adopt more of a deliberative approach, eg the Monetary Authority of Singapore, they remain actively engaged with market participants to ensure that they have a good working knowledge of what is going on in the industry. In respect of the market for digital assets (in its broadest sense – not merely unbacked crypto currencies), this is obviously a challenging exercise, because the nature of the industry involves a multiplicity of actors, from established firms, some of whom are already regulated in certain product areas, to the communities of individual developers that are writing code and innovating with new applications for the blockchain(s) that they are aligned with. Some of these communities are loosely known as DAOs (decentralized autonomous organisations).

What is the scale of activity in this latter space? The Electric Capital Company produces regular analyses[1] of the number and distribution of self-employed develo-

---

1 https://github.com/electric-capital/developer-reports/blob/master/Blockchain%20Developer%20Geography%20Analysis%202023.pdf.

https://doi.org/10.1515/9783111340937-007

pers working in the 'Web 3' space, and the latest report indicates that there are over 23,000 coders working across a number of different blockchains, and that the US share of these is reducing to other jurisdictions. These numbers only relate to those working on open blockchains (as opposed to forked), and does not include coders working in established firms. The Annual Report for 2022, published in January[2] identified an average of 471,000 code commits per month, and a growing number of coders having joined each of the communities (Bitcoin, Ethereum, Solana etc) despite the 'crypto winter'. All of which is to say that policy makers have a lot of ground to cover, if they are truly to stay across the pace of development, and especially whilst the world is distracted by other issues like the emergence of AI.

It is worth bearing in mind that engineers are generally guided by two goals: shipping the product and getting 'product market fit' (PMF), through scaling adoption. If it becomes clear that getting to scale is not going to happen, despite best efforts (marketing, partnerships, code tweaks, etc), then products tend to get deprecated. If you are a regulator that has spent resources on rushing out new rules at the earliest sign of a new product (or, even, just a White Paper), only to see that product disappear, whilst you may be relieved, you are more likely to feel that it might have been better to wait a bit longer. Working with industry to ensure that new products can be developed in a way that protects consumer interests and upholds wider policy objectives, including promoting innovation, is the central challenge today. The pace of change requires more focus and resource from policy makers for this.

In my view, it is incumbent on policy makers to take a lead here and find new and better ways to engage with the broadest cross-section of actors in the industry. One regulator that has set a new benchmark for others to follow is CFTC Commissioner Caroline D Pham, who announced the creation of new sub-committees for the Global Markets Advisory Committee on 28 February[3], including a new Digital Assets Sub-Committee. Let's hope that other regulators find inspiration in this approach, which will serve them and all of us better in understanding the fast pace of potentially bewildering innovation, some of which will never scale or, therefore, trouble regulators.

---

2 https://www.developerreport.com/developer-report.
3 https://www.cftc.gov/PressRoom/PressReleases/8668-23.

Cecilia Skingsley
How should we approach Crypto Assets

The crypto ecosystem has received a great deal of attention recently. I would like to briefly lay out couple of facts. First, over the past year the sector witnessed catastrophic price falls, bankruptcy, and allegations of fraud. Second, over a one year time period, while the S&P 500 is down approximately 14 %, the crypto market is down 53 % and counting. These developments have highlighted the challenges and structural limitations inherent in the crypto markets. But they have also added a sense of urgency for authorities to act. Let me suggest that there are three potential lines of action drawing from the Bank for International Settlements (BIS) research in this area.

First, ban specific crypto activities. Second, isolate crypto from traditional finance (which is now apparently known as TradFi) and the real economy. And third, regulate the sector in a similar manner to TradFi based on the similarities between the activities involved.

The **first option** is to ban crypto, which is the most extreme one. It would have the benefit that potential harm to the financial system would be eliminated. On the other hand, potentially useful innovation from crypto could be lost or delayed. The **second option** is to **make crypto a niche activity**. This could be done by limiting the flow of funds into and out of the traditional finance sector. The advantages of this approach would be that authorities could avoid giving crypto a regulatory "seal of approval" and could prevent crypto from damaging the real economy. But this approach has also challenges. First of all, a fully effective firewall may not be feasible in practice. The new standards issued by the Basel Committee on Banking Supervision on banking sector activities in crypto are a significant step in the right direction. They show that this approach might work for banks, but there are other entities with less constrained investment mandates that could still be drawn into the crypto world, lured by the promise of high returns.

This bring me to the **third approach** which is to **regulate crypto in a similar way to traditional finance.** To pursue this approach, authorities could map activities performed in crypto markets to traditional finance and then use similar guiding principles to regulate them. For example, last year CPMI-IOSCO published guidance on how the Principles for Financial Market Infrastructures (PFMIs) could apply to systemically important stablecoin arrangements. This guidance encourages the stablecoin arrangements to observe the PFMIs and key considerations related to governance (P2), the framework for the comprehensive management of risks (P3), settlement finality (P8) and money settlement (P9).

Of course, this approach has also challenges. One is to establish an appropriate map between activities and entities in crypto and their traditional finance counter-

https://doi.org/10.1515/9783111340937-008

parts. Another one is enforcement – given the lack of clear reference points, whether these be firms or individuals, in some cases in decentralised finance. The public response that is being developed as we debate these issues also needs to be related to an accurate assessment of the value of the new forms of technology that underpin crypto and distributed finance in general. I believe that there is merit in them, but we need to know more about what improvements they can actually bring to the financial system.

This brings me to my daytime job. We at the BIS Innovation Hub are doing our part to inform policy makers about what technology can do. Among other things we are experimenting with distributed ledger technology. But we are also comparing this with what can be achieved by using traditional rails. In any case, a central aspect in these experiments is cyber security. We are seeing that technological innovation can create new opportunities for efficiency and scalability, but at the same time it creates new vulnerabilities related to cyber attacks.

III. NBFIs

Tobias Adrian
Policy Approaches towards NBFI Vulnerabilities

After the 2008 Global Financial Crisis, regulatory reforms increased the resilience of the banking system, as we saw during the pandemic. However, risks have not disappeared. For example, the rapid and significant growth of nonbank financial intermediation, or NBFI, in intermediating global credit and cross-border capital flows indicates that risks have moved to other parts of the global financial system. Vulnerabilities in the increasingly significant NBFI sector have also been amplified by incentives for investors to take on additional risks during the period of low interest rates and low asset price volatility that followed the Global Financial Crisis.

These developments contributed to some of the recent episodes of financial market turmoil and stress that originated from, or were magnified by, NBFI. The most prominent examples of these episodes were the "dash-for-cash" of March 2020 and the UK pension fund crisis last year. Both events also highlighted how information gaps are impinging upon effective market monitoring and supervisory horizon scanning and stability surveillance. This has hindered timely imposition of market discipline and policy action that could attenuate the build-up of vulnerabilities and amplification of shocks by NBFI, eventually forcing central banks to intervene to preserve financial stability when shocks occurred.

At the current juncture, the goal of normalizing monetary policy imposes constraints on central banks in providing liquidity to capital markets for financial stability purposes. This makes addressing vulnerabilities following shocks difficult and increases the onus on action early on to maintain stability, including importantly, through closing information gaps, enhancing horizon scanning, and strengthening prudential regulation.

Let me give you one example that we examined in depth recently in the context of our surveillance and policy work: the **liquidity mismatch** between open-end funds' asset holdings and their liabilities.

Investing in relatively illiquid assets, such as high-yield corporate bonds, have made open-end funds vulnerable to investor runs during times of market stress. This is because while investors can redeem shares daily, at a fixed price, it can take fund managers significantly longer to sell underlying assets to meet these redemptions during times of stress. In a market with falling asset prices, this can translate into investors redeeming at prices significantly higher than those reflecting the full trading costs, and this can generate an incentive for them to redeem and demand liquidity before others do. The resulting spike in investor redemptions can materially amplify liquidity imbalances and depress valuations in financial markets when they force funds to sell assets quickly in stressed markets.

https://doi.org/10.1515/9783111340937-009

In our 2021 *policy paper on Investment Funds* and the October 2022 *Global Financial Stability Report,* we argued that the **liquidity mismatches of open-end funds can contribute to fragility in asset prices and deserve policy attention.** For example, a decline in fund liquidity similar to that seen in March 2020 can increase bond return volatility by more than 20 percent.

What can policymakers do to address this vulnerability? Several liquidity management tools are available—including swing pricing, anti-dilution levies, in-kind redemptions, and redemption gates. However, their use may fall well short of optimal. **A key limitation** is that decisions regarding whether, and when, to use these tools is usually vested with fund managers and not with regulators. Nor is it mandated under regulations. Where private incentives and financial stability goals are not aligned, this will imply that available tools will not be used optimally.

Authorities should ensure that **liquidity management tools are available *and used*** by funds. They could mandate use where necessary, as well as provide guidance to encourage use of the tools and mitigate possible stigma effects. Finally, **matching the redemption terms that are** offered to end-investors to the liquidity of underlying assets—especially where market liquidity is low—is also an option worthy of further exploration.

Liquidity mismatches of open-end funds are an important issue given that these funds' holdings represent about one-fifth of assets intermediated by NBFI. But there are certainly **other vulnerabilities** related to the NBFI sector that we should be concerned about as well. Take, for example, *liquidity spirals* that result from a combination of leverage and low levels of market liquidity—which are a dynamic we have seen at play in the recent episode of financial market turmoil centered around UK pension funds.

Another important characteristic of the NBFI sector that is especially relevant to financial stability is its interconnectedness—for example, with global systemically important banks, which can provide a key shock transmission and spillover channel across financial institutions and asset markets. We saw this interplay of crowded trades, excessive concentration, and the interlinkages between NBFI and global systemically important banks at work in amplifying the stress impact of the default of Archegos Capital in 2021.

At the IMF we are actively working on improving our understanding of these vulnerabilities, and on providing guidance to policymakers on how to address them.

In this context, addressing data gaps is paramount. In the NBFI sector, these gaps are significant even for regulators, hindering access by both regulators and market participants to timely and adequate information to address risks and vulnerabilities appropriately. This indicates that priority needs to be given to enhancing the quality and timeliness of market disclosures and regulatory reporting by NBFI. Practically, this may need an iterative process where supervisors engage in risk assessments and identify key improvements needed in data availability. Based on improved data and risk assessments, stress tests of subsectors with high systemic risk potential could become a powerful supervisory tool. Regulators can also take an indirect approach to NBFI vulnerabilities. For example, banks that provide leverage and liquidity to high-risk nonbank intermediaries can improve the risk management of their NBFI exposures—the lack of which was evident in the Archegos and UK Liability-Driven Investment cases. Transparency of leverage and consistency of its measurement, which also need to be improved, could significantly improve the situation here.

In sum, as a first line of defense, robust surveillance, regulation, and supervision of NBFI is vital. Priorities should include closing key data gaps, incentivizing risk management by NBFI, setting appropriate regulation, and intensifying supervision.

In addition, well-designed central bank tools for the provision of liquidity can potentially support the necessary pace of monetary policy normalization while mitigating the risks of widespread market dysfunction. A framework to consider **when** and **how** central banks should support NBFI entities experiencing liquidity problems is needed. If strains emerge in financial markets, the availability of additional tools aimed at providing liquidity and supporting financial stability may help improve tradeoffs, particularly in an environment of high inflation.

Program design is crucial. It must address the source of the problem while mitigating moral hazard, containing the risks to the central bank, and providing incentives for market-based financing to resume. This means that the bar for direct central bank support should remain high. And if intervention is warranted, there is a need for a clear framework to ensure that support is targeted and temporary.

Regarding the type of central bank interventions, there are three broad categories: (1) discretionary marketwide operations, (2) standing lending facilities, and (3) discretionary provision through lender of last resort (LOLR) arrangements.

First, discretionary marketwide operations may be required to deal with broad market liquidity stress events. "Marketwide" refers to asset-purchase and lending operations aimed at re-establishing proper functioning of a market segment (such as government bonds), or to cope with stress in a NBFI segment (such as money market funds). "Discretionary" means that the timing and amounts of the operation are decided by the central bank. Lessons from previous stress events highlight that such operations should be (1) temporary, (2) targeted at those segments of the NBFI ecosystem where further market dislocation and disintermediation could have adverse macro-financial stability implications, and (3) designed to restore market functioning while containing moral hazard (King and others 2017). In the past, programs have been "time-bound" if the amount announced is sufficiently large to influence market expectation. Alternatively, the program could be "state-contingent" and "self-liquidate" to facilitate exit once market stress abates. In addition, central banks should guarantee that appropriate risk mitigation measures are in place.

Regarding the timing of discretionary marketwide interventions, early provision of liquidity may be preferable to avoid contagion and lessen solvency risk, although it risks increasing moral hazard. A framework based on "discretion under constraints" should be in place. This means data-driven metrics should guide the decision to intervene (the constraints), while policymakers ultimately retain the discretion on whether to intervene. The metrics may be based on a heatmap of indicators—such as funding spreads, premium in relation to a risk-free benchmark, margin requirements, trading volumes, bid/offers spreads, and price volatility—with appropriate thresholds. This can be complemented with more sophisticated methods based on forecasts of the short-term distributions of these indicators. The thresholds should ensure that the central bank will contemplate intervening only to respond to extreme tail risks. While these metrics are important guideposts, policymakers' judgment remains crucial in the decision to provide liquidity and ameliorate systemic risk.

Second, access by NBFIs to central banks' standing lending facilities could be granted to reduce the risk of fire sales and spillovers to the financial system. In contrast with discretionary marketwide operations, standing facilities are permanently available at the initiative of the eligible counterparties. Importantly, the bar for such access should be very high to avoid moral hazard. Central banks should coordinate with NBFI regulators to ensure that the appropriate regulatory and supervisory regimes are in place proportionate to the risk profiles of the different types of NBFIs, some of which may not qualify because of a high-risk profile. The central bank should also charge a sufficiently high rate to discourage recourse to the facility in normal times (IMF 2020).

Third, in case of idiosyncratic (not marketwide) stress at a systemically important NBFI, central banks should be prepared to act as LOLR. In some cases, an ex ante designation of a systemically important NBFI may be in place with accompanying appropriate supervisory and regulatory guardrails (in nonsystemic cases, the institution may be left to the relevant resolution/bankruptcy procedures to instill market discipline). General LOLR principles applied to banks or standard counterparties provide the template for responses in such cases. The principles affirm that lending should be at the discretion of the central bank, after exhausting other liquidity support options, only to solvent firms, at a penalty rate, fully collateralized, and with more intrusive supervisory oversight (Dobler and others 2016). To compensate for the higher risk taken by the central bank, including possibly because of lower-quality collateral and large exposure, conditions could be imposed on the borrower. These might include conditions on the use of the funds and conditions that the measures taken should have a clear timeline to reestablish the liquidity of the institutions. Extra attention is also needed to protect the central bank through loss-sharing arrangements with the government. Finally, LOLR may be necessary even when standing lending facilities are available. For example, this may happen if a systemically important institution has exhausted its eligible collateral: the LOLR may provide emergency liquidity against lower quality collateral, but with tighter risk-mitigation measures and conditionality.

Transposing LOLR principles to NBFIs is challenging. Criterion for solvency and viability are not as clearly defined for NBFIs as for banks. LOLR could be provided only to institutions fully in the surveillance perimeter of the central bank, which supposes full information transfer from the NBFI regulators and enough capacity at the central bank to process this information.

Finally, clear communication is critical. In the current high-inflation environment, central banks may be perceived as working at cross-purposes during periods of market stress—they may need to provide liquidity to restore financial stability while bringing inflation back to target, both by hiking the policy rates and possibly by shrinking their balance sheets. In these circumstances, central banks should use separate tools aimed at price stability and financial stability, if available. A clear separation of tools may support communication and strengthen the effectiveness of policy action. The communication should clarify the source of the stress; the objectives of the intervention and its modalities; the time horizon of the intervention, if appropriate; and the time and threshold for exit that preferably does not overlap with the timing of monetary policy operations.

Joanna Cound
We need a holistic Perspective on Liquidity Stress

Introduction

In the years following the 2007–08 Global Financial Crisis (GFC), we have seen repeated bouts of market-wide liquidity stress in fixed income markets coinciding
with shocks external to the economy and financial system, such as the pandemic or
Russia's invasion of Ukraine. Much of the commentary on this phenomenon focuses
on the changing composition of the financial system over this period, which has
seen an increase in the proportion of non-bank financial intermediation relative to
bank-based intermediation. Some commentators suggest structural vulnerabilities
in particular parts the non-bank sector are a cause of liquidity stress. This article
will set out why the current focus is unlikely to identify the root causes of liquidity
stress, and aims to offer a more holistic perspective.

The Composition of financial Intermediation

The value of global financial assets has risen significantly since the GFC. Figure 1
shows that in the decade up to 2021, total assets increased from approximately
$267 Trillion to $516 Trillion – driven by an increase in issuance and the valuation
effects of monetary policy. Over the same period, the share of non-bank financial intermediation increased from 44 % to 49 %.

End-investors in markets – retail investors, pension funds, insurance companies, corporates, official institutions, plus endowments, foundations, and charities –
choose between managing their investments themselves, or using the services of asset managers. Figure 2 shows that a minority – 27 % – of global financial assets are
managed 'externally' by asset managers.

End-investors using the services of asset managers can use either separately
managed accounts, or choose to invest in collective investment schemes – like
open-ended mutual funds (OEFs). Zooming in further, where we have data, we can
see that OEFs are typically minority investors in fixed income markets: figure 3
shows the proportions of US fixed income security issuance held by OEFs.

https://doi.org/10.1515/9783111340937-010

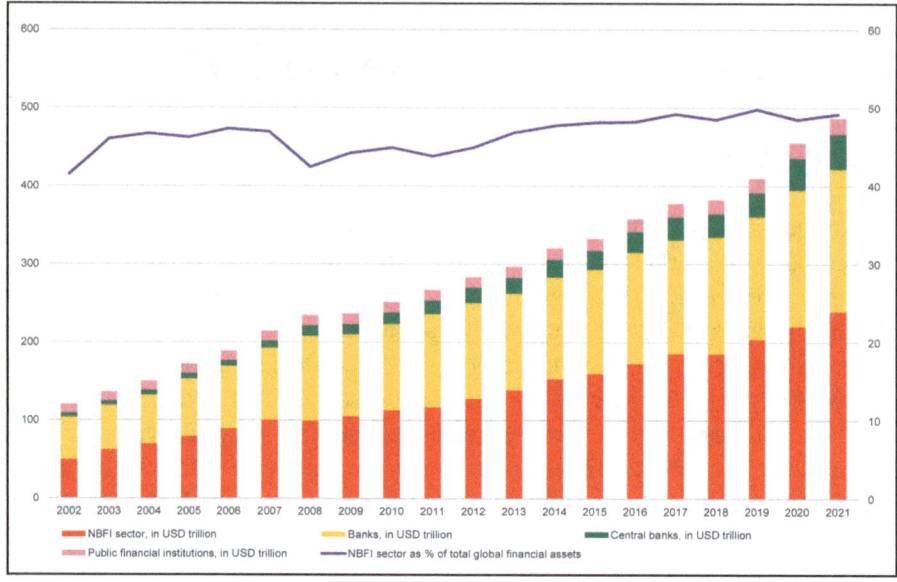

Fig. 1: Total global financial assets by sector, 2002–2021 (Source: Financial Stability Board Global Monitoring Report on Non-Bank Financial Intermediation, December 2022).

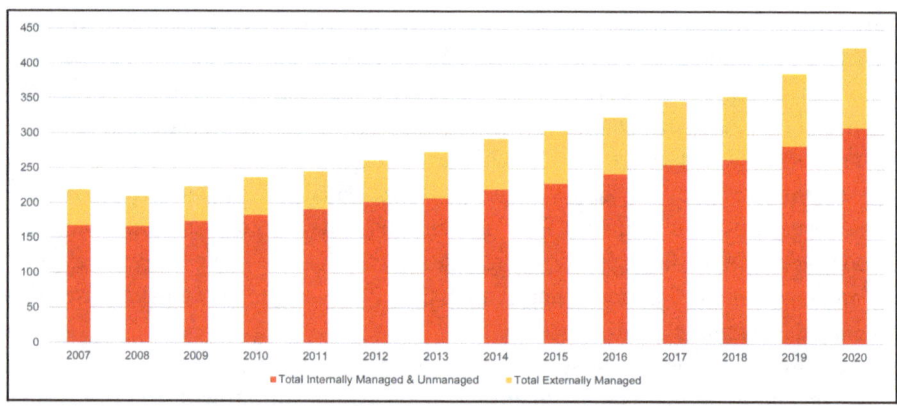

Fig. 2: Global Financial Assets managed externally by asset managers, 2007–2020 (Source: McKinsey Performance Lens Global Growth Cube).

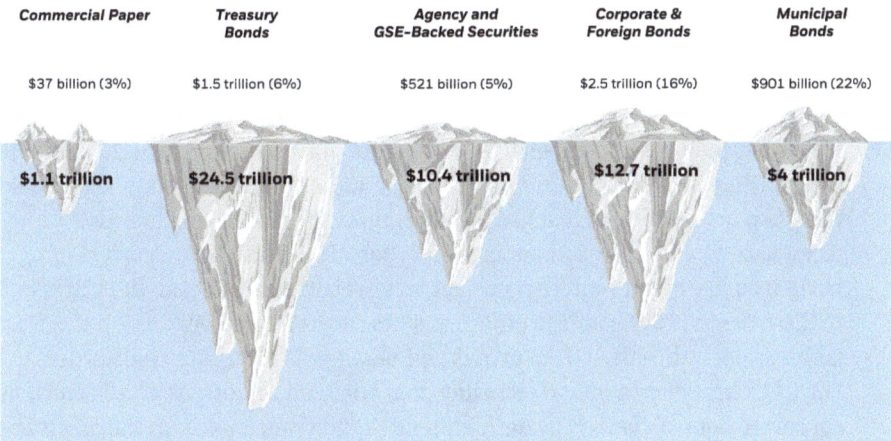

Fig. 3: Mutual funds in US fixed income markets (Source: Federal Reserve Z.1 Financial Accounts of the United States, as of 8 June 2022. Mutual fund data excludes ETFs).

Open-ended Funds as a Source of liquidity Demand

Discussion of liquidity dynamics in the non-bank sector of the financial system often centres on OEFs. In part, this is because OEFs are very transparent: they are required to make frequent detailed reports on their holdings and activities, which is often not the case for the range of other types of end-investors in markets.

However, some commentators have suggested some OEFs may generate liquidity demands and amplify market movements disproportionately to their relative market share – which they put down to a 'liquidity mismatch' in some types of OEFs offering daily liquidity; and a risk of 'first-mover advantage' incentives arising from the collective investment structure.

Before discussing each concern, it is worth recapping some fundamentals: OEFs do not face bank-like run risk. Bank depositors hold a debt obligation on the bank, their principal must be returned at par, and bank runs can occur when depositors demand their money back in short order.

By contrast, OEF investors have an equity stake valued according to their pro-rata share of underlying fund assets and bear all investment risks. Redemptions are generally met by selling a representative sample of fund assets, rather than relying on cash or near-cash assets. OEFs therefore face redemption risk: that is, the risk of difficulty in meeting investor requests to redeem shares for cash within the time-frame required without negatively impacting remaining shareholders. These risks are considered at the fund design and portfolio construction phases, as well as on an ongoing basis; OEFs are designed to ensure their dealing and pricing terms are consistent with the assets they invest in:

- OEFs investing in inherently illiquid assets present a liquidity mismatch if daily dealing is offered – this covers assets that do not trade frequently and are not traded on public markets, such as real estate, infrastructure, or other private assets. OEFs invested in these assets should not offer daily dealing and should integrate notice periods that are appropriate to the underlying market.
- Some securities – for example certain types of asset-backed security – might trade frequently but require more upfront preparation to do so. OEFs invested in these assets may be able to offer investors redemptions every day, but should make use of notice periods to allow fund managers to prepare trade orders.
- For OEFs invested in public securities that trade on an intraday basis (such as corporate bonds), there is by definition no liquidity mismatch (as the assets are priced and traded continuously) and daily dealing is suitable, since it matches the underlying market.

As long as the trading frequency of an asset corresponds with the dealing frequency of an OEF, no liquidity mismatch exists, given the investors in the fund are equity shareholders and loss absorbing. But OEF managers should account for the fact that the cost of accessing liquidity might vary with market conditions – and take steps to mitigate any adverse impact trading has on the fund's remaining investors, for example through measures such as swing pricing, discussed below.

Liquidity Cost and 'First-Mover Advantage'

Variation in asset liquidity means OEF managers must consider liquidity risk at the fund design phase as well as on an ongoing basis. Asset liquidity and tradability should be considered alongside fund dealing terms, and the fund price offered to end-investors should incorporate liquidity costs through anti-dilution mechanisms like swing pricing.[1]

Anti-dilution mechanisms are a means by which OEF managers can mitigate first-mover advantage risk arising from the collective investment structure of OEFs, which may occur when one set of investors are motivated to transact ahead of others to gain a better price, negatively impacting or 'diluting' the positions of re-

---

1 Swing pricing is one example of anti-dilution mechanisms. In the US, significant changes to the fund ecosystem would be required for funds to implement it. For further discussion see BlackRock's response to Open End Fund Liquidity Risk Management Programs and Swing Pricing; Form N PORT Reporting, File Number s7 26 22.

maining investors. This is particularly important if funds are invested in asset classes where liquidity costs are more variable, or where prices can be slower to adjust.

Robust liquidity risk management removes any first-mover advantage arising *within fund structures* by making sure the investor(s) who want to trade in or out of the fund bear the cost of doing so. But first-mover advantage *in markets* – the ability for some market participants able to utilise available market liquidity ahead of others – will continue to exist irrespective of investment vehicle. In short, as long as appropriate liquidity risk management tools are in place, OEFs do not place disproportionate liquidity demand on markets.

Sidebar: What counts as a liquid asset?
Some assets – like real estate or private debt – are inherently illiquid and cannot be traded at short notice. At the other end of the spectrum, large-cap equities and sovereign bonds like US Treasuries trade frequently at high volumes intraday on all trading days. Within this spectrum, some assets – like asset-backed securities – trade frequently but have unique market structures that require special consideration; while others – such as High Yield or Emerging Market bonds – trade frequently but with variable liquidity cost (see figure 4). Judgements about asset liquidity must therefore be informed by observations of trading volume as well as trading costs.

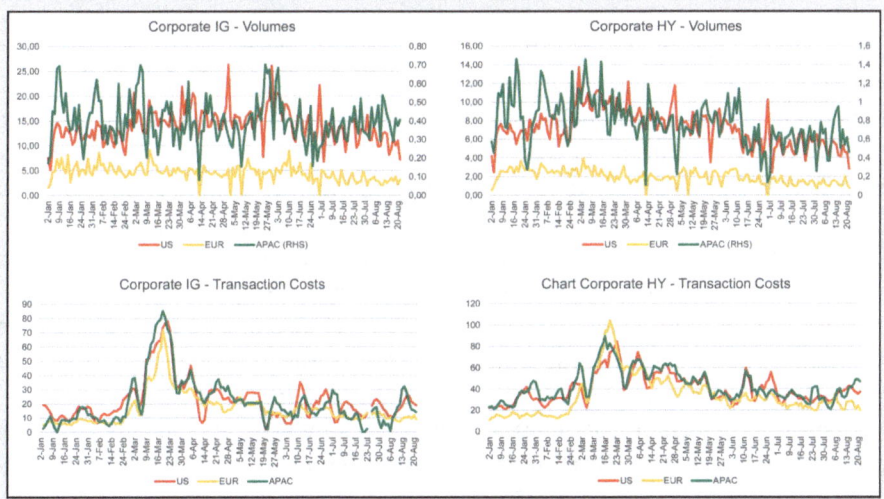

Fig. 4: Trading volumes and costs for corporate bonds during 2020 (Source: MACP+, IDC CEP, Tradeweb, TRACE (US); AxessAll, IDC CEP, Tradeweb (EU & APAC)).

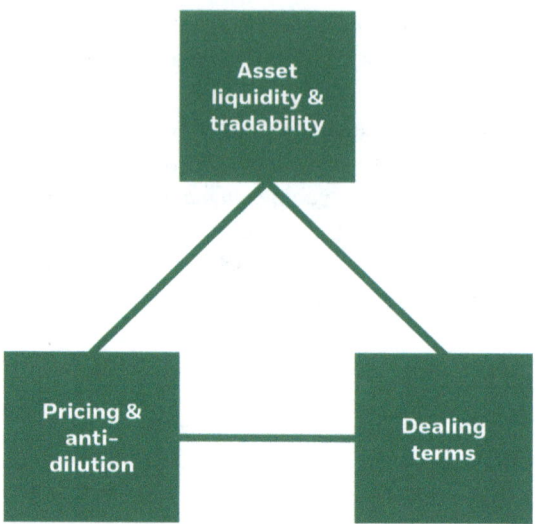

Fig. 5: Liquidity risk management considerations.

Policies to address liquidity stress

More can be done to enhance OEF liquidity risk management and mitigate first-mover advantage in funds. Policymakers should ensure all asset managers have the full liquidity management toolkit at their disposal and are operationally able to use it. But care must be taken to avoid restrictions on OEFs that compromise their ability to hold and trade assets on a level playing field with other types of investors and take advantage of first mover advantage *in markets* – for example by unduly limiting the range of assets that can be held in daily dealing funds.

Addressing market-wide liquidity stress requires, however, a market-wide perspective. This means looking holistically at all investor types, and considering the strong influence regulation, intermediaries, market structure, and transparency have on liquidity dynamics.

Post-GFC regulation continues to impact liquidity demand and supply during market stress events. Central clearing and collateralisation mandates have mitigated counterparty risk and poor transparency, but replaced them with liquidity risk: market volatility is reflected in heightened demand for cash to post as margin, increasing liquidity demand on the system. At the same time, capital and liquidity requirements have made banks more resilient, but curtailed their ability to warehouse risk and move cash through the system, hampering intermediation capacity liquidity supply.

It is for policymakers to decide whether the right balance has been struck between the measures taken to promote resilience post-GFC, and the structural changes they have embedded into the financial system.

That said, given global fixed income markets grew by more than 50 % in the ten years up to 2021, while market intermediation capacity has remained flat, policymakers should consider whether systemic liquidity supply could be improved by targeted guidance on the usability of banks' prudential buffers. Beyond this, trading in bond markets could be improved by – for example – improving availability of fixed income post-trade data, and standardising bond issuance to allow for more bonds to trade on all-to-all platforms, and larger, more liquid issuances; and creating conditions for better integrated bond markets.

On the other side of the equation, policymakers could consider whether excessive liquidity demand could curbed. Reviewing collateral eligibility for central clearing counterparties (CCPs) could lessen market participants' need to sell down assets to meet margin calls. For example, money market fund units could be deemed eligible collateral for margin and transferred directly between end-investors and CCPs, avoiding a situation where MMF units are redeemed by one investor only for funds to be transferred and reinvested into an MMF by the receiving party.

Martin Moloney

Building the financial Stability of Investment Funds

Abstract: This article argues that the Financial Stability Board's ('FSB') policy mak-ing process to manage the potential amplification of financial market shocks by in-vestment funds shows all the characteristics of a pragmatic, progressive and conser-vative approach to policy making as would be indicative of an awareness of the bounded rationality characteristic of this policy making process.

It is argued that the available analysis of the March-April 2020 COVID-related market events supports such a bounded rationality perspective on this policy issue because the available analysis is characterised by numerous points of evidently in-adequate understanding.

However, the published FSB documents also present the FSB as engaging in a more comprehensively rational policy making process. It is argued that these fea-tures are inessential to its core purposes and those elements of the presentation are best understood as being there for legitimate aspirational signalling reasons about the policy making process and in support of emerging financial economics work on investment fund redemptions, but may not be the most persuasive presentation of its policy conclusions.

Paradoxically, the presence of features suggesting a more nuanced and author-itative reasoning makes the FSB's publications on this matter apparently susceptible to criticism, while actually leaving its core analysis and arguments untouched. This observation is illustrated by going into the merits of reasoning to policy conclusions which involve assuming the existence of a first mover advantage.

On this basis, I conclude that the FSB policy making process with regard to open-ended Investment Funds is a strong example of good policymaking at a global level with potential for being presented in an improved way which might improve its persuasiveness.

Introduction

The purpose of this article is to examine the changing mix of financial economic reasoning and policy analysis in the policy work of the Financial Stability Board on

Note: The views expressed in this article are perspectives developed by the author and do not indicate the policy positions of IOSCO or any of its member organisations. Notwithstanding any glosses on the analysis presented by the FSB, the article should be understood as agreeing with the core analysis and conclusions presented by the FSB.

https://doi.org/10.1515/9783111340937-011

promoting the financial stability of investment funds over the last ten years. The article should not be read as a contribution to financial economics but as a contribution to the understanding of the policy making process and its public presentation. The author was a policy -focused rather than an economics-focused participant in this process. While there is an extensive academic literature on public policy making, I avoid any engagement with that by making the intentionally naïve assumption that policy making, whatever else it may involve, involves, a phase of presentation of rational analysis in which policies are recommended and reasons put forward as to why those policies are in the public interest.[1]

The background to the particular policy making process reviewed here is that in 2013, the Financial Stability Board (hereafter 'FSB') which had been established in 2009 by the G20 in response to the 2008 financial crisis, published high level recommendations on what was then termed 'shadow banking' but which has come to be collapsed into a broader concept of 'Non-bank Financial Intermediation' (hereafter 'NBFI'[2]) since then.[3]

In its 2013 Recommendations, the FSB indicated a two-pillar approach of creating a monitoring framework to monitor the build-up of leverage and risks outside the regulated banking system, what we might call growing 'systemic vulnerabilities', and to identify policy recommendations to strengthen the existing regulatory frameworks which already applied outside banking. The purpose of this latter stream of activity was to tackle what the FSB calls 'structural vulnerabilities'. (I will

---

1 For an easily available and useful basic overview of the many issues in the analysis of public policy, using the example of Obamacare and with extensive references to further reading, see Kimberly Martin, Keith E. Lee and John Powell Hall (n.d.) *Public Policy, Origins, Practice and Analysis*, University of North Georgia, *public-policy.pdf (ung.edu)*. In Harold Laswell's well-known taxonomy of the stages of policy making, set out there, the presentation of the reasons for a policy seem to me to be involved mainly in the policy formulation stage of the process, but are also closely connected to the legitimation stage of the policy process.
2 The FSB defines 'NBFI' as made up of "*a diverse set of financial activities, entities and infrastructures. Non-bank financial institutions – comprising investment funds, insurance companies, pension funds and other financial intermediaries – have different business models, balance sheets and governance structures, and are subject to distinct regulatory frameworks within and across jurisdictions.....*". *Non-Bank Financial Intermediation – Financial Stability Board (fsb.org)*.
3 See Financial Stability Board: *Strengthening Oversight and Regulation of Shadow Banking An Overview of Policy Recommendations*, 29th August 2013. The transition from the use of the term 'shadow banking' to the use of the term 'Non Bank Financial Intermediation' occurred in conjunction with a widening of focus away from the arbitrage involved in banks creating non-bank structures within which to hold lending assets towards a more comprehensive focus on the sale of assets by investment vehicles during periods of market stress, which then amplify the stress caused by some initial triggering event. The transition was, I think, one from a focus on regulatory arbitrage and leverage to a focus on liquidity management in stressed market conditions.

come back later to the question of how we should understand these terms 'systemic vulnerabilities' and 'structural vulnerabilities'.)

In this article I focus on one aspect of the follow up work of the FSB to enhance the regulation of securities trading and intermediation[4] so that financial stability concerns inform the regulation of such intermediation. There are a number of important aspects of that work on securities trading and intermediation that I do not look at, but to which this analysis might be extended.[5] The first of those is, arguably, the most important aspect of the post-crisis reforms, which is the creation of regulatory requirements to clear or margin certain tradeable financial instruments in order to reduce counter-party risk in the system. The second area I do not look at is the role of insurance companies and pension funds. The third area I do not look at is 'shadow banking' as originally conceived, namely the generation of leverage at the initiative of banks but located intentionally outside the regulated banking requirements. The fourth area I do not look at in any detail is the work of the FSB on Money Market Funds and short term funding markets. While that work is closely related to the matters covered here, there are a number of details about that work which would divert us from the core theme of this article. The area of FSB work I do look at is investment fund (to be more precise, open ended investment fund[6] sometimes referred to by the acronym 'OEF') policy making.

It is argued in the pages that follow that the process of presenting the justification of the FSB's global policy recommendations for open-ended investment funds is a classic example of what Herbert Simon described as 'satisficing' (an invented term by Simon which can usefully be thought of as intended to contrast with both 'satisfying' and 'optimising' and referencing 'sufficient').[7] It is argued that this can be seen

---

4 By intermediation I refer to the role of professional financial firms in 'intermediating' between end-investors and securities markets. Intermediation in this sense not only includes the provision of services to investors (investment advice, trade execution, securities custody, management of securities lending etc.) but also includes a number of activities, notably market making and other forms of principal trading, where financial intermediaries trade on their own account, as well as providing services to investors.

5 However, the presentational phenomenon which is examined here as it arises with regard to investment fund policy making by the FSB arguably does not occur or does not occur to the same degree in the other areas of the work of the FSB on NBFI. That phenomenon as explained later is the overlay of a rational choice meta-narrative within the published policy document using putative economic analysis.

6 *Open-Ended Fund: Definition, Example, Pros and Cons (investopedia.com)*

7 Simon, Herbert A.(1956). *"Rational Choice and the Structure of the Environment"* (PDF). *Psychological Review*. **63** (2): 129–138. Without delving into the extensive literature, this article by, Gerd Gigerenzer and Daniel G. Goldstein (1996) *Reasoning the Fast and Frugal Way: Models of Bounded Rationality*, Psychological Review 103(4), 650–669 illustrates nicely by comparative study that bounded rationality can come up with as good if not better outcomes than more classically ambitious reason-

from the fact that the process is one of finding a sufficient response to the identified threat to financial stability from the mechanisms of financial market shock amplification. Where the reasoning articulated identifies a plausible understanding of the sources of fragility and a policy approach that is likely to provide some shock absorption, thus reducing the intensity of the fragility, it has achieved as much as can be expected. I contrast this kind of reasoning with an alternative which would seek to develop a simplified model of non-bank financial markets such as would indicate an optimal solution to that open-ended liquiidty transformation funds issue.

In other words, it is argued that this FSB policy making process with regard to investment funds is evidently a policy development process based on inadequate information, incomplete arguments, limited theoretical diagnostic frameworks and incomplete policy solutions. Because of those unavoidable characteristics of this policy making process, seeking a sufficient solution is a wiser course than seeking an optimal solution. But presenting the process as having these weaknesses has proven challenging and this paper identifies the public presentation of the reasons for the FSB's recommendations as displaying features that suggest that the process is more robust than it seems currently to be.

While these features of inadequate information and incomplete theory are often thought of as sources of weakness in policy making processes, they are not fatal precisely because only a sufficient solution is aimed at. Such bounded rationality, I suggest, is not an endogenous weakness within the policy making process that is readily capable of being improved on by better policy making processes but is, rather, an exogenous feature imposed on the policy making process by the character of the topics under consideration.

The key hypothesis presented here is that FSB publications display an overlay of a meta-narrative[8] seeking to suggest that the policy making process is supported

---

ing. http://web.mit.edu/curhan/www/docs/Articles/biases/Gigerenzer_Goldstein_Reasoning%20Fast%20and%20Frugal.pdf.

8 I use the term 'meta-narrative' to refer to the statements within the relevant FSB policy publications which describe the standards of justification that are aimed at and any theoretical frameworks which structure the perspective applied in the policy-focused reasoning within that published analysis. The hopefully uncontentious view of what is going on is that a policy document of the kind the FSB tends to publish will contain three elements: a set of recommendations (i.e. the 'proposed policies'), a presentation of an analysis which gives the reader at least a summary of the reasoning which has led the FSB to make those recommendations (i.e. the reasoning for the proposals) and thirdly an explanation as to why the publication of those policy proposals and that reasoning meets the mandate of the FSB in regard to the specific matter (the meta-narrative). I have not sought to ground this use of the term 'meta-narrative' in any deeper academic discipline of examining public policy reasoning as to do so would add significantly to the burden on the reader. The use of the term meta-narrative is, hopefully, reasonably self-evident merely by the addition of this footnote.

by theoretical insights and analytical processes which are actually not relied on. The addition of this meta-narrative affects the reception of the FSB proposals because that meta-narrative is more susceptible to criticism than what I term here the 'core reasoning' within the FSB's policy making process on this topic.

I begin by characterising the core reasoning as based on managing the financial fragility generated by search for yield by investment funds. I then characterise the restraints on reasoning about investment fund financial stability as substantially exogenous and not open to being dispelled by a better policy making process, at least in the short term. This is intended to constitute a characterisation of the kind of reasoning actually being used. After that I identify two interlinked presentational features of FSB's 2022 Report, which I call the Excess Redemptions Hypothesis and the First Mover Advantage Hypothesis, I trace their origins in the 2017 Report and in the research referenced there. I seek to establish advantages and disadvantages of these presentational features of the FSB reports and indicate how the concept of first mover advantage, in particular, might be robustly used in the presentation of FSB policy reasoning in a manner characterized by strong consistency with the core reasoning.

The FSB's 'Core Reasoning' with regard to the Financial Stability Risk attaching to open-ended Investment Funds

The relevant documents here are a 2017 set of Recommendations and a 2022 review of progress in the implementation of those 2017 Recommendations which doubles as an assessment of their effectiveness. The core reasoning of the 2022 report depends upon and refers back to what the FSB had said in 2017.

In 2017, the FSB published *Policy Recommendations to Address Structural Vulnerabilities from Asset Management Activities* (the "2017 Recommendations").[9] That earlier report sets out fourteen policy recommendations to address 'structural vulnerabilities' from asset management activities that could potentially present financial stability risks. These covered not only the suggested liquidity mismatch in open ended investment funds, but also leverage, operational risk and securities lending activities. The focus of this paper is on the recommendations with regard to liquidity mismatch.

One section of the 2017 Report, Section 2.1, was devoted to explaining how 'liquidity mismatch' could be a structural vulnerability and it is worth looking in a lit-

---

9 *Policy Recommendations to Address Structural Vulnerabilities from Asset Management Activities (fsb.org).*

tle depth at that succinct text. This section of the Report observed that open ended investment funds offered daily liquidity to investors (i.e. the ability to redeem their investment 'daily'[10]). It further observed that asset management activities had increased significantly over the previous decade (i.e. 2006–16), including through open-ended funds that offer daily redemptions to their investors. It observed that there was increased investment in some less actively traded assets. It explained that because of *"... accommodative monetary policy...investors may reach for yield and under-price...liquidity risk"*.[11] It was the combination of these features which created what was described as a structural vulnerability in open-ended investment funds.

Overall, this picture was quite clear: low interest rates leading to search for yield, leading in turn to underestimation of liquidity risk and weak liquidity planning,[12] leading in turn to a sudden realisation of exposure to liquidity risk within investment funds and an enhanced proclivity to exit from the investment in funds in the face of prospective price falls *"....to minimise further negative returns"*.[13] This sudden exit could – when occurring after a shock to financial markets – amplify that shock because the funds would sell securities into a falling market and accelerate and intensify the fall in the prices of those securities being sold.

---

10 While the use of the term 'daily' by the FSB is in accord with common usage, this does not necessarily mean you will get your investment back on the same day. For example the USA SEC describes the situation with regard to mutual funds as follows:- " *Mutual fund shares are "redeemable," meaning investors can sell the shares back to the fund at any time. The fund usually must send you the payment within seven days.*" https://www.investor.gov/introduction-investing/investing-basics/investment-products/mutual-funds-and-exchange-traded-1.

11 Section 2.1, Ibid. The 'reach for yield' referred to here (more often described as 'search for yield' phenomenon) as it affects monetary policy is discussed usefully in Ugo Albertazzi, Bo Becker, Miguel Boucinha (2018) *Portfolio rebalancing and the transmission of large-scale asset programmes: evidence from the euro area* , ECB Working paper Series No. 2125, https://www.ecb.europa.eu/pub/pdf/scpwps/ecb.wp2125.en.pdf. The policy intentionally incentivises investors to move into assets that are less liquid and more risky.

12 This concept of liquidity planning involves both demand and supply management and is itself complicated by the fact that John Kay is almost certainly correct to observes that when looking at liquidity of supply that is a supply security concept and not just a trading volume concept. See John Kay (2013) *A fixation on liquidity is not healthy for financial markets* Financial Times September 17th 2013. https://www.ft.com/content/5e70c3b8-1f83-11e3-aa36-00144feab7de#axzz2fXhskUqR. This would suggest that to plan your liquidity means to improve your reasoned confidence that you can find supply in a wider range of market conditions by preparatory actions. It is notable that the weaker the microstructures of a market, the more liquidity planning pays off. The concept of liquidity is thus often a concept of resilience of supply. These kinds of preparatory actions have a cost. A legitimate concern for policy makers is that rather than incur this expenditure, some market participants will just assume that public purse liquidity – usually from central banks – will be forthcoming to save them from their own failure to take care of the interests of their investors.

13 2017 Recommendations, Section 2.1.

The FSB also acknowledged that historical evidence suggested that open-ended funds generally had not created financial stability concerns in recent periods of stress but said that growth in the sector and increasing holdings of less liquid assets by investment funds suggested that risks may have increased in recent years. Thus, the financial stability risk was linked primarily to the conjuncture, to the kind of assets invested in and the motives of those investing, rather than to the structure (i.e. contractual terms on which open ended fund shares are purchased) of open-ended investment funds as such.

Consistent with this, the emphasis of the recommendations was on increasing transparency to authorities of what assets the funds were invested in and in promoting good liquidity risk management by the funds. Those 2017 Recommendations were subsequently implemented by IOSCO in a separate set of Recommendations to relevant authorities and asset managers to improve the design of funds, the management of liquidity and the management of crises.[14]

It is fair to say that the 2017 Recommendations were carefully caveated, emphasising the distinction between bank deposits and investment funds and only tentatively suggesting such funds were a risk to financial stability and only offering tentative suggestions as to how best to understand that risk, emphasising most strongly the liquidity of assets held. The FSB made its recommendations notwithstanding that degree of countervailing influences promoting the stability of the open-ended investment fund sector which it had acknowledged; it presented itself as making recommendations out of caution. As that report put it *"It is important to address these vulnerabilities before they manifest themselves as realised threats to financial stability"*.[15] The 2017 Report goes on to explain that it is particularly important to address these potential vulnerabilities because open-ended funds are becoming a bigger part of the market and because dealers have more constrained balance sheets.

That the precautionary character of the policy making and the bounded reasoning is emphasised in the 2017 report is evident: these funds are a big part of the system and their assets are less and less liquid and for that reason something must be done, notwithstanding our difficulties understanding the mechanics of the market. This, I suggest is the bounded character of the core reasoning of the 2017 Report on which the 2022 report is built.

That said, it is possible to differentiate three distinct causes of fragility mentioned in the 2017 document, although each is only tentatively presented, consistent

---

14 https://www.iosco.org/library/pubdocs/pdf/IOSCOPD590.pdf.
15 2017 Recommendations, Section 2.1.

with that overall bounded and precautionary approach to reasoning and policy making.

The first cause of fragility is that set out above which we might call the 'search for yield' reasoning and that is part of the core reasoning. This sets out a reasonable narrative as to how the difference in the liquidity profile of the assets held by comparison with the liquidity offered can sometimes lead to significant asset sales by open ended funds. When this is significant relative to the size of the asset market, it can push prices of illiquid assets down and thus amplify shocks. It is probably fair to say that this characterisation of the problem is not strongly supported by cited empirical evidence and relies mostly on the common-sense character of its reasoning and the wide spread acceptance within the financial sector that a 'search for yield' phenomenon did indeed exist.

The second cause of fragility given is herding behaviour. In acknowledging this driver, the FSB provides no further details itself, but rather refers to some work by the IMF.[16] It might better be formulated as the idea that the more a fund manager

---

16 The reference is to the April 2015 edition of the regular IMF publication, *the Global Financial Stability Report*, where the IMF explain first how contagion can arise: "… *if fund managers become more risk averse in response to past losses, and if they are evaluated against their peers or benchmarks, they may be induced to retrench to the benchmark in response to losses. This behaviour, in turn, can induce the transmission of shocks across assets and result in momentum trading (Broner, Gelos, and Reinhart 2006). See Calvo and Mendoza (2000), Chakravorti and Lall (2003), and Ilyina (2006) for other types of models linking benchmark-based compensation to contagion*". The IMF then go on to explain how the separate phenomenon of 'herding' can arise: "*Evaluation [of the performance of As-set Managers for investors] relative to average performance tends to induce risk-averse portfolio managers to mimic the behaviour of peers (Scharfstein and Stein 1990; Arora and Ou-Yang 2001; Maug and Naik 2011). Incentives to herd are reinforced because end investors can exit funds quickly, and mutual fund managers cannot afford to wait until their peers' private information is revealed and incorporated fully in asset prices (Froot, O'Connell, and Seasholes 2001). Vayanos (2004) shows that when fund managers lose AUM because of poor performance, "flights to quality" may occur. Feroli and others (2014) construct a model in which performance evaluation relative to benchmarks creates incentives for fund managers to join selloffs during downturns and chase yield during upturns. Buffa, Vayanos, and Woolley (2014) discuss theoretically how such benchmark-centric assessments can contribute to the build-up of bubbles.*" . It is notable that these mechanisms, although well supported in the literature, are no longer highlighted in the 2022 FSB assessment as significant features of the market to be addressed by FSB Recommendations. The IMF document also usefully differentiates between sources of fragility arising from the intermediation process and sources of instability arising from incentives for end-investors to 'run' from investment funds in certain circumstances in ways that may prefigure the excess redemptions hypothesis from the 2022 Report set out in the next section. In this regard, the IMF cites Elliott, Douglas. 2014. "*Systemic Risk and the Asset Management Industry.*" Economic Studies at Brookings, Brookings Institution, Washington, systemic_risk_asset_management_elliott.pdf (brookings.edu). Elliot does indeed argue that "*…It is critical to determine whether the existence of an asset manager causes the total level of systemic risk to be significantly*

believes that investors in his market will herd the less convinced he will be that liquidity of supply of the assets he is invested in will remain robust because he will fear that all trading will become 'one way' for a period. Not only will the fund manager come to believe that she or he has underestimated the liquidity risk of the managed portfolio but will come to believe that other portfolio managers are drawing the same conclusion. It is clear, however, that this cause is presented by the FSB as supplementary to the first.

The third is a very caveated presentation of the idea that there may be some cases where something called 'first mover advantage' might play a role. It is worth quoting this in full because the argument of this paper is that, like the herding argument, this was not a part of the core reasoning in 2017. Unlike the herding argument, it reappears in the 2022 Report in a strengthened version. The full observation in 2017 is as follows:

> There may also be cases in which open-ended funds could create incentives for investors to redeem ahead of others (i.e. create a "first-mover advantage"). This could occur in situations where the redeeming investors do not bear the full cost of redemptions, and instead these costs are borne by remaining unit holders. However, there are several countering factors that may mitigate any first-mover advantage. Such factors include investment strategy constraints on what assets a fund may sell; many investors' long-term investment horizon and relatively firm investment allocations; application of liquidity management tools to address or mitigate first mover effects; or fund operator fiduciary duty considerations.[17]

---

higher than it otherwise would be..." (P.5) He argues: " *It will generally be ineffective to try to reduce systemic risk at the asset manager level in those cases where the real determinants are decisions by end-investors.*" He provides no source or evidence for this claim which he seems to consider self-evident. It is not clear why it would be ineffective. He goes on to observe that: "One *might argue that it may be appropriate to regulate asset managers even if they simply transmit risk. One could create restrictions to reduce systemic risk, essentially using the convenience of asset managers as entities that can be regulated to deal with risks that arise from the underlying investors.....However, I believe this type of approach would be a mistake. It is likely to push investors' money into channels that are not restricted in this way, dampening socially useful asset management activities and creating new regulatory risks....*" (P.7) Elliot's claim here of this being an undesirable policy is entirely dependent on the degree of potential for transference of investor money to channels that are not restricted in this way and that would occur if regulators were to use the convenience of mutual funds being regulated to help dampen financial fragility. The key consideration is that if a substantial number of investors just would not invest in securities at all if not done through mutual funds (for tax reasons or research cost reasons or numerous other constraints), then Elliot's fear is unfounded and in the meantime is unsupported by modelling or significant empirical evidence. If policy makers can use this convenient access point to financial markets (i.e., asset management) to add stabilising features to markets and investors cannot escape the effect of their regulatory initiative, then the policy would be akin to taxing commercial activities that cannot move outside a jurisdiction: a tried and trusted approach to policy making.

17 2017 Recommendations, Section 2.1.

There are a couple of important points to note about this: in 2017, the FSB was tentative about this idea, did not see first mover advantage as ubiquitous and saw first mover advantage, when it occurs, as subject to a number of significant countervailing factors that are listed. At that time, the concept of first mover advantage was a gloss on the core argument and the policy conclusions evidently did not rely on it. Rather that policy conclusion relied on an alternative argument not so much about the inherent structure of open-ended investment funds but about an emerging systemic relationship between asset quality and liquidity management in the context of a low-for-long monetary policy.

So much for the 2017 Report; some years later in the 2022 document the FSB then looks at whether the FSB 2017 Recommendations were implemented and how effective they had proven to be in the March 2020 (COVID-related) market turmoil that led to substantial central bank provision of liquidity across jurisdictions to stabilise markets. The question to consider is whether the reasoning in the 2017 Report is significantly amended in 2022 work.

With severe data limitations and while acknowledging that it is generalising across potentially significant jurisdictional differences, the FSB found in 2022 that:

- On an absolute basis, open ended funds have increased their holdings of less liquid and illiquid assets since 2017 ;
- Open ended funds, including those that invest in less liquid and illiquid assets, have generally continued to offer investors daily dealing ;
- Overall, open ended funds that predominantly hold less liquid and illiquid assets appear to have decreased their allocations to cash and advanced economy government bonds between 2016 and 2019, before increasing allocations in 2020 and 2021 (likely due to a combination of expectations of elevated redemptions and macro-financial uncertainty during the March 2020 'dash for cash' episode) ;
- Funds with investment strategies that tilt towards holdings of less liquid assets tend to also maintain higher allocations to cash than funds exposed to more liquid instruments ;
- Taken together, these results suggest that there has been no measurable reduction in the degree of structural liquidity mismatch across the OEF sector.
- At regulatory level, the 2018 IOSCO Recommendations on Liquidity and Leverage (which implemented the FSB 2017 Recommendations) were generally implemented in most major jurisdictions but less comprehensively in other jurisdicitons ;
- Liquidity management tools are generally available in jurisdictions examined
- The use of price-based liquidity management tools was widespread but did not necessarily capture all the costs of redemption
- Quantity-based liquidity management tools were rarely used in 2020.

Overall, this is a picture which suggests that regulation has improved significantly, liquidity management has improved notably, crisis management has shown some strengths, but fund design has hardly improved at all. As the report puts it, this constitutes 'meaningful progress' by authorities but further steps can be taken.

The 2022 report goes on to suggest further clarification of the FSB Recommendations to differentiate between funds holding different types of assets would be helpful. It argues that more clarity is needed for funds that invest more than 30–50 % in illiquid assets or funds that invest in assets that are significantly less liquid than *"certain listed equities, certain government bonds and certain other assets that can be readily converted into cash"*.[18] It goes on to suggest that an either/or approach should be developed: either funds investing in these types of assets show that they are going to pass on the cost of redemption to redeeming investors in both stressed and normal times or they should reduce the liquidity offering to investors by reducing redemption frequency or by implementing longer notice or settlement periods. Where a fund does not fall clearly into either category, its managers should be *"able to demonstrate to authorities (…) that their determinations are appropriate…"*[19] This refinement of the 2017 approach is to be further elaborated in precise recommendations to be developed in 2023.

The most reasonable interpretation of this 2022 Report is that it is a well justified doubling down on the 2017 approach, effectively seeking to refine those 2017 Recommendations. It is of course – like any policy reasoning – susceptible to critique. Perhaps criticism of the nascent additional recommendations should wait until the FSB has finalised those. As to the analysis which underpins these recommendations, the assessment of the analysis would be likely to fall into three parts: firstly the overall assessment of the way the 2022 report looks at whether the prior Recommendations have been effective, secondly the understanding of what the events of 2020 tell us about the correctness or otherwise of the 'search for yield' hypothesis (and with what degree of certainty) and, thirdly, assessment of whether the 2017 Recommendations have been implemented. This last stream of potential criticism would be likely to focus on the related IOSCO thematic review of it's Liquidity Risk Management Recommendations (2018), on which the FSB relies.[20] All these potential streams for commentary are reasonable and should form part of a good policy making process, although my own view is that the 2017 and 2022 documents add up to a mutually coherent and sensible policy analysis.

---

18 P.25, FSB (2022), https://www.fsb.org/wp-content/uploads/P141222.pdf.

19 P.26, FSB (2022) https://www.fsb.org/wp-content/uploads/P141222.pdf.

20 https://www.iosco.org/library/pubdocs/pdf/IOSCOPD721.pdf.

The exogenous character of certain restraints on Investment Fund Policy Making

However, it might appear that this core reasoning across both reports itself amounts to a rather weak set of arguments for quite substantial and potentially costly policy recommendations which are now to be doubled down on. One could argue that it is significant that there is limited data to support the analysis, there are evident data gaps to which both the FSB and IOSCO have each themselves drawn attention, there is no overwhelming consensus among financial economists to show that this search for yield is a long-term phenomenon or how it can be addressed without changing monetary policy. Surely, it might be argued, it would be better to come up with better peer-reviewed theoretical frameworks, more comprehensive data and a more convincing argument that the proposed recommendations will resolve this huge fragility in the market.

However, in the opinion of this author that would be an unwise counsel of perfection and the kind of precautionary and tentative reasoning displayed by the FSB is actually characteristic of good policy making and, indeed, essential in order to avoid an excessive hesitation to act in the face of a build-up of risks. But it is important to admit the weaknesses and assess whether they are capable of being remediated as part of the policy making process or whether we should treat them as exogenous to the policy making process and as constraints which should lead us to accept that we must and indeed should engage in the kind of severely bounded reasoning we find in both the relevant FSB publications.

It is, in this regard, evident that the FSB, like all others who study the question, have great difficulty in defining the target we are aiming at: financial stability remains a vague concept and no-one that I am aware of has convincingly defined what a sufficiently stable financial market would look like.

It is possible to define an alternative goal rather than financial stability as a substitute for the goal of financial stability. That would perhaps involve avoiding market situations where asset price movements are having a sufficiently severe impact on the real economy so that central banks need to intervene to provide liquidity from the public purse. While this has a lot of merits, articulating such a goal with any clarity would raise significant moral hazard issues for central banks, because markets participants would seek to adopt trading positions that would profit from that point being reached and putting such trading positions in place might make that trigger point more likely to be reached rather than easier to avoid.

From this I draw the conclusion that financial stability is not only an inherently vague policy target to aim at but attempts to clarify it will come quickly into conflict with a bigger policy commitment to combine having some degree of publicly financed liquidity available in times of crisis while also allowing private persons and entities to trade for their own advantage by taking trading positions which pay out if future market conditions deteriorate, but without distorting that behaviour.

We have even greater difficulty estimating the likelihood of our chosen responses working sufficiently to meet any such target. We have entirely inadequate information to model the behaviour of any market, but on top of that, many of the markets we are speaking of – particularly for short term assets, bond assets and alternative assets – lack the microstructures characteristic of markets for listed equities and are interconnected with related markets in ways which make modelling the response of markets to regulatory initiatives very difficult. Not only do we lack the data and lack the market structures to facilitate modelling, but modelling is also done primarily by economists who seek to simplify away from the complexities of market structure, participant psychology and other such factors.[21]

This difficulty is strongly illuminated when a subsequent market event occurs, and we prove in a weak position when it comes to determining what that event tells us about how well our prior policy has worked. This is the case for the events of March-April 2020.[22] While much can be said about those events, it is fair to say that neither the FSB nor IOSCO nor any other analyst has authoritatively accounted for why the flight to quality assets which was a rational response to the uncertainty triggered by the emergence of the COVID global pandemic, should have turned into a large scale 'dash for cash' and the widespread dysfunction of short term funding, certain treasury and other markets that actually occurred.

In the face of these limitations, the global policy making process with regard to financial fragility of open-ended investment funds has proven to be one, in part, of weighing the importance of the various constraints under which we operate. The precautionary approach adopted by the FSB in 2017, in other words, remains valid. This means that the process is significantly less rigorous than a policy making process might be if the goals could be more clearly defined and if the available information allowed for better modelling of the complex market realities to be influenced by the policy choices.

Many of the boundaries on our insight into these issues are themselves the consequence of policy decisions already made over decades and strongly embedded in our financial system. Some of those are quite fundamental and hard to reverse, such as the creation of legal frameworks which allow risk to be traded as it currently is. Some of those constraints seem less fundamental but still challenging, such as the

---

21 The scale of the challenges are well set out in straightforward language in Mandelbrot, Benoit R. *The (Mis) Behaviour of Markets*, Profile Books, London, 2008.
22 *Holistic Review of the March Market Turmoil – Financial Stability Board (fsb.org).* See also FSB (2022) *Assessment of the effectiveness of the FSB's 2017 recommendations on liquidity mismatch in open-ended funds*, P. 8 for a list of information challenges in assessing what happened in March 2020.

limitations on the range of information available to policy makers about what is happening in markets. But even these data limitations can prove hard to ease. The collection of data is expensive and arguably only displaces the issue from collection to analysis. This is because the behaviours of market participants can be quite complex, collecting the data can sometimes achieve little more than highlight our ignorance.

For that reason, most of the constraints on our reasoning seem better seen as exogenous rather than endogenous. What I mean by this is that if a constraint is seen as exogenous to the policy making process, then it makes sense for the policy makers to accept the constraint on their capacity to reason and to proceed with particular caution, knowing that they are incapable of comprehensively modelling, identifying costs and benefits and of identifying an optimum outcome. Rather, in those situations, a cautious approach which prioritises the avoidance of harm rather than the achievement of reform is likely to be wise, but this should not amount to inaction in the face of a potential risk from a major part of the global financial system. Rather, a progressive approach which first initiates the minimum change credible and adds to that only in the face of evident need is also likely to be wise. Furthermore, the identification of policy tools that have the desired effect notwithstanding there being a variety of market mechanisms potentially at work seems also to be a desirable approach. The primary challenge for policy making will be to assess additional information so as to recalibrate apparently sufficient recommendations proportionately so that they operate in a slightly better way. At its core, the 2022 report does exactly that by refocusing with increased attention on the 'search for yield' analysis and zoning in on those funds with the least liquid assets.

An Excess Redemptions Hypothesis

All that said, it is not always evident that the FSB work on open ended funds is engaging in that kind of self-consciously bound, precautionary, progressive, and cautious approach. Admitting that the constraints being operated under in making policy are significant can be problematic for any policy maker. Some comments in the 2022 Report in particular suggest a somewhat different understanding of what is being done. In particular the 2022 report has a somewhat less tentative and narrower approach to creating a meta-narrative of what is going on.

In the 2022 Report the following suggestion – underlined and quoted in context for ease of reference – is made:

> Open ended funds offer short-term (often daily) liquidity to their investors, notwithstanding that the liquidity of fund investments varies across different open-ended funds and over time

for any particular fund. Some fund investors may overestimate the liquidity of the assets held by the funds in which they invest and may not expect the additional cost or difficulty associated with funds exiting their positions or rebalancing their portfolios. As a result, *in anticipation of large losses stemming from a quick deterioration in underlying market prices and the costs of selling portfolio assets, some investors may decide to make redemptions that are larger than if they were directly responsible for liquidating portfolio assets.* In the presence of liquidity mismatch, investors might have additional incentives to redeem shares if they anticipate that other fund investors will redeem shares and that remaining investors will bear the costs of those redemptions. To the extent that proper valuation or LMTs do not remove this expectation, a first-mover advantage may give rise to excess redemptions, especially in stressed market conditions. Funds' sale of portfolio assets to meet these excess redemptions could result in greater market volatility with the potential to result in negative spill overs.[23]

Echoing Elliot, the underlined text, seems to bring to bear what appears to be a very precise hypothesis. Let us call this important text the 'excess redemptions hypothesis'.

As I read this hypothesis, it suggests that there is a supposed degree of surplus redemptions arising solely from the open-ended character of investment funds. At a notional level that may not seem contentious, but I take it as implied in 2022 – although not stated in 2017 – that there is a precise goal of policy making to eliminate this surplus liquidity. This is an interesting but problematic hypothesis. I will briefly say something about why this is not a good goal for policy making at this time.

It is somewhat difficult to engage with this argument because it is only mentioned in passing.[24] A similar idea was present in the original 2017 FSB Recommen-

---

23 Financial Stability Board (2022) Assessment of the effectiveness of the FSB's 2017 recommendations on liquidity mismatch in open-ended funds, P. 5, underlining added. https://www.fsb.org/wp-content/uploads/P141222.pdf The hypothesis is restated on P. 9.

24 It is also a claim that is always going to be difficult to engage with because it is a subjunctive conditional – a counterfactual – which relies on the exercise of rational imagination to assess it, see Byrne, Ruth M. J., 2005, *The Rational Imagination: How People Create Alternatives to Reality*, Cambridge, MA: MIT Press. In brief using counterfactuals in this way involves claiming that if investments had still occurred but not through the mutual funds then there is a portion of the subsequent crisis-driven sales of the assets invested in which would not have occurred. There is quite a strong reason to believe that treating the scale of investment as invariant in this way is so unrealistic as to render the whole argument irrelevant. The challenges in verifying such a claim are immense. For different views of the issues with such counterfactuals in general see Pearl, J., (2000) *Causality*, Cambridge: Cambridge University Press and Lewis, D (1986) *The Plurality of Worlds*, Oxford: Blackwell. A review of this methodological literature will, I think support the conclusion that the use of this counterfactual-based attempt to determine causality in relation to sales by investment funds into falling markets is unlikely ever to produce proofs that are going to be compelling for cautious policy makers dealing with global financial sector policy issues. In brief, the more speculative the invariance projected to apply in the possible world, the less convincing a counterfactual is. In this case, the sug-

dations on this topic but was present in that document to a modest degree. It is more strongly affirmed in 2022 that it was in 2017. There is one relevant sentence in the 2017 Report which occurs as part of an explanation of the preconditions that would have to apply for liquidity transformation in open-ended funds to lead to amplification of a risk to financial stability. The sentence reads as follows with a critical phrase in parenthesis left out for a moment:

> There would need to be a significant redemptions from funds (.....) together with significant asset sales by those funds (....). Finally, those asset sales would need to be significant enough, either relative to total assets or normal trading volume in particular market segments, to lead to material price declines or increases in price volatility in the secondary market that would be serious enough to impair market access by borrowers...[25]

The logic of this is clear: in effect it is saying that the asset sales from funds have to be large enough to influence the market and they have to have been caused by the pressure on the fund of redemptions or anticipation of fund redemptions; if those two conditions are not met then we cannot say that the movement in the market price was caused by the liquidity mismatch in the fund. So far so good.

However, the 2017 Report did add a caveat within the brackets which I have left out of the above quotation, and which does not seem to follow from the overall observation, and it is this: – *".... from funds (and greater redemptions than would be the case if investors had invested directly in the markets) together with...".* The rest of this paragraph is evidently true because fund sales can't be an amplification mechanism if they are not large enough to influence price and a liquidity mismatch can't be the cause if neither actual redemptions nor – I would add – the fear of redemptions didn't drive the sales. But this phrase in parenthesis adds a significant new idea, namely a counterfactual of what would have happened had the same investors invested directly.

In support of this, the 2017 Report cites a number of papers[26]. As the 2022 Report does not give citations, it is important to look at those underpinning the 2017 origins

---

gested invariance is of a wide range of investors investing directly in illiquid assets, notwithstanding under-developed market micro-structures and high denomination sizes, if investment funds did not exist. This is quite unlikely and, furthermore, is directly linked to the matter being studied, i.e., investment and redemption cost. Strong caution in the face of this kind of plausible but weak argument seems appropriate. However, I don't want to rule out entirely the possibility the financial economics could prove me wrong in this regard and come up with a credible rationale for the excess redemptions hypothesis.

25 FSB (2017) Section 2.1.

26 One paper can no longer be identified because a link is given to a Harvard Business School website but no paper title is given and that website page has continued to be updated to more recent papers.

of this idea. One of these is *The Role of Institutional Investors In Propagating the Crisis of 2007–08* by Manconi, Masada and Yasuda.[27] What that paper actually shows is that there was a transmission channel through mutual funds which held both securitized bonds and corporate bonds. Because the later were more liquid, the mutual funds sold the somewhat more liquid corporate bonds, although the redemption pressure arose from the deteriorating quality of the securitized bonds; thus, the mutual funds mediated an amplification mechanism from securitized bond markets to corporate bond markets. But had those investors invested directly in both securitized bonds and corporate bonds, it seems to me they would still have faced the same problem that the mutual fund faced and it is not evident that they would have behaved differently than to sell their more liquid holdings, namely the corporate bonds.

Reference is also made to a paper by Ellul, Jokastri and Lundblad entitled *Regulatory pressure and fire sales in the corporate bond market.*[28] which shows that insurance company holders of bonds are more likely to sell downgraded bonds if more constrained by regulation. Once again, it does not seem to support this idea that if mutual funds only sold on the same scale as direct holders, then this would not constitute liquidity transformation-driven amplification.

Reference is made to a third article by Gilchrist and Zakrajsek entitled *Credit Spreads and Business Cycle Fluctuations*[29] which is concerned to decompose corporate bond spreads into a firm-specific and an 'excess' element monitoring of which, they argue has a certain predictive power, because an increase in the excess bond premium appears to reflect a reduction in the risk-bearing capacity of the financial sector, which should lead in turn to a contraction in the supply of credit.

None of these papers throws light that I can see on the idea in parenthesis. There is a tautological sense in which a phrase similar to that in brackets must be true, namely that if the investors invested directly there just would be no mutual fund liquidity transformation; but this cannot be the meaning of the point being made because the phrase refers to the level of redemptions having to be greater as well as the holdings having to be held indirectly. In other words, this difficult-to-understand phrase in parenthesis seems to suggest that even if the mutual funds faced redemptions and this drove them to redeem only to the same (unknown) level as would have occurred if the assets had been held directly and sold off, then this

---

27 Journal of Financial Economics, Vol. 104, No. 3, pp. 491–518, June 2012, see also https://ssrn.com/abstract=2235923.
28 Journal of Financial Economics Volume 101, Issue 3, September 2011, Pages 596–620, see also https://www.sciencedirect.com/science/article/abs/pii/S0304405X11000857.
29 American Economic Review, Vol. 102, No. 4, June 2012 pp 1692–1720, see also *Credit Spreads and Business Cycle Fluctuations – American Economic Association (aeaweb.org)*.

would not constitute liquidity mismatch-driven amplification. The point being made seems to be like saying that if I am knocked down by a car and then get a heart attack and die, the car is not actually part of the causation of my death if I was doomed to get a heart attack anyway. There seems to be a quite subtle point being made here which is perhaps moot, since I can't know whether I would have had a heart attack anyway just as I can't know what the level of sales by investors would have been had they invested directly. This is particularly so given that many of them would not have invested at all without the benefits of the cooperative investment option that is available because mutual funds exist.

It is quite possible that I have simply failed to have the imagination to see the point being made or that I have failed to notice an elaboration of the point in one of the papers cited. But in any event the point seems to me entirely unnecessary for the force of the argument in the 2017 Report and the 2017 cited papers do not seem to justify the stronger formulation of this hypothesis in 2022.

If, after this diversion, we return to the 2022 Report, what we notice is that the underlined passage above arises from the interpolation of the concept in parenthesis from the 2017 text into an explanation very similar to that presented in the 2017 text of the search for yield hypothesis, but with the reference to monetary policy no longer present. Instead of the concept of an excess operating as a limit on when liquidity transformation has an amplificatory effect, the phrase now operates not as a (difficult to understand) limiting condition but as a potential scenario. Arguably, this transforms the explanation and certainly suggests a new structural element to the argument that was not present in 2017.

The apparent purpose of the argument, namely, to delimit the target for regulatory intervention, is an attractive one. It is Elliot's argument (see footnote 17 above). This argument would be that investment fund regulation should only be adjusted to deal with issues that are particular to investment funds as a structure, namely excess redemption rates. It would perhaps claim that it is inherently unfair to investment funds to seek to dampen their rate of sales into a falling market below the level of other investors in order to stabilise the market. But this is not clearly stated.

There are at least three potential counterarguments: i) that imposing constraints on fund disinvestment to a greater degree does the fund or its investors no inherent harm by contrast with any comparable alternative investment route for those investors since investors in investment funds will mostly not invest directly in such illiquid high denomination assets and therefore the question of fairness does not arise, ii) that there is a separate investor protection reason to put obstacles in the way of investment funds selling into a falling market because to allow it harms the more persistent investors and this means there is a desirable synergy available of imposing constraints that work both to improve financial stability and to protect investors and that synergy makes this kind of policy proportionate and iii) that there is an over-riding public interest in the expediency of making use of the regula-tory touch points that exist to help stabilise markets, even if there is some resulting disadvantage to investors investing through the investment fund route. However, as the arguments for confining the role of the FSB to tackling excess redemptions has not been made in any detail, it is difficult to work through these issues to a rounded assessment.

First Mover Advantages

What we do need to assess, however, is the implications of the next addition in 2022 to the meta-narrative: "...... . *To the extent that proper valuation or LMTs do not re-move this expectation, a first-mover advantage may give rise to excess redemptions, especially in stressed market conditions.....*"[30]

What we see here is the Excess Redemption Hypothesis being linked to another more powerful hypothesis, that of first mover advantage. What is meant here by first mover advantage I take to be what Nobel Prize winners Diamond and Dybvig mean by first mover advantage.[31] By that I mean, roughly, that as between two de-positors, or in this case investors, one will decide to move now in order to assure themselves that they can exit before other depositors/investors, because if they don't and the others then do, the outcome for remaining investors will be worse. While I suspect this does not work both ways (i.e., the First Mover Advantage Hy-pothesis does not necessarily imply the Excess Redemptions Hypothesis), it seems evident that the Excess Redemptions Hypothesis only makes sense as an effect of the instability supposedly inherent in the mutual fund structure because of first mover advantage.

Diamond and Dybvig developed their elegant model in 1983 in a way that showed well that there was no institution-specific liquidity management solution to the threat of bank runs which would work quite as well as a deposit protection guarantee from the State. To underpin this claim that public money (or rather pub-lic guarantees) was the optimal solution to the financial stability problem of runs on banks by depositors, they modelled a particularly challenging bank run in which the only motive for the depositors to withdraw their deposits was the concern that others might withdraw theirs. Their work illustrated that this was an intractable

---

30 FSB (2022) P. 5, https://www.fsb.org/wp-content/uploads/P141222.pdf.

31 Diamond, Douglas W., and Dybvig, Philip H. "Bank Runs, Deposit Insurance, and Liquidity." J.P.E. 91 (June 1983): 401–19 https://www.bu.edu/econ/files/2012/01/DD83jpe.pdf. See also Douglas W. Dia-mond, Raghuram G. Rajan, *Liquidity Risk, Liquidity Creation, and Financial Fragility: A Theory of Banking | Journal of Political Economy: Vol 109, No 2 (uchicago.edu).*

scenario if viewed from the perspective of optimising the quality of the liquidity management by the banks. Nothing a bank could do to be – and to show that it was – responsibly managing its leverage would eliminate the risk of this kind of a run. This kind of risk is inherent in the bank-depositor contract, given what banks do with depositor's money. Only deposit guarantees will stop this kind of run.

Unsurprisingly this argument has generated a rich debate. That debate has focused on whether it is best to see actual financial instability events as a consequence of an instability inherent in the structure of financial intermediation or whether financial instability is driven primarily by deterioration in the quality of lending or, by extension investment.[32] The detail of that rich debate does not concern us here and I would not be qualified to comment given the terms in which the debate must be conducted. What does concern us is the fact that, right or wrong, Diamond and Dybivg's conclusions are not intuitive because intuitively we tend to see bank runs as driven by weak lending standards by banks.

For these reasons, to support the first mover advantage hypothesis with regard to open-ended investment fund merely be analogical thinking with the Diamond & Dybvig model would create a significant degree of weakness, by contrast with our intuitive understanding, in the degree of persuasiveness of the FSB's policy recommendations. That lack of persuasiveness does not substantively arise from any limitations on the persuasiveness of the Diamond and Dybvig model itself for the purposes for which it was formulated – for which it is highly persuasive. The lack of persuasiveness arises from two distinct frames of reference that arise, namely trying to explain bank runs as such, rather than justifying deposit insurance, and secondly extending the argument to investment funds. I will come back to the reasons why extension to investment funds is problematic in a moment.

On the other hand, there is a tantalising attractiveness to adopting first mover advantage. The most attractive feature of it is from the point of view of financial economists. If Diamond and Dybvig can be extended to investment funds, mutatis

---

32 Thus, Diamond and Dybvig comment: *"...a bank run in our model is caused by a shift in expectations, which could depend on almost anything, consistent with the apparently irrational observed behaviour of people running on banks. "* Ibid, P. 404 For a useful reference giving a sense of this debate, see Edward J. Green and Pin Ling, (1999) *Diamond and Dybvig's Classic Theory of Financial Intermediation: What's Missing?* Federal Reserve Bank of Minneapolis Quarterly Review Volume 24, No. 1. The intuitive concern on the part of those who have questioned the Diamond & Dybvig approach is that bank runs seem almost invariably to be linked to rational concerns about bank lending standards. It is such concern, it often seems, that stimulates a focus on the inevitable losses which arise – and which are baked into the Diamond and & Dybvig model – when a bank is liquidated and its lending assets sold at a discount. On one reading of the Diamond & Dybvig approach it seems to allow the possibility that bank runs might just be random events. In my opinion, despite the comment above, it is not saying that.

mutandis, then it promises an integrated framework for approaching financial instability in numerous financial intermediation mechanisms. A second reason may perhaps be that it promises a desirable clarification of the goal of financial stability policy making with regard to investment funds. Rather than having a general policy goal of making investment funds contribute less to amplification, there is a more specific goal of targeting this first mover advantage. It is a little difficult for a member of the public reading this FSB document to work out what this means.[33] However, unless we have regard to these considerations, the strengthening of the presentational status of the concept of first mover advantage by comparison with the presentation of the search for yield hypothesis seems unmerited.

---

33 It is useful to read the USA Office of Financial Research (2013) paper on *Asset management and Financial Stability* https://www.financialresearch.gov/reports/files/ofr_asset_management_and_financial_stability.pdf which also refers to a potential for "...*investors in mutual funds with portfolios of securities with varying levels of liquidity to have a "first-mover advantage" to sell early, if they believe cash on hand and maturing assets are insufficient to cover redemption requests and that more liquid assets may need to be sold to meet redemptions*" and who in turn refers on to Chen, Goldstein, and Jiang (2010) "*Payoff Complementarities and Financial Fragility: Evidence from Mutual Fund Outflows.*" Journal of Financial Economics 97, (2010): 239–262, https://www.fdic.gov/analysis/cfr/bank-research-conference/annual-7th/chen-goldstein-jiang.pdf. That impressive and influential paper presents evidence which suggests that funds with illiquid assets exhibit stronger sensitivity of outflows to bad past performance than funds with liquid assets. They also find that this pattern disappears in funds where the shareholder base is composed mostly of large investors. While this paper finds empirical support for the idea of investors – particularly smaller investors – seeking a first mover advantage, it does show this effect most strongly present in the most illiquid funds, in terms of assets. In policy terms, this seems to mean that whether investors are seeking advantage over each other or repositioning from illiquid assets to cash because they need the cash – having mis-estimated their own liquidity management needs in the face of low for long monetary policies – amounts to the same policy challenge: how to get funds with illiquid assets to sell less into falling and illiquid markets in ways that amplify shocks. Furthermore, they caution themselves against reading their results as applying to the average investor; they clarify that the results apply only to the marginal investor and are not an explanation of runs on mutual funds (see footnote 3). The significance of the fact that the paper works off a data base of funds investing in equities is unclear as is the lack of a full, separate model for investment fund runs to underpin the hypothesis being tested. My sense is that this paper has inspired a growing number of attempts to look for evidence of first mover advantage in run-like market stress events. On the one hand this literature is welcome in that it trawls through the available data. On the other hand, if this literature is framed as endeavouring to extend the Diamond & Dybvig model to mutual funds, it faces an evident concern of confirmation bias.

Why First Mover Advantage is not persuasive

To say of a scientific argument that it is not intuitively persuasive is not necessarily to condemn it since science often uncovers counterintuitive realities that people are surprised by.[34] But I am suggesting that that lack of intuitive persuasiveness does raise a distinct issue with regard to the choices to be made in presenting the reasoning for policy choices, particularly if the scientific hypothesis is weakly supported. When it comes to policy making reasoning, my own preference would be to rely on hypotheses from financial economics when they are counterintuitive only when they are very well established. That is not the case here, although empirical work continues to be written on the topic. The reasons why it is not the case seem quite substantive.

On the face of it, the problems are that it doesn't align with the day-to-day experience of market participants. The first of the evident problems with extending this idea to investment funds is that it isn't always the case for all investors that they want to avoid valuation losses at points in time. There is a dependence on the time horizon for investment returns to define a sub-group of investors who want to avoid unrealised losses at any point in time.[35] Secondly, the scale of the anticipated valuation losses seems likely to be highly relevant to actual decisions to demand redemption from mutual funds. Thirdly, where the disinvestment is done to hoard cash as a crisis management technique, the exiting investor is also unlikely to be very sensitive to the price of exiting.

However, I think we can analyse a little more the character of the challenges for the first mover advantage thesis in order to understand this lack of persuasiveness. I identify below two different classes of problem: the first arises from the concept of a first mover advantage. Analytically, some kind of first mover advantage seems to arise whenever there is some degree of equivalence of access to a resource that is limited in supply. The precise character of the advantage will depend both on the terms of the equivalence of access and the nature of the resource. But that means

---

34 For example, Newton's first law of motion would not have been considered intuitive in claiming that an object will remain in motion at a constant velocity unless impacted by an unbalanced force.
35 This depends both on the accounting treatment, the remuneration structure of portfolio managers and the kind of investor. It is well understood in markets that there are certain investors who, knowing that prices are about to move downward, will stay invested because they perceive that markets go up and down and they should hold until their investment horizon is reached. Excessive churning of investments can cost more than responding to partial understanding of likely market developments. It should be acknowledged that the original formulation of the first mover advantage hypothesis by the FSB recognised "counter factors" along these lines but gave no indication as to how those interacted with the posited first mover advantage, see Footnote 18 above for the relevant reference.

that because securities trading involves i) market structures (defining equivalence of access among traders), ii) intermediation structures (defining equivalence of access among clients) and iii) multiple different asset (and related proxy and asset derivative) markets, we actually have a whole range of first mover advantages at play in markets. Secondly, the Diamond & Dybvig model deals with a very precise situation, modelling key aspects of bank deposit lending some of which evidently don't translate easily across to investment fund investment.

First Mover Advantages in traded assets

Turning to the first of these, there is at least one scenario in which it seems necessary to mention first mover advantage which has come strongly to light in the 2017–22 period. It is where we also assume that the fund is willing to take some action to prevent a continuing outflow of investors in a period of market stress. We might a little awkwardly call this a 'Dynamic Repayment Policy First Mover Advantage'. If the fund is willing to change its approach to redemptions in a period of market stress, that potentially brings into existence a first mover advantage. Once it is an option that the fund may limit the capacity of investors to redeem (by what is called 'gating') or might impose a price penalty of some sort for redeeming (by what is called 'swing pricing' or a similar mechanism), there is an evident first mover advantage for those who get out of the fund before that option is exercised by the fund, provided they have a reasonable expectation that the change in approach to redemptions will occur.

In the separate area of Money Market Funds recommendations, the FSB and IOSCO have had to acknowledge that previous recommendations did indeed create an undesirable first mover advantage and the FSB has moved promptly in light of the 2020 events to urge jurisdictions to end or limit that first mover advantage.[36] The lesson of that experience is that it is possible to create a 'cliff effect' which in turn creates a first mover advantage. But – and it is perhaps an argument for another time to work through this in detail – if the regulatory intervention to push mutual funds to change their redemption practices in times of stress is unpredictable for investors in its effect, then perhaps no actionable first mover advantage arises. It is surely reasonable to observe – although this is not clearly stated – that the current working assumption of the FSB is that this can be achieved by leaving asset managers a degree of discretion (and unpredict-

---

36 P.21 *Policy proposals to enhance money market fund resilience: Final report – Financial Stability Board (fsb.org).*

ability) as to when to change their redemption policies and/or by changing their approach in both stressed and normal market conditions (for example by imposing swing pricing at all times).

This first example of a first mover advantage might well be better understood as a market structure first mover advantage. Regulation would then be understood as redefining the market structures investors face. The advantage sought by high frequency traders may perhaps be seen as another market structure first mover advantage that can be sought.

There seems to be a second type of first mover advantage that is already present in all market conditions, namely the first mover advantage of getting out of an asset whose price is likely to fall earlier than others. We might call this the asset class first mover advantage. In its inverse form it is the first mover advantage of getting into an asset before its price rises. Arguably this first mover advantage is fundamental to markets and a lot of policy work focuses on ensuring the efficient circulation of market sensitive information and integrity of trading to allow market participants to seek this advantage. It is what drives the price discovery process in markets. In countering Elliot's suggestion, I have argued above that there are circumstances – rare circumstances – in which authorities will wish to curtail the operation of this first mover advantage to keep markets stable. Further argumentation on this point is outside the scope of this article. It is a type of first mover advantage that is increasingly complicated by the emergence of interdependencies between markets, the market for a particular asset, the market for close substitutes for that asset, the market for derivatives commonly applied to that asset and the market for the shares of mutual funds and exchange traded funds that invest in that asset or shares that depend on the value of that asset. It is arguably, by far, the most impactful first mover advantage.

There is a perhaps also a third type of first mover advantage, which is the advantage of getting cash in a period of stress before it becomes harder to accumulate.[37] This arises if it is the case that cash as an asset is about to come increasingly into demand and cash is about to become expensive to procure. Much more could be said about this also. This might be seen as the first mover advantage in markets

---

37 I understand this type of first mover advantage may be what is being somewhat acknowledged in the Footnote 10 on P. 9 of the 2022 Report: *"Competition for finite asset liquidity among different types of investors that hold overlapping portfolios has the potential to produce first mover advantage at a market-wide level. This form of first mover advantage is not the focus of this assessment, which has concentrated on potential vulnerabilities stemming from an OEF's structure. See, for example, Stahel (2022), Strategic Complementarity among Investors with Overlapping Portfolios."*. One would need to debate whether this is solely a process of competition for liquidity or perhaps also competition for purchasing power.

inversely correlated with the asset invested in or perhaps more generally as the first mover advantage in the assets not already invested in.

So far, we have a picture of three first mover advantages, those arising from market structure, those arising from getting into and out of the investment target asset and those arising from other assets. The latter two might be thought of as exercising pull and push influences on the investor.

But we are concerned with a fourth, overlapping type of first mover advantage based on avoiding costs of redemption. Perhaps we might call this 'liquidation cost first mover advantage'. There is a difficulty with trying to conceive of liquidation costs in funds and banks as similar. Diamond & Dybvig observe of their model that it would also apply where there are sales costs arising from illiquidity.[38] But in their model there are no transaction costs. By contrast, in relation to funds we are asked to think of the liquidation risk as predominantly a matter of transaction costs. Banks invest liquid funds in illiquid assets and, nevertheless, provide liquidity back to depositors on demand. Thus the 'cost' being avoided by early movers in a bank run is the cost of premature sale of the banks' assets on liquidation of the bank. But when it comes to investment funds, the reason why a collective investment occurs is to get the benefits of investing together which are sharing management costs and avoiding or minimising transaction costs, which will most obviously be broker fees but can also include taxes and may include the full impact on each investor of the bid-ask spread and, potentially the impact of trading on the market price.[39] The liquidation cost involved seems to be the costs of this type that would occur if the fund were wound up. These costs vary with the type of asset invested in, but they are also close to being capped in a way that bank liquidation costs are not. Indeed, bank liquidation cost redemption seems, for practical purposes, identical with an

---

38 " ... *The analysis would be the same if the asset were illiquid because of selling costs: one receives a low return if unexpectedly forced to "liquidate" early. ...*" Diamond & Dybvig (1983) P. 403. Because, unlike Diamond and Dybvig we are talking about investment funds we are generally talking about traded assets – unlike bank debt which is only tradeable in limited circumstances – and therefore we are speaking about market liquidity when talking about 'liquidity'. This has its own highly complex analytical framework not considered here, see Thierry Foucault, Marco Pagano and Alisa Roell (2013) *Market Liquidity: Theory, Evidence and Policy*, Oxford University Press for a comprehensive and authoritative introduction and chapter 9 in particular for liquidity and market stress.
39 See Blackrock, (2021) *Swing Pricing: Raising the Bar*, Blackrock Whitepaper, https://www.blackrock.com/corporate/literature/whitepaper/spotlight-swing-pricing-raising-the-bar-september-2021. pdf and Borkovec, M., Serbin, V., Zhou, Z., (2016) *Swing Pricing 101: A Closer Look at the Dealing Costs of Investment Funds Across the Globe*. The Journal of Investing, P. 77–89. See also Ulf Lewrick and Jochen Schanz (2017) *Is the Price Right? Swing pricing and investor redemptions*, BIS Working Paper no. 664 which represents an interesting attempt to produce a model of the incentives for redemptions in mutual funds.

asset class redemption first mover advantage. Only when it comes to traded assets can we distinguish between them.

From these observations we might conclude that liquidation costs first mover advantages are specific to the business model of the intermediary. Perhaps what we are dealing with here is a financial intermediation first mover advantage. But I can only tentatively suggest this idea as it would require significant more thought to bottom out this issue.

If this kind of analysis were accepted, tentatively identifying four different types of first mover advantages in traded, intermediated markets with multiple assets, it would suggest two key points: firstly there are invariably a complex number of first mover advantages at play and any empirical testing is going to have to decompose the incentives to act if it wishes to get a refined understanding of the different first mover advantages at play. This is invariably going to be difficult, particularly in markets where different first mover advantages are aligned so that more than one of these first mover advantages incentivises the same behaviours. Decomposing two influences hidden in data may often be achievable, but decomposing four, some of which can be quite complex, is always going to be challenging. That, in turn, means that understanding markets where less detailed data is available is going to be particularly challenging. The significance of this point is underpinned by the likelihood that financial intermediation or liquidation cost first mover advantage is going to be larger – and maybe comparatively larger compared to other first mover advantages at work – in markets with weak microstructures.[40]

But it seems also true that if more than one first mover advantage can be a source of instability at any one time and that a countermeasure can be agnostic as between different first mover advantages (or one that also doubles as an investor protection measure), this is likely to be useful. Paradoxically, in the face of complexity, a less targeted countermeasure is more likely to have greater impact in stabilising markets.

---

[40] I think there may be an argument which would run that all first mover advantages must attach to an asset class and that the variation that can occur is that more than one structure can influence the character of that first mover advantage. Thus market structure might be seen as one influence determining how the first mover advantage in that asset class works if it is a traded asset, but the structure of intermediation can also determine the structure of a first mover advantage. That would mean that market structure and intermediation can combine to co-determine how the first mover advantage for an asset class operates for some or all of its investors or potential investors. I have not pursued this idea as it seems unnecessary to the point of this article.

Thus, we identify two specific and substantial boundaries to using first mover advantage as a tool for policy work: the complexity of first mover influences and the desirability from a policy perspective of focusing on stabilising markets rather than on devising tools to influence individual mechanisms within markets.

Weaknesses of the Argument by Analogy

Refining our understanding of first mover advantage in this way and identifying these persistent boundaries to reasoning about first mover advantage allows us to go back to the argument by analogy to Diamond & Dybvig's model with increased focus. The reason why Diamond and Dybvig's model is so compelling as a public policy argument for deposit insurance is that the first mover advantages it focuses on are very difficult to dispel by any improvement in management practices. It is such a compelling argument in relation to the policy issue of deposit insurance that it is intuitively desirable to seek an analogous first mover advantage along the lines of that studied by Diamond and Dybvig that is inherent in any entity which offers unconditional redemption rights to each of a number of co-invested individuals. The formal similarities seem substantial, but they have their limits.[41]

On that argument, as long as funds offer on-demand redemption they create a first mover advantage to manage; this supposedly makes them fragile in the face of any shock. This argument, if accepted, would change the policy focus. In support of this perspective one can argue that the Diamond and Dybvig model is accepted for banks and can be applied by analogy to investment funds to draw the conclusion that there must be a 'first mover advantage' in any investment funds which has a character similar to that which the acceptance of the Diamond and Dybvig model indicates is present in banks.

But argument by analogy is always a perilous activity. It is almost always an inconclusive form of reasoning, at best ampliative. It suggests that because similarities of one type exist between two different things, that an additional similarity exists.[42] Furthermore economic models are a very specific type of model and one whose legitimate use should be narrowly constrained. The whole question of how to

---

41 It is a little inconvenient for this intuition that Diamond & Dybvig in their paper explicitly contrast the banking deposit contract with other financial contracts as more unstable than those.

42 As explained by Hesse M.B.,1966, *Models and Analogies in Science*, Notre Dame: University of Notre Dame Press, a key challenge for arguments by analogy is how to judge well which characteristics are essential to each of the relevant objects of the argument. In this case, there is a counterargument often articulated that a deposit and an investment are so essentially different that this argument by analogy cannot hold.

avoid the misuse of models in economics is a very large one.[43] But there are a number of obvious difficulties with this attempted use which will give policy makers pause for thought in relying on the analogy. I can do no more here than give a colloquial summary of some of those difficulties to illustrate the policy maker's problem.

The first is that a number of the defined functions within the model, notably the consumption function of depositors in Diamond and Dybvig, seems significantly different than for investors in a fund. Depositors are modelled as seeking the utility of using their funds to consume, but subject to two characteristics: some only want to

---

[43] My understanding of the force of the Diamond and Dybvig model is that its force does not rely on empirical verification of any suggestion that bank runs are always, usually, or often driven by sudden and uncaused panics responding to the inherently unstable structure of deposit taking. Rather I understand its force, from a policy making perspective, as deriving from identifying the optimal policy conclusion by outlining the hardest case. Diamond and Dybvig might themselves go further and think that their model describes widespread empirical realities. From my point of view, it does not need to do that to have useful policy implications. There is a related general issue in economics with how models are understood to relate to empirical realities. See Dani Rodrik (2015) *Economics Rules: Ther Rights and Wrongs of the Dismal Science* W. W. Norton & Company New York and London, where Rodrik discusses that economists tend to become and remain supporters of one model of an economic reality even when this does not serve the policy goal well. He observes: "...*accepted practice does not require economists to think through the conditions under which their models are useful....The standards of the profession require that the modeler make only some general claims about how what he or she is doing is relevant to the real world....*" (P.172). *Economics Rules: Why Economics Works, When It Fails, and How To Tell The Difference (hzu.edu.in)* The Diamond and Dybvig model has been called unfalsifiable, George Elgin (2022) *Diamond and Dybvig and the Crisis of 1907,* Blog Post *Diamond and Dybvig and the Panic of 1907 – Alt-M.* This comment echoes an analysis made more formally in Gorton (1988) *Banking panics and business cycles,* Oxford Economic Papers 40, 751–781. Whether Diamond and Dybvig is strictly unfalsifiable in the Popperian sense is arguable, but the charge alone indicates its problematic relationship to any procedure of empirical verification. That point is sufficient to conclude that it is problematic to use Diamond and Dybvig to draw policy conclusions which are overly focused on eliminating first mover advantage. [The traditional view of the role of models in economics is that they stylise reality to create testable hypotheses, see for example Sam Oulians (2011) *What are Economic Models,* Finance and Development June 2011, Volume 48, No. 2. Chen, Goldstein, and Jiang (2010) display a welcome focus on this issue of verification as it affects finding empirical evidence for redemptions and provide the strongest empirical approach to testing the existence of first mover advantage that I have reviewed. This work does not suggest that the first mover advantage hypothesis is impossible to verify, but it does suggest that it is difficult to verify empirically and that models which include runs as arising from bad fundamentals in terms of underwriting and investment choices are likely to be as consistent with empirical evidence. [Few studies of how economics interacts with policy making focus on this problem of models in the interface between economics and policy making. See for example, Erik Angner (2023) *How Economics Can Save the World,* Penguin Business, or Abhijit Banerjee and Esther Duflo (2020) *Good Economics for Hard Times,* Penguin Books which each emphasise the importance of empirical testing and discuss the role of values assumptions in economic studies.]

consume later and all could store funds themselves without cost. The requirement of fund investors for cash in a crisis and their sensitivity to the current valuation of the assets of the fund seems fundamentally dissimilar to the depositors in the Diamond and Dybvig model.

Secondly, deposits are repaid at a fixed valuation (the value at which they were initially taken as deposits) and this is not true of investment fund shares, except accidentally. In investment funds, what I get back is always subject to a valuation process, not just in the event of liquidation, and the valuation can go up as well as down. In a deposit taking institution, the advantage I seek is the full return of my deposit at par, which will not happen to later investors because lending assets will have had to be liquidated at a discount. The Diamond and Dybvig model is quite specific to providing one's funds to an entity which holds assets which – for a time – cannot be redeemed at the price at which they were taken onto the balance sheet and yet I expect at par redemption of my deposit. This is built into the model.[44] The first mover advantage being sought is, arguably, to distribute that inevitable discount on revaluation at the point of liquidation to other depositors by getting out first.

By contrast, it is quite sensible to imagine an investment fund where there is, let's say, one trading asset and ten investors. If they start to panic for whatever reason and seek advantage over each other by leaving, they will all get their investment back at the same valuation unless the trading price of the asset happens to move over the period of time it takes them all to lodge their demand for repayment. The fact that they would get back different amounts only if the asset price moves suggests that the first mover advantage, they achieve is not one created by their common investment mechanism, but a first mover advantage arising at the level of the asset class. Furthermore, the early redeemers get an advantage over all holders of that asset, not just their fellow investment fund members and they share that advantage with all other early exiting investors from that asset, irrespective of whether they had invested through an investment fund or not.[45] This discount on liquidation for banking assets does not exist for investment assets: there is no inherently low valuation to be avoided. It is notable that where funds such as private equity funds do something similar to what banks do (i.e., investing in untraded com-

---

44 *"This is because the face value of deposits is larger than the liquidation value of the bank's assets"* Diamond and Dybvig (1983) P. 409.

45 It is acknowledged that the situation is more complex if the fund sales are a sufficiently large portion of total transactions to move the price of the asset. But that is a complication, one of many that can be added to the scenarios under consideration. This is not the situation modelled by Diamond & Dybvig where assets sold 'early' (i.e., in response to illiquidity within the fund caused by redemption demand) are invariably sold at a loss.

mercial assets), they impose a closed ended structure which eliminates much of the analogous first mover advantage, which clearly does exist.

The third issue with the use to which Diamond and Dybvig's model is put is the apparent psychologization of a model that is not implied in it and which often occurs in order to apply that model beyond the issue of analysing the merits of deposit guarantee schemes. The problem arises when an attempt is made to use the Diamond and Dybvig model in a naturalist way as descriptive rather than analytical. This psychologization of the Diamond and Dybvig model – by which I mean claiming that persons engaged in a run have the psychological attitude of seeking to get a timing advantage over other investors (as distinct from acting in ways indistinguishable from having that attitude) – has been a significant source of confusion for market participants with many testifying at consultative roundtables and other events that it is just not true that they withdrew their investment out of concern that others would exit before them. If we were dealing with the policy issue that Diamond and Dybvig addressed, such discordant reported subjective mental states would not be a difficulty because the force of the model was not that it described any actual bank run but rather that it set out the hardest case to deal with. The hardest case indicated that public intervention was optimal. However, when our purpose is to reduce the need for public intervention we do, on the contrary, need to understand more about those psychological states of mind of the withdrawing investor because we are trying to persuade them not to withdraw their investment or we are trying to persuade the investment fund asset manager not to allow them to withdraw their investment.

Taken together, these points are, I think, sufficient to argue that the argument from analogy is not self-evident and is problematic from a policy reasoning presentation perspective.

A Policy Making Narrative?

Drawing all this together what we find is two complex ideas presented briefly and in an intermingled way: the Excess Redemptions Hypothesis and the First Mover Advantage hypothesis. They are presented without a strong supporting framework of academic references which we can consult to explore how well supported they are, although this literature is developing. Taken either together or singly they have the implication of fundamentally shifting the goal of FSB policy making recommendations to the management/elimination of a posited specific feature of investment funds, whether that is the excess rate of redemptions, or the first mover advantage investors are supposedly subject to or both, by contrast with the established mandate of the FSB to promote financial stability. In a moment, I want to come back to why we might give financial intermediation or liquidation cost first mover advantage some weight in a policy making process provided we abandon the idea that it is sufficiently well supported to shift the overall purpose of the policy making exercise. But first I need to consider why, if we don't have such a theoretical framework well established, do these hypotheses get aired in an FSB policy document?[46]

One consideration worth entertaining is that this theoretical framework gets articulated because of an almost instinctive desire to create a credible narrative for the work. It can be seen – reasonably – as a kind of benign virtue signalling, setting out a framework within which – in a more ideal world – policy analysis would happen. In particular, it might be seen as indicating support for the emerging work on investment fund redemption patterns within financial economics. More generally, in terms of the public and legislators, it is arguably reassuring to be told that the FSB is targeting excess redemption levels and a first mover advantage in investment funds that it has identified, rather than to hear that it is trying somehow to shore up the financial stability of the sector in a tentative and hopefully adequate way.

However, to label this merely as 'virtue signalling'[47] would certainly do a disservice to the extensive efforts made by the FSB across its policy making horizon to set itself standards for how it analyses policy issues and develops its approach. That said, it is an approach which runs into significant difficulties where potential for reasoned policy making is as constrained as it is in relation to this topic. In particular, because this meta-narrative about the theoretical framework underpinning the policy work is significantly more susceptible to criticism than the core reasoning, the addition of this kind of aspirational theoretical framework opens the policy making process up to criticisms to which the conclusions can be immune.

That can in turn lead to the odd situation of a body publishing policy documents that are vulnerable to forceful criticism while the core reasoning is not impacted by those criticisms. It can be hugely difficult for a third party to differentiate between criticisms of the meta-narrative and criticisms of the core reasoning. Thus, a policy document can appear to be strongly refuted when in fact its policy and core reasoning is substantially unaffected by the criticisms. Furthermore, adopting a concept of first mover advantage primarily by analogy as just described is in danger of acting,

---

46 I don't want to give the impression that no work is being done by economists in this area, only that it is as yet in an early stage of development and inconclusive.

47 The term virtue signalling is often used in quite a pejorative way. I do not intend that here. It seems to me that the virtues being signalled are desirable, although perhaps unattainable because exogenous to the process as discussed already. However see the following piece for the more critical perspective on virtue signalling: Olivia Eriksen (2021) *Virtue Signalling: What is it and why is it so dangerous*, Blog, https://www.realclearenergy.org/articles/2021/08/02/virtue_signaling_what_is_it_and_why_is_it_so_dangerous_788208.html.

paradoxically, as an obstacle to understanding better how first mover advantages actually works in relation to investment funds. In seeking confirmation of a possibly misconceived analogy one can fail to look objectively at the balance of factors that are influencing financial fragility.

In favour of FMA after all

All that said, it is one thing to decline to base one's whole policy making process on an unproven analogy, it is quite a different thing to affirm that there is no motive (other than the asset price first mover advantage common to the whole market for a particular asset[48]) for one investor in an investment fund to get out ahead of others. While it may not be at all practical to disaggregate the various effects, surely it is reasonable to think that if I have two investments, one directly in an asset and a second an investment in the same asset through a mutual fund and I have decided to exit at least one of them, I will tend to decide to exit the mutual fund investment first if the costs of doing so are lower than exiting the direct investment?

I can see nothing wrong with this idea that there is a 'financial intermediation or liquidation cost first mover advantage' in mutual funds if they don't charge the redeeming investor the full cost of redemption. But if there is such an effect, then the difficult question is how it should fit into the policy making reasoning if we cannot isolate its impact and if dealing with it does not fully meet our FSB mandate?

I think there is a way to do so. To explain how, I first summarise the relevant meta-claims by the FSB about how it does policy making. The heart of the FSB approach is to identify 'vulnerabilities' in the way NBFI operates and then suggest 'policies' that are likely to reduce the impact of those vulnerabilities. These policies can be either discretionary policy tools or, more usually, policies which it recommends being hard-wired into regulatory frameworks in jurisdictions (i.e. either 'ex ante' or ex post').[49]

---

48 Obviously in a real period of systemic market stress, a first mover advantage of getting out of a whole range of assets can emerge simultaneously, usually intensified by the rising uncertainty as to which assets actually have an increased risk of falling in price.

49 It is important to note that the FSB has always recognised that a focus on individual vulnerabilities was not entirely satisfactory, and it has set itself the task of moving from a focus on key vulnerabilities to a broader 'systemic' view. That requires developing a picture of the interconnections in the NBFI sectors and their connections with other sectors. NBFI resilience then depends both on the behaviour of different types of NBFI entities *and* on the 'inter-connectedness' between those entities and other parts of the financial system. This arguably involves three layers of analysis:

1) The identification of vulnerabilities that would lead to increased liquidity demand under adverse market conditions (arguably already done) and the identification of liquidity providers

The 'vulnerabilities' in the NBFI sector are usually described by the FSB as 'structural'. This is certainly the case in relation to investment funds. To understand the significance of this word 'structural' it is useful to refer to a summary of the way financial stability issues are generally approached which can be found in a joint IMF/FSB/BIS paper *Elements of Effective macroprudential Policies*.[50] While financial stability policy with regard to the NBFI sector is somewhat broader than 'macroprudential' policy, the points the paper makes about how to look at systemic risk are a useful indicator of the significance of this vocabulary. As it explains, systemic risk is understood within the macroprudential tradition of thinking as made up of 'vulnerabilities', vulnerabilities arising from the build-up of risk over time and vulnerabilities arising from the web of interconnections of providers of financial services at any point in time. Vulnerabilities that would arise over time are understood as 'systemic vulnerabilities' while vulnerabilities arising from interconnectedness are understood of as 'structural vulnerabilities.

It is an important part of the narrative with regard to open-ended Investment Funds that their so-called 'liquidity transformation' is seen as a structural vulnerability.[51] In other words, it might be seen as analogous to the 'To Big to Fail' problem

---

that might meet that demand and the identification of policy stances that might either increase supply or reduce demand;

2) The identification and quantification of inter-connections which might create consequential effects by triggering the use of liquidity buffers, pledging additional collateral for repo, redeeming fund investments, asset sales, or drawing down lines of credit, and

3) An assessment of the potential interaction of vulnerabilities and interconnections, and their implications for the liquidity of core markets that underpin the functioning of the global financial system that connects real economy borrowers and lenders.

This ambitious goal, arising from a fully systemic approach, would integrate the understanding of structural vulnerabilities and emerging systemic risk issues into an overall assessment of systemic risk. However, it is quite challenging even to conceive how this might be done in the real financial world of limited data, multiple markets, differing market structures and differing intermediation structures with costs attaching to market access and access to intermediaries. It is at risk of becoming another part of an aspirational but vulnerable meta-narrative.

50 *Elements of Effective Macroprudential Policies: Lessons from International Experience; jointly by IMF-FSB-BIS; August 31, 2016.*

51 Strictly speaking, while this is often described as a 'transformation', it is not necessarily a 'transformation' from less liquid fund assets to more liquid fund shares. It is quite possible that the fund assets are at times as liquid as the fund shares, or even more liquid. For example, I can, in certain jurisdictions get my money back on a direct investment in equity shares far quicker than I can get my money back on a mutual fund investment in those shares. The point is that the liquidity of the fund shares and the fund assets are not necessarily correlated. It is not the case that as the liquidity of assets deteriorates in a period of stress in markets, the liquidity on offer from the fund for fund shares is automatically reduced or its price (the 'swing factor') automatically increased. Thus, the liquidity of the assets may be more, less or then same as that of the fund shares depending on the

in banks if that is seen as something inherent in those banks over time rather than as something appearing and disappearing across the cycle. As such, it is considered not so much a matter of monitoring for a build up of systemic risk, but rather a question of altering or reducing the interconnectedness, which needs to be tackled irrespective of the point in the economic or financial cycle that has been reached.

Based on identifying a range of such vulnerabilities, the FSB framework originally identified five specific areas in which policies are needed to mitigate the potential vulnerabilities associated with NBFI.[52] These were originally bank exposures to the NBFI sector;[53] money market funds (MMFs);[54] securitisation; securities financing transactions (SFTs); and – as a catch-all – policies to mitigate systemic risks posed by other non-bank entities and activities. The work on investment funds falls into this last category.[55]

The narrative, therefore, is that work on mitigating the impact on markets of the liquidity offering attaching to investment fund shares is one of a range of structural and systemic vulnerabilities which much be addressed in a range of ways. But we might legitimately ask, which one: is the issue of liquidity transformation a structural or a systemic risk?

---

point in time. The vulnerability is the unstable relationship between the liquidity of the assets and the liquidity of the liabilities of a fund. What counts is that the relationship is unstable and changes in periods of stress. The use of the term 'transformation' appears to arise by way of analogical thinking to the existence of maturity 'transformation' as an inherent feature of 21st century bank balance sheets, a context in which the term 'transformation' makes sense and something which is also correctly understood as a vulnerability of the banking system. It makes less sense when considering differentiated liquidity terms in a mutual fund as between its assets and its liabilities; but because each side of the fund balance sheet is created under different terms and conditions, one can still think of the fund as 'transforming' liquidity terms and conditions as between the two, i.e., as between the assets and liabilities of a fund.

52 The policy framework was set out in *Policy Framework for Strengthening Oversight and Regulation of Shadow Banking Entities* (August 2013) and was previously reviewed in *Thematic Review on the Implementation of the FSB Policy Framework for Shadow Banking Entities* (May 2016) and in *Assessment of shadow banking activities: risks and the adequacy of post-crisis policy tools to address financial stability concerns* (July 2017).

53 The policies to address this include enhancements to consolidation rules for off-balance sheet entities; stronger capital rules for banks' exposures to non-banks (higher risk-weights for exposures to unregulated financial entities, risk-sensitive capital requirements for banks' investments in the equity of funds, and a standard for measuring and controlling large exposures); and guidance on the identification and management of step-in-risk.

54 See Footnote 35 above.

55 While margin requirements (cleared and non-cleared) were not originally listed they are now considered.

I want to suggest that the best answer to this is: both. On the one hand financial intermediation or liquidation cost first mover advantage arises from an inherent feature of the open-ended investment fund contract. It will always be there and continually characterising the inter-connections of parties connected to each other under the terms of the open-ended fund investment contract. On the other hand, the 'search for yield' is a phenomenon that increases systemic risk, precisely because monetary policy applies across the system for so long as it occurs.[56] If we were to deal with the vulnerabilities in investment funds as 'systemic' rather than as 'structural' we would need to consider whether the drivers of the search for yield were likely to continue beyond a single cycle. The FSB approach has been to see these risks as 'structural' and this tends to focus attention on the terms of the open-ended fund investment contract which is deemed inherently unstable in the absence swing pricing. We might also see the degree of investment in illiquid assets as 'structural' (i.e. as persistent) even though it can have cyclical drivers. In other words, we are unlikely to reach a state where open-ended funds invest only in robustly liquid assets.

But do we lose part of the story if we fail to acknowledge the systematic element of the risk? To put this another way, it is puzzling that the debate around Diamond & Dybvig's model has not settled on the view that banking runs have both a risk element and a contractual element in their causation. Perhaps I am too pragmatic and abductive in this perspective. But it seems the obvious answer to that debate that neither heightened riskiness nor contractual instability is a sufficient cause of a bank run but that both need to be present. A bank run will, almost invariably, have both a systemic and a structural element.

By extension, subject to persuasive modelling, one might say that runs on open-ended funds arise both when there is an asset price first mover advantage and a financial intermediation or liquidation cost first mover advantage. While this might not be entirely persuasive,[57] it would at least provide additional encouragement to policy makers to address financial intermediation or liquidation cost first mover advantage because it would also be in the interests of dulling the effect on open ended investment funds of asset price first mover advantage. It is notable from a bounded rationality perspective that introducing swing pricing may be an excessive reaction

---

56 It is worth noting that if one concluded that mutual funds always look for an illiquidity premium because of a principal-agent problem of asset managers mispricing the risks of investing in illiquid assets because they are seeking to give the impression of a higher rate of return on assets invested, one might also say, I think, that the search for yield has a structural element when it comes to all delegated investment management, including both mutual funds and managed accounts.
57 In common sense terms, it seems quite likely that some runs on investment funds will occur no matter what swing pricing penalties are imposed.

to a minor first mover advantage, but even if so, introducing swing pricing will dampen the responsiveness of the investment funds sector to all first mover advantages as well as providing an additional investor protection measure for continuing investors who do not redeem.[58]

In terms of modelling, this kind of perspective could observe that abstracting away from the conjunctural and risk-focused determinants of runs was precisely the correct thing to do for Diamond and Dybvig because they were explaining why the radical option of deposit guarantees was optimal. But where one does not have that policy purpose *"to eliminate the problem of runs"*,[59] their model is no longer the best one to rely on. On the contrary, focusing exclusively on financial intermediation or liquidation cost first mover advantage – if one rules out an investor guarantee policy as I think we should – is going to lead towards policy conclusions to the effect that the open-ended fund investor contract is the problem. But this radical view would require very substantive justification. When one is trying to reduce the likelihood of a marginal behaviour rather than to exclude the possibility of an unlikely but hugely damaging event and when one is aiming only for a policy that satisfices rather than optimises, the focus needs to be on altering the balance of incentives for the marginal behaviour. That means that what is required for this policy purpose is a model which focuses on something else, probably on either the extent of the incentives for portfolio managers to seek an illiquidity premium or, perhaps using a behavioural economics analysis, the best way to design regulatory imperatives to impede redemptions so that we don't create a market structure or Dynamic Redemption Policy First Mover Advantage. Perhaps some combination of the two would be particularly helpful.[60]

---

58 Extending Elliot's fairness argument could lead to it being suggested that this is unfair to redeeming investors if the redemption cost first mover advantage is not the main cause of the amplification threat from the investment fund sector. The counterarguments set out above to the effect that there is an over-riding public interest etc. apply as does the argument that the prior approach of many mutual funds over recent decades was so unfair to continuing investors that the balance of fairness is with the swing pricing policy anyway, irrespective of whether swing pricing is the correct solution to the financial stability issue.

59 Diamond & Dybvig (1983) P.410.

60 I am assuming that there is no viable policy option of managing asset class first mover advantage or of influencing the tendency of markets to herd. I am unclear in my mind as to whether the literature on pledgeability could be useful. Personally, I find an analogy with the engineering of weirs on rivers as a flood control device a useful way to think about the policy issue of investment funds and financial stability. Weirs are open structures built on rivers and other waterways to control but not stop the flow of water. They raise the water level upstream by operating as an impediment to the flow of water. They are appropriate in situations where the flow of water is usually low. A weir can be contrasted with a dam or a barrage. In effect, they operate to lengthen the amount of time it takes water to flow into a flood plain, in the event that the volume gets higher than a defined level. Weirs

Conclusion

The analysis set out here is not that of an informed financial economist, but only the reading available to a relatively uneducated (in financial economics) policy maker. My own suggestion is that the way the FSB has presented the matter needs to be judged as a presentational device by contrast with another presentational way to present the process. That other way to present the analysis would be to acknowledge and be guided by the bounded character of any potential analysis. Doing so would inject an important element of caution and conservatism into the policy making process. It would suggest that we proceed slowly and even 'gingerly' because we are aware of our own limited technical capacity to create targeted outcomes within the complex ecosystem of financial markets. It might also place the policy focus on the behaviour of the marginal redeeming investor in a mutual fund.

Perhaps the most famous writer on financial stability, Walter Bagehot, emphasised a point similar to my suggestion that we should present ourselves as engaged in a bounded form of reasoning when he pointed out of his own hugely influential policy proposals for managing market panics that "*...we must I think have recourse to feeble and humble palliatives such as I have suggested. With good sense, good judgement and good care, I have no doubt that they may be enough. But I have written in vain if I require to say now that the problem is delicate, that the solution is varying and difficult and that the result is inestimable to us all*".[61]

---

are designed based on defining this 'subcritical flow', i.e. a rate of flow of water below which the engineers are happy for the rate of flow to be determined by upriver conditions (in my analogy, market conditions) and the rating curve, i.e. the amount of flow that passes over the weir which depends on three aspects of its design: the length of the weir, the height of the water level above the crest of the weir, and the geometry of the weir, which determines this coefficient. In my analogy, the policy question is at what point one wishes to allow at least some sales to facilitate price discovery and valuation of portfolios so as to cap the build-up of uncertainty in markets which in turn feeds contagion by herding. Perhaps we are looking for a policy analogous to how a V-notch weir works, a weir which allows water to flow through without impediment for so long as that flow doesn't rise above a certain level and then places strong impediments to additional volume, up to a point where water overflows the weir structure. *What is a Weir? — Practical Engineering*.

61 Walter Bagehot, (1896) *Lombard Street A Description of the Money Market*, Kegan Paul, Trench, Trubner & Co, London, P. 336 https://archive.org/details/lombardstreetad00bagegoog/page/n350/mode/1up, originally published in 1873. It has been observed that the ideas presented by Bagehot so famously had already been articulated by others, notably Henry Thornton fifty years earlier (Charles Goodhart (1999) *Myths about Lender of Last Resort*, International Finance Journal, 2(3) Blackwell Publishers, P 339–59 also available in google books here: https://books.google.es/books?id=2486Jp8TjEcC&pg=PA227&lpg=PA227&dq=Myths+about+Lender+of+Last+Resort,&source=bl&ots=uX2yElm77Z&sig=ACfU3U3d24OE2xYUG8wH2MJjuUjDOi2QPQ&hl=en&sa=X&ved=2ahUKEwir2fGxoq79AhXNDewKHTyVBJ0Q6AF6BAgFEAM#v=onepage&q=Myths%20about%20Lender%20of%20Last%

However, it should be recognised that formulating the Excess Redemption Hypothesis and the First Mover Advantage hypothesis actually also injects a certain conservatism into the process, but in a different way: each of those hypotheses has the implication that the FSB should only target a limited impact on investment funds. Under the Excess Redemption Hypothesis, the bulk of selling by investment funds into the market in a period of crisis would be considered acceptable, irrespective of what its impact on financial stability was because it would be only proportionate to the size of the investment funds sector within the overall profile of investors. Under the First Mover Advantage hypothesis, if the full cost of redemption is transferred to the redeeming investor across the globe and they still choose to exit, this is probably an acceptable outcome.

Each approach can be seen therefore to have some advantages in limiting the ambition of the FSB. In addition, the reliance on hypotheses as outlined here implies an ambition that the policy making process will be rational in character and driven by the science and the data to the extent that it is available. By contrast the 'bounded rationality' approach can be seen as advocating a certain irrationalism or at least a willingness to draw policy conclusions without strong supporting data and opening up the policy makers to criticism for making up policy without appropriate scientific underpinnings.

One concern with the hypothesis-focused approach to presentation of its policy conclusions is that it might be seen as inconsistent with the broad mandate of the FSB. The FSB could be seen to be narrowing its role and accepting potentially higher degrees of market instability caused by amplifying selling, just because it isn't 'excess' selling or just because it is not motivated by financial intermediation or liquidation cost first mover advantage. However, the FSB makes its thinking clear to the G20 and if this narrowing were unacceptable then arguably it would be for the G20 to say so.

Perhaps the deciding question is to ask which of the two approaches to creating a meta narrative for this policy making process promotes greater degrees of engagement and acceptance? In this regard, the answer would, I suspect be quite different if the Excess Redemptions hypothesis or the First Mover Advantage hypothesis were well grounded in extensively articulated economic theory. That is not to suggest that financial markets participants simply defer to economists in understanding their own sector. But it seems to me uncontentious to suggest that the scope for a common-sense scepticism is reduced the better developed the theory is.

20Resort%2C&f=false). Bagehot's success in giving longevity to these ideas was probably because both to the timing of his work, just after a major banking crisis in the UK, and because of the quality of his presentation. Diamond and Dybvig's 1983 article is also notably well presented.

In the absence of good empirical verification or well-developed models, I would see strong merits in emphasising the bounded character of the process of policy making that is being undertaken. Without a doubt, however, that is going to be a problem in those jurisdictions where there is an obligation on policy makers – particularly regulators – to provide comprehensive analytical foundations for policy changes or face legal challenge. To have global standard setters stating that they are making policy recommendations which are the least worst option on the basis of limited insight would surely increase the legal risk of subsequent challenge in at least some jurisdictions. Perhaps that is the deciding factor. However, one should prefer a situation where financial economics made the choice of meta narrative a little easier by providing a better-grounded theoretical framework for policy making. That is not to discount the value of the work done by many, some of them cited in this paper which in recent years has perhaps begun to build towards a better understanding. On the contrary, it is because that work is emerging that there is still some reason to hope that the financial intermediation or liquidation cost first mover advantage will in the end have a well-grounded position in policy reasoning in this area.

There is, however, one other potential twist to this argument. One could argue that precisely because in making policy in such a complex and untransparent topic, our capacity to reason authoritatively is limited, that we should engage in putting forward plausible conjectures even when those are not underpinned with well-developed peer-tested analysis and – where relevant – empirical testing.[62] There is some strength to this argument for a heterodox approach to the presentation of reasoning in a complex policy area like this. Each hypothesis has some plausibility whether because of apparent analogy to better developed theories or because of some consistent statistical evidence. This kind of presentation seems to have its strongest persuasiveness within the academy. What is striking about the two hypotheses articulated in this 2022 report is that these hypotheses only have the strength of plausibility with regard to economic science rather than with regard to

---

62 It is for example possible to argue that the somewhat stronger performance of ETFs than open-ended investment funds in March 2020 was because their structure is more stable and has less first mover advantage. But there is a counterargument that firstly they are more stable but not because of the absence of redemption cost first mover advantage and, secondly, that if there had not been central banking intervention the ETF sector would also have become stressed and that their greater stability, at best, delayed the stress temporarily. The empirical evidence is inconclusive. As observed by the financial journalist Patrick Jenkins in noting the controversy in academic papers on such matters, "*the complexity* [of corporate bond ETFs] *is underpinned by practical but problematic reasoning.*" See Patrick Jenkins (2023) *Reality of Corporate Bond ETFs differs from the Appearance*, Financial Times, 28 February 2023. He further usefully suggests that: "*...bond ETFs are not what they seem: in effect they are derivative products, reliant on complex structures that may be open to abuse.*"

day-to-day experience. Is that really the most useful kind of plausibility to aim for in a public report rather than in a scientific paper, particularly when those hypotheses seem to contrast strikingly with everyday experience of traders on markets? The way one might reconcile all this is to say that the FSB is operating with a particularly open way of presenting the reasoning backing policy proposals in that it is presenting tentative hypotheses and discussing the evidence supporting those, while only relying on a core part of the presented reasoning.

None of this takes from the evident fact that the FSB has been particularly diligent and careful in its work to date on investment funds. Directly and through IOSCO it has engaged in extensive consultation and detailed review of available evidence. Its latest set of proposals indicate a careful and cautious approach. However, as a society we seem uncomfortable with the necessarily tentative character of any such complex policy initiative. As discussed here, we see signs of that discomfort reflected even in the pages of the FSB's own publications, sitting beside what this author judges to be well framed core arguments and proportionate policy recommendations consistent with an asset-quality focused approach to promoting financial stability.

Patrick Kenadjian

Reforming MMFs and Bond OEFs is good, but providing reliable Liquidity to the Treasury Market is better

Introduction

The third panel of the January 24, 2023 ILF conference on where the next systemic financial crisis might come from was devoted to non-bank financial institutions (NBFIs). The topic is a vast one and the panel decided to concentrate on a particular area of it, money market mutual funds (MMFs) and open-ended funds which invest in bonds (bond OEFs). This was consistent with the recent focus of the Financial Stability Board (FSB) on these institutions in the aftermath of what has come to be called the "March 2020 market turmoil" or the "dash for cash". The panelists had extremely cogent views on the roles of MMFs and bond OEFs in the market turmoil and on consequent proposals to reform them. I agree with many of them, but would like to focus this article on another aspect of the March 2020 market turmoil and to advance the view that while MMFs and bond OEFs would no doubt benefit from some of the proposed reforms, these reforms do not address the central problem of March 2020.

That problem was a market dysfunction due to the structure of the markets for government securities worldwide and for US Treasuries in particular, which results in serious periodic liquidity squeezes and which I believe can best be resolved by addressing a fundamental structural problem of these markets. These markets have grown exponentially since the Global Financial Crisis (GFC). According to the FSB's October 2022 report on Liquidity in Core Government Bond Markets, outstanding government debt as a percentage of GDP grew in the decade from 2010 to 2020 from 90 % to 131 % in the US, from 87 % to 113 % in the euro area, from 80 % to 137 % in the UK and from 174 % to 238 % in Japan. In contrast, the balance sheets of the traditional intermediaries in these markets, market makers largely affiliated with regulated banking institutions, have not kept pace. In fact they have mostly done the opposite, they have shrunk. Consequently they are no longer in a position to intermediate effectively in those markets in stressed situations.

This leaves only the central banks, backed by their sovereigns' treasuries, as intermediaries of last resort. All other reform proposals can contribute to improve-

Note: The views expressed in this article are my own.

https://doi.org/10.1515/9783111340937-012

ments, but most of them will take time to agree and implement and do not resolve the central problem, which has manifested itself in the US Treasury (Treasury) market in September 2019 and March 2020 and in the UK government securities market in October 2022, each time triggered by a different conjunction of circumstances and actors. I believe there is a fairly straightforward solution, partly already in place in the US, but needing expansion, a standing repurchase facility of the Federal Reserve (the Fed) for Treasuries, open to the broadest number of market actors, including MMFs and bond OEFs. This solution can be implemented rapidly since a more limited version of it already exists. It is, however, only a first step, in that repos are considered to be debt and MMFs, in general, are not allowed to leverage themselves, but it is an important one, pending a more complete solution, which would involve the Fed fully embracing the role of purchaser or market maker, as well as lender of last resort, which I believe the evolving structure of the markets requires it to take.

Background

NBFIs, which we used to call "shadow banking" when we were unclear what we were talking about or looking for, refer to a very broad category of financial activities outside the scope of traditionally regulated financial institutions which, in the wake of the GFC, we realized might make up 40–50 % of the financial sector, at least in the US and the EU.

Since the GFC, the importance of non-bank financial intermediation has only increased, as the size of the traditional banking sector has shrunk while the reliance of our economies on debt has only increased. So NBFIs have been a focus of attention from the FSB for years. Initially the FSB cast a very wide net, urging collection of information on a broad Monitoring Universe of Non-Bank Financial Intermediation (MUNFI) measure of assets of other financial intermediaries (OFIs), insurance companies and pension funds, before introducing a narrower "economic function" measure in their 2015 Global Shadow Banking monitoring report. This was meant to focus on those institutions most likely to give rise to systemic risk, focusing on non-bank credit intermediation involving maturity or liquidity transformation, imperfect risk transfer and leverage.

According to the FSB's 2022 NBFI Survey, this narrow measure amounted to $67.8 trillion worldwide, of which 76.2 % (or $51.6 trillion in assets), labeled EF1, was made up of collective investment vehicles with features which, according to the FSB, make them susceptible to runs, including MMFs, fixed income funds, mixed funds, credit hedge funds and real estate funds. According to that same report, that segment was also the part of the narrow measure which exhibited the most growth in

2021. Two important parts of this segment, MMFs and OEFs investing in bonds, received the most regulatory attention under the auspices of the FSB as a result of the "market turmoil" of March 2020, during which the market for US Treasury debt was severely dislocated.

As described in the Group of 30's 2021 report entitled "U.S. Treasury Markets, Steps Toward Increased Resilience", "[a]round March 11, the Treasury market became essentially dysfunctional. Heavy investor demands to liquidate Treasury securities overwhelmed the capacity of dealers to intermediate the market. Investors demanding large amounts of cash in exchange for Treasuries included relative-value hedge funds, mutual funds and foreign central banks." (p.3) The report concluded "[i]n short, U.S. Treasuries did not serve their traditional safe-haven roles. Instead, dysfunction in the Treasury market exacerbated the crisis." In a word, March 2020 involved what might be called a market failure in a systemically important market. This generated the need for massive intervention by the Fed to restore liquidity to the market. The Fed purchased nearly $1 trillion in Treasuries within a three week period beginning March 16. The Fed and other key regulators also took regulatory action to help other market actors to provide liquidity to the market, by temporarily exempting Treasuries and reserves held at the Fed from the Supplemental Leverage Ratio (SLR) under the Basel III capital adequacy rules.

Why focus on MMFs and bond OEFs?

The initial international regulatory focus was on MMFs which had played a role in the market dislocations which followed the Lehman Brothers bankruptcy in the Fall of 2008. There had been U.S. Securities and Exchange Commission (SEC) reforms in 2014 to deal with the perceived causes of the 2008 events, namely how the fixed net asset value (NAV) of the MMF shares was calculated. The process allowed first movers to redeem their shares at what was in effect a fictitious price, based on the prior day's closing value. This was seen as incentivizing institutional investors to redeem early before other investors in the funds became aware of a potential change in the value of the underlying portfolio. The 2014 SEC Rules also allowed MMFs to impose redemption gates (temporary suspensions of redemption) and liquidity fees for redemptions in stressed situations to reduce these incentives. The latter set of liquidity management tools (LMTs) were not used in March 2020 and the new valuation rules clearly did not suffice to reduce first mover advantage (FMA).

Regulatory attention also expanded to other OEFs, in particular bond OEFs. The analysis was that they suffered from serious structural flaws which also made them vulnerable to FMA, and thus to runs. Namely, like MMFs they offered their investors daily redemption in cash, but invested in long-term assets which were often hard to liquidate quickly. Thus the funds were seen as suffering from liquidity mismatches which exposed them to the danger of having to sell assets in a fire sale mode, to meet redemptions regardless of whether they sought to sell a representative sample of fund assets by asset type and maturity, i.e. selling portfolio assets proportionately to the portion of the portfolio they represented, so as to maintain risk-consistent positions over time across their portfolio, or opted to sell down their most liquid assets, such as Treasuries.

It is important to note that the MMFs and the OEFs did not originate the selling pressure in March 2020. They sold to meet redemptions by their investors who were either short of liquidity themselves (non-financial entities whose sources of revenue were drying up as a result of COVID) or who needed to rebalance their portfolios as a result of sharp movements in the value of different asset classes. And they were not the only sellers. Foreign central banks and sovereign wealth funds were also major sellers. But the funds clearly acted as amplifiers of a crisis which originated elsewhere, and the question the FSB and national regulators have asked is what kind of reforms would be needed in their structure and regulation to prevent a recurrence of this.

The focus on these two sets of market actors is consistent with the approach of the FSB throughout its examination of NBFIs, which has tended to focus on the actors much more than on the markets in which these entities operate. The MMFs, having been a factor of propagation of the GFC in 2008 and already a target for reform in the aftermath of the GFC, easily belonged to what Captain Renault, in the film Casablanca referred to as "the usual suspects" and bond OEFs, which share structural features with MMFs were logically assimilated thereto. Of course, in analyzing the March market turmoil the FSB did look closely at the mechanics of that market but their overall default setting is to focus on individual market actors rather than the broader question of whether the markets themselves are in need of reforming.

Why not focus on the market itself?

Not all markets can be examined in detail, but I would suggest that the most important ones, those for government debt securities, merit examination, since they constitute the basis for the pricing of all other debt markets. As the Group of 30 Report noted, the Treasury market is "the single most important financial market in the world, as Treasury rates are a fundamental benchmark for pricing virtually all other financial assets ... it is critical to the stability of the global financial system." (p.1). The central recommendation of the Group of 30 in its 2021 report is that the best way to avoid a repetition of March 2020 would be for the Fed to set up a liquidity facility in the form of a standing repurchase (repo) facility open to a broader segment of market actors than just prime dealers and depositary banks. This would include NBFIs. A repo facility has a number of advantages over open market interventions from a financial stability point of view. Its use does not directly move the price of the securities involved, while fire sales followed by large scale central bank open market purchases do move prices. It sterilizes itself, rather than resulting in a permanent growth in the central bank's balance sheet. And a standing facility provides a reliable backstop to the market and its market makers. Also, as a standing facility, there is no need for an announcement that it is being used to intervene in the market. It is simply there to be used at the initiative of the eligible counterparties. So, no need for carefully calibrated announcements which can be misinterpreted by the market.

A repo does have at least one disadvantage from a market participant's point of view: the buyer normally applies a haircut to the market value of the securities involved, so they do not receive the full value of the securities sold. A second point to make is that since repos are akin to secured borrowing, any entity which is limited in the degree to which it can incur leverage may not be able to take full advantage of such a program. This should not be a problem for bond OEFs or, subject to certain limitations, for European Union law Undertakings for Collective Investments in Transferable Securities (UCITS), but the entities' constituent documents and applicable law will need to be checked and MMFs, while they are active repo lenders, do not incur repo liabilities, as noted in a useful 2021 US Securities and Exchange primer.

At the January 24, 2023 conference I suggested this as a possible solution, especially in view of the problems experienced in the markets for UK government bonds known as gilts in September 2022. These problems were not caused by MMFs or bond OEFs but by so-called liability driven investment (LDI) strategies followed by UK defined benefit pension plans pursuant to which they pledged UK gilts to generate funds to purchase higher yielding securities to enhance their returns. When there was a sharp decline in the value of the GBP in reaction to the UK mini-budget on 23 September and a resulting sharp rise in yields on gilts, this resulted in a significant fall in the net asset value these funds and of their pledged assets. Some slower moving pooled funds were unable to mobilize additional funds in a timely manner and had to sell assets to reduce their leverage at a speed which exceeded the normal capacity of the gilt market to absorb the additional trades. The Bank of England intervened decisively, for a limited period of time, to restore liquidity to the market before the selling pressure could reach fire sale proportions and result in a downward spiral. Sarah Breeden of the Bank of England, in a very illuminating speech of November 7, 2022 to ISDA explaining the mechanics involved and in her excellent contribution to this volume, concedes that the market was unable to absorb these sales, but attributes the problem to poorly managed leverage by those funds rather than to a market dysfunction.

Not surprisingly therefore, Ms. Breeden rejected my suggestion at the conference. In this she was joined by Tobias Adrian of the IMF. Both essentially based their position on the fear that to so would lead to "moral hazard". Tobias used the term. Ms. Breeden did not, but couched her position in terms of market actors needing to provide "self-insurance" before benefiting from central bank intervention, which should only be "a backstop, not a frontstop". Her position was that the central bank should not provide liquidity to entities who were not willing or required to take appropriate measures to provide their own liquidity. Regulated financial institutions, such as banks, subject to prudential regulation, are compelled to do so. NBFIs are not. The implications of this position are made quite clear in Chapter 3 of the International Monetary Fund (IMF) April 2023 Global Financial Stability Report. In order for NBFIs to receive liquidity support they must be made subject to "adequate and comprehensive regulatory standards" and to "appropriately resourced and intrusive supervisory oversight." (p. 78)

I think this is too narrow a view for two reasons. First, it does not make what I believe is a necessary distinction between providing liquidity to individual borrowers in traditional lender of last resort operations, where moral hazard has traditionally, and rightfully, been a concern and providing liquidity to a market, where I believe moral hazard is much less relevant. Second, Axel Weber, who was on the Group of 30 panel which made the recommendation, made the excellent point at the conference that this position harkens back to the days of "constructive ambiguity" as the dominant policy of central banks, where they sought to leave the market in the dark as to how they might react to a crisis. In his view, these days are, or at least should be, over and the best way to deal with market instability is not to have to improvise in the midst of a crisis, but to have a clear strategy, thought out and articulated in advance. He thus suggested pursuing "constructive clarity" instead. "Constructive ambiguity" in any case was a strategy meant to leave the market in doubt as to whether a particular financial institution might be rescued or allowed to fail, not whether a whole market, especially a systemically important one, would be allowed to collapse, without the central bank seeking to intervene. Common sense suggests that the latter possibility is unrealistic. And, in any event, in a crisis, to quote Timothy Geithner, former President of the New York Fed and later US Secretary of the Treasury during the GFC, "plan beats no plan."

The object of a predetermined policy or plan would not be to allow NBFIs to take more risks because they knew they would be bailed out, so much as to stabilize a systemically important market, among other things by encouraging other market participants, primary dealers and regulated financial institutions, who hesitated to provide liquidity to the market in March 2020, to step in because they could see that there was a stabilizing back up to their interventions. As I note below, the existing market makers in the Treasuries markets are too small, acting alone, to stabilize these markets in period of stress, but if they were to step in, rather than sit on the sidelines, as they did in March 2020, crises might not develop so easily or so fast.

The debt markets, and especially the markets for sovereign debt, have grown so much since the GFC and the reforms of the financial system post GFC have reduced the ability of most other market actors to provide the needed liquidity in stress situations, so that only a government backstop is a reasonable solution. The FSB's Liquidity in Core Government Bond Markets Report from October 2022 contains an excellent analysis of why other market participants did not provide sufficient liquidity. It was primarily due to uncertainty caused by the pandemic, followed by large one-sided flows and their internal risk management. (p. 2, 18–19). A January 2021 speech by Andrew Hauser, Executive Director, Markets of the Bank of England, contains two illuminating charts comparing the stock of US and UK government bonds relative to bank/dealer balance sheets showing the striking disparity in size between the two in the US and the UK:

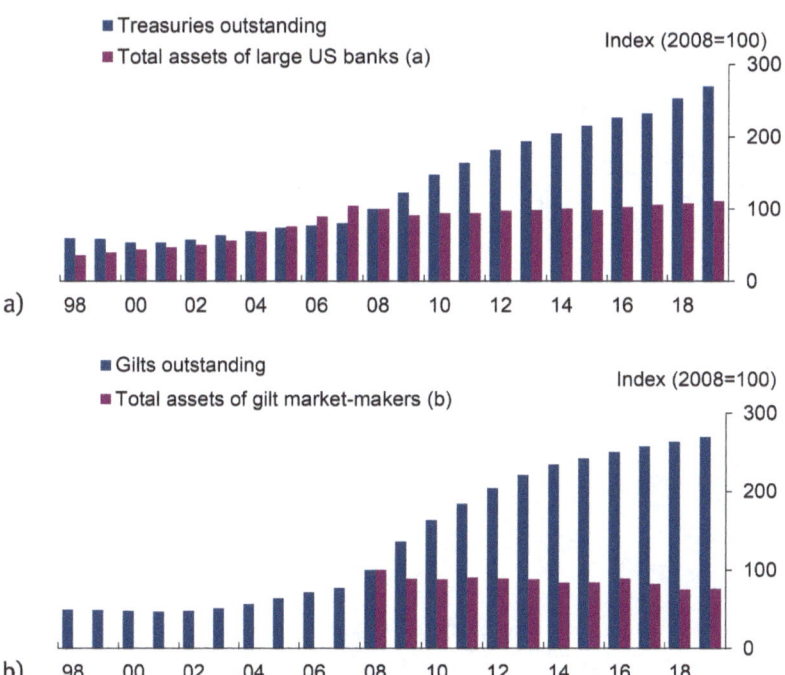

Fig. 1: Stock of US & UK government bonds relative to bank/dealer balance sheets
(a) Total assets for the holding companies of Bank of America, Bear Sterns, Citigroup, Goldman Sachs, JP Morgan Chase, Lehman Brothers, Merrill Lynch, Morgan Stanley and Wells Fargo.
(b) Based on quarterly averages available from 2008, excluding assets of banking entities authorised. to operate in the UK through branches. Gifts outstanding as of end-March 2020.
(Sources: https://www.brookings..edu/wp-content/uploads/2020/05/WP62_Duffie_v2.pdf;
UK Debt Management Office; Bank of England Regulatory Returns and Bank calculations)

They illustrate the growing and, I would hazard to add, irreversible imbalance between the size of key markets for government securities, and the balance sheet capacity of banks and dealers who have traditionally helped transfer risk smoothly between investors and borrowers. This disparity is even greater when one considers the fact that only a fraction of the bank and dealer balance sheets can at any time be used for market making in the government securities markets.

An even more graphic display of the problem can be gleaned from a US Treasury report to the Treasury Borrowing Advisory Committee (TBAC) for Q3 2022 showing Treasury market developments since 2015. The tables below track the decline in bank capital as against the increase in the Treasury market size since 2008 to below 5% at the end of 2020 and indicate that primary dealers' transactions are now just a little over 2% of the market, down from 14% in 2008.

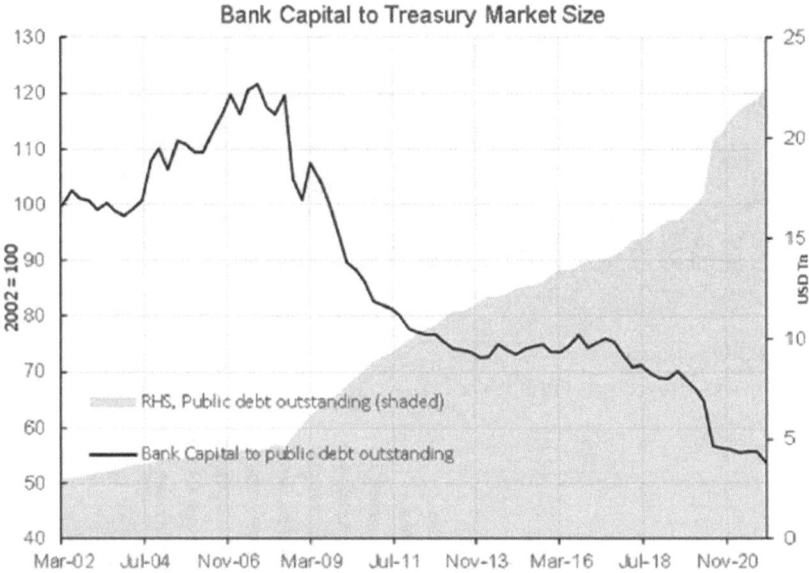

Fig. 2: US Treasury market growth has outpaced the growth in bank capital
(Sources: U.S. Treasury, Federal Reserve, Haver Analytics)

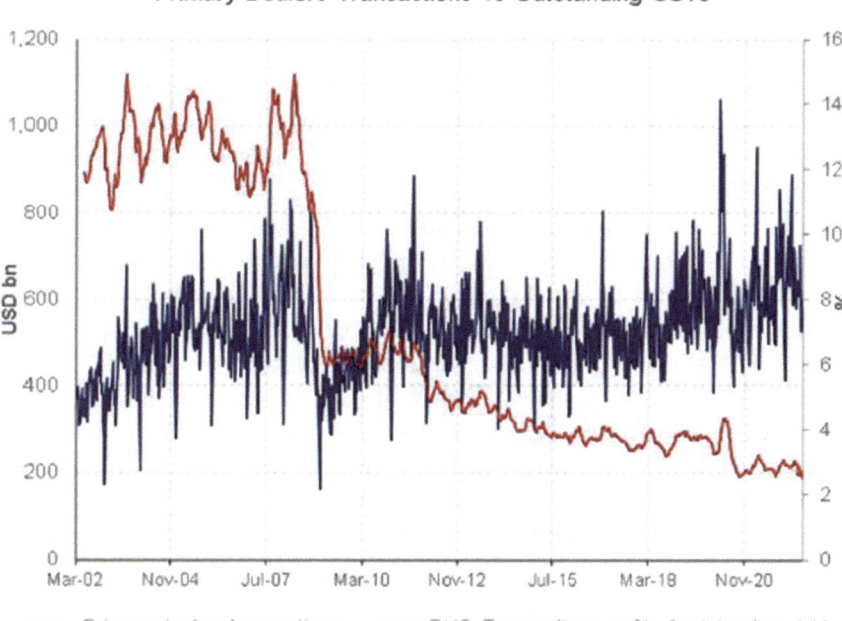

Fig. 3: Dealers' transaction volume falling as % of debt outstanding
(Source: U.S. Treasury)

The report comments that the growth in the market and changes in regulations have impacted intermediation capacity and that various metrics suggest dealers face binding constraints resulting in low participation relative to the growth in the market. It cites increased volatility and well known regulatory changes as having reduced dealers' intermediation capacity. These regulatory changes include the supplementary leverage ratio as a constraint on balance sheet growth of banks, the GSIB capital surpluses and the SA-CCR stress capital buffer as regulatory constraints, plus VAR constraints which reduce risk appetite at times of heightened volatility.

It is worth noting at this point that the foregoing discussion and conclusion apply principally to the Treasury market in the US. Not all markets are structured in the same way. In the European Union (EU) there are two significant differences. First, there is no equivalent to the Treasury market to be stabilized, since the EU has not issued any significant amount of bonds itself. Instead there are a myriad of smaller markets, built around sovereign bonds of the various Member States, in particular, those of Germany, the so-called Bunds. Secondly, in the EU banks are a much larger source of credit than in the US, so that it is possible that, as an April 2023 European Central Bank (ECB) Working Paper 2805 concluded, providing funds to the banks, and not to non-banks, may provide sufficient "trickle down" credit to help funds meet redemptions of the kind they faced in March 2020. The banks would therefore act in effect as intermediaries between the ECB and the non-banks, through the repo market. As noted above, US banks and their related broker-dealers do not have sufficient size and heft to transmit enough buying power in the US and all the literature on central bank intervention emphasizes the importance of the size of the central bank's commitment to their success. Diluting that strength by straining it through the sieve of the limited capacity of these intermediaries would be counterproductive. Hence my suggestion to cut out the middleman there.

Now back to the US and, I think, UK markets; if we do not look to stabilize the markets themselves, I fear we are condemned to play repeated rounds of "whack-a-mole" with ever changing new sources of financial stability. I think the title of Sarah Breeden's ISDA speech cited above, which she reprises in her contribution to this volume, says it well: "how did a small corner of the pensions industry threaten financial stability?" How, indeed, and where will the next small corner of the financial sector be which generates the next threat to financial stability? As Sarah notes in her speech and in her contribution to this volume, the size of the sector has little to do with its potential to cause mischief: "around £200 billion pooled LDI funds threatened the £1.4 trillion traded gilt market, which itself acts as the foundation of the UK financial system underlying around £2 trillion of lending."

Other Proposals

I agree that some changes will have to be made in the regulation of MMFs and bond OEFs, so that an examination of the proposals advanced for MMF and bond OEF reform, as was conducted by our panel and is reflected in the other panelists' contribution to this volume, is also in order. In particular liquidity mismatches between portfolio asset duration and the promise of daily liquidity to investors and share redemption prices which do not reflect the full cost to the fund of liquidating assets to meet redemptions are issues which should be dealt with. There are a number of sensible proposals to do that, which would reduce the extent to which these funds contribute to amplifying shocks originating elsewhere. However I simply believe that they are not central to solving the market failures we have repeatedly seen in the sovereign debt markets.

An excellent tool for evaluating these proposals is provided by the FSB in its October 2021 report on Policy Proposals to Enhance Money Market Fund Resilience. While these criteria were developed to evaluate MMF reform proposals, with a little adaptation to the different objectives of other bond OEFs, they can also be used to evaluate proposals to reform them as well. The criteria I find most relevant amount to asking the following questions: (i) would the proposal reduce the cash-like character of the fund; (ii) would it reduce FMA and thus diminish the incentive to redeem preemptively; (iii) would it impose liquidity restrictions on investors in normal market conditions and not just in stressed conditions; (iv) would it have a positive effect on the resilience of the fund; and (v) would it overall diminish the attractiveness of this kind of fund and reduce the diversity of funding sources for borrowers and thus make short-term funding more costly? If we omit point (i) and the reference to short-term in point (v), I think we have very useful criteria for evaluating proposals for bond OEFs as well as for MMFs.

That said, I must add an important caveat. Martin Moloney's thoughtful article in this volume examining in depth what we think we know about bond OEFs, together with Joanna Cound's empirical analysis of what actually happened during the "dash for cash" in March 2020 have made me more cautious about whether I know enough about the area to be certain of how regulation should best be changed in the area, or whether I have not been victim of certain appealing narratives about the actors and their motivations.

The second recommendation to enhance stability of the Treasuries market which the Group of 30 made in its 2021 report was to mandate central clearing of these securities. Darrell Duffie of Stanford also advocates central clearing as a solution. I am a little more cautious about central clearing. On its face it is an appealing idea, as it promises enhanced transparency and reduced counterparty risk. But I believe the structure of CCPs is more fragile than it appears. That was the conclusion of our 2019 conference on Resolution in Europe and the recent problems at the London Metals Exchange (LME) in 2022, which had to cancel trades in order to prevent what it termed a "death spiral" which would have led to the simultaneous bankruptcy of multiple clearing members, provide a recent example of this potential for fragility. It is possible that a CCP for Treasuries might be more robust, just based on the nature of the assets traded there, but I fear that the fundamental structural weaknesses we identified back in 2019 as obstacles to their successful resolution along the lines applicable to banks in case of failure remain. As I wrote at the time, unlike a bank or an insurance company, which are large institutions with assets and liabilities susceptible of being restructured along traditional lines, a failing CCP is a relatively small place with a failed risk model and not much to restructure. The panic around the LME tends to confirm that judgement. Also, mandating such a change in the market and implementing it will clearly, like most other solutions, take time and in the interim we will continue to live with the underlying market conditions which made the market so fragile in September 2019 and in March 2020.

Andrew Hauser's January 2021 speech provides a useful way to think about the issues involved in moving central banks from lender to last resort to market maker of last resort in the form of a triangle, depicting what he sees as the three steps –

I would say areas of focus – necessary to strengthen market functioning: (1) reforms to strengthen the resilience of private NBFIs to liquidity shocks, under which would come to various proposals to reform MMFs and bond OEFs, (2) strengthened market-wide infrastructure, under which would come the various proposals for central clearing of government securities and (3) better targeted central bank backstops, under which would come the expanded standing repo facility I advocate. (p. 4). He suggests they be seen as three presumably successive steps. I agree that they cover the fundamental issues involved, but I disagree with the implied order. I would start by focusing on his third part, because it is key to dealing with a market dysfunction.

There is a structural Problem in the Market for Treasuries that needs to be addressed directly

March 2020 involved a market dysfunction basically caused by the volume of Treasury issuances having vastly outstripped the capacity of traditional private sector market makers to intermediate effectively in stressed situations. Neither side of this equation of growing debt outstanding and shrinking broker/dealer and regulated bank balance sheets has reversed since then, nor is either likely to in a material way in the near future. The TBAC report cited above makes that clear. Focusing on the role of two categories of market participants, MMFs and bond OEFs, while useful in itself, will not solve the fundamental issue of market structure. Formulating, adopting and implementing reforms for these two sets of market actors will take time, no matter how far regulators and supervisors have advanced their thinking since March 2020. An idea of the extent and complexity, including the need for international cooperation, which could be involved can be gleaned from p. 78 of Chapter 3 of the IMF Global Financial Stability Report referred to above. Meanwhile, the next market stress is just as likely to come from another source, as it did in the Treasuries market in September 2019 or in the market for UK Gilts in the fall of 2022.

In September 2019 two seemingly anodyne factors, the withdrawal of quarterly tax payments from banks and MMFs on the same day that $54 billion of long-term Treasuries settled, resulted in drawing about $120 billion in cash out of the market over two days. As a result the primary dealers who purchased the Treasuries which they expected to finance in the repo market, found that the market was simply not able to provide the required liquidity. The strains in the repo market quickly spilled over into the Fed funds market. The Fed had to intervene by offering a total of $225 billion in overnight repos against US agency and agency MBS collateral and by adjusting two of its administered rates. Full details are available in an excellent February 2020 FEDS Notes.

Can we really afford to wait and see where the next source of stress comes from, once again be surprised at its source and yet again have to rely on an ad hoc response from the Fed, the Bank of England or any other central bank to deal with the situation, effectively and at the least cost? Or would it not be better to set up a system in advance to deal with potential market stress, so that they do not result in a crisis? With time to reflect on what the best features of such a system would be, what adverse consequences it should be designed to guard against, would we not be better off? The underlying market structure has not improved since March 2020. A November 2022 Liberty Street Economics blog from the Federal Reserve Bank of New York analysed the liquidity of the Treasuries market in 2022 and concluded that it had been relatively illiquid. In particular they found that the order book depth was the lowest it had been since March 2020, that volatility had also been high and that liquidity has tracked volatility. The blog concludes that "Treasury debt outstanding continues to grow. Moreover, lower-than-usual liquidity implies that a liquidity shock will have longer than usual effects on prices and perhaps be more likely to precipitate a negative feedback loop between security sales, volatility and illiquidity".

Happily, we do not have to start from scratch in designing such a system. One already exists, it just needs to be expanded to cover more of the key market actors. The Standing Repo Facility (SRF) is the Fed's overnight repo facility for US Treasury and agency bonds, which the Fed established in 2021 in response to the recommendation of the Group of 30 mentioned above, which was also one of the recommendations made in a December 2020 Hutchins Center working paper co-authored by Nellie Liang, then at the Brookings Institution and now Under Secretary of the US Treasury for Domestic Finance. That facility has a number of excellent features. It is a backstop facility designed to support the effective implementation of monetary policy and smooth market functioning. As a backstop facility, its minimum bid rate as of February 23, 2023 was set at 5.00 %, so above the pricing in the overnight repo market under normal market conditions. This is meant to insure that it will not be used under normal market conditions. A useful Liberty Street Economics blog from January 2022 notes "since pressures in overnight markets can be difficult to predict and are harder to tamp down once they emerge, a key benefit of the SRF is its ability to forestall rate pressures before they develop into larger disruptions. This characteristic should enhance market confidence...even if the SRF is little used." This latter trait is common to successful central bank interventions: they need to be large enough to impress the market (Hank Paulson's "bazooka") but if they succeed in doing this, the take up is often much lower. The Bank of England's intervention is the gilt markets in October 2022 is a good example of this phenomenon.

The SRF is limited in amount ($500 billion), in duration (overnight repos only) and, most important, in the number of its eligible counterparties (primary dealers and deposit taking institutions regulated in the US). I am not competent to pass on the amount or the limitation to overnight repos, but I do want to comment on the limited number of counterparties. As of April 8, 2022 the list had a grand total of 17 names on it, representing 14 bank groups. It is consistent with Nellie Liang's paper, but it means that the SRF excludes the NBFI sector entirely, so that the facility has to rely on the eligible regulated intermediaries to use it and then pass on its benefits to other market participants, even though these intermediaries have no legal obligation to do so, their internal risk management systems may counsel against use of the facility, as they counseled against increased market making in March 2020, and their balance sheets are demonstrably too small to provide the liquidity the Treasuries market needs in stressed situations. It is instructive to compare the 17 eligible counterparties for the Fed's repo program with the 148 eligible counterparties for the Fed's overnight reverse repo program, for an indication of who holds the securities involved.

The FSB's 20 October 2022 report on Liquidity in Core Government Bond Markets includes a good graphic depiction of the relative size of government bond holders by type:

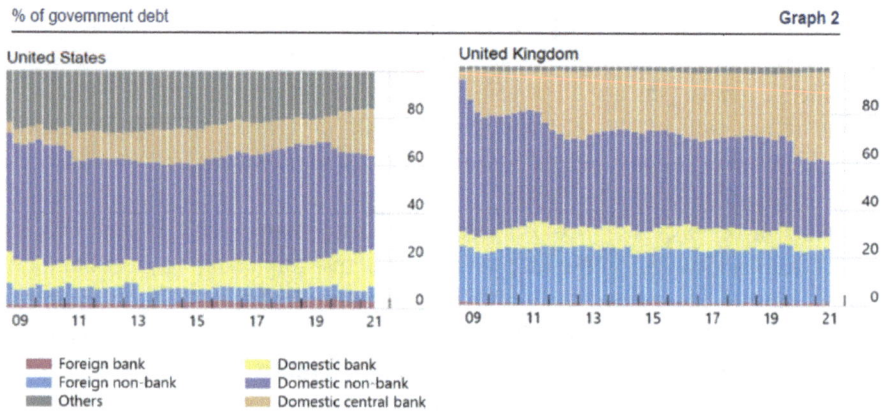

Fig. 4: Government debt by type of holder (Sources: IMF, FSB calculations).

The Fed's current standing repo facility is open only to the narrow yellow band in the graph above. I would like to expand it to the broad blue band above that. Thus, my suggested solution is to follow the Group of 30's recommendation and expand the Fed's existing repo facility to the broadest possible group of market participants who have eligible collateral. This proposal has been made implicitly by the Group of 30 in their July 2021 report (where they recommend "very broad access" (p. 9)) and explicitly by the Fed's then Vice Chairman for Financial Stability, Randal Quarles (in a speech in May 2020 at the Hoover Institution). The authors of the January 2023

ESRB report discussed more fully below are also explicit: while lending operations should be limited to supervised counterparties, "[a]s an MMLR, buy from all sellers, insisting on delivery versus payment." (p. 30) This notion does not find favor with central bank staff and traditionalists, who believe central banks should only provide liquidity to regulated financial institutions subject to prudential regulation and supervision, in order to avoid "moral hazard".

Before turning to the question of moral hazard, I would like to refer the reader to the analysis by Stuart Graham in this volume of the interconnections between NBFIs and regulated financial institutions. In his article on key risks faced by global banks he details the connections, both direct and indirect, between NBFIs and regulated banks. Looking at direct connections alone, he sees financing flows of $6 to 7 trillion in both directions. His firm estimates that the leading global US, European and Japanese banks have exposures to NBFIs equal to on average 165 % of CET1 capital and that in some cases the exposure is as high as almost 400 % of CET1 capital. He also notes indirect risks stemming from the fact that the banks own many of the same assets as the NBFIs, so that fire sales by NBFIs may also affect the value of regulated banks' assets. It seems to me that this degree of interconnection should not leave central banks indifferent as to the results that failures of NBFIs could have on the regulated banks they supervise.

Moral Hazard, LOLR and MMLR Interventions

Objections based on "moral hazard" are most justified where the central banks intervention takes the form of their traditional lender of last resort (LOLR) intervention, where they are taking credit risk of a particular borrower, especially if the collateral for these LOLR loans is anything other than government securities. But where the intervention takes the form of purchases of securities, especially of Treasuries, in what, since a seminal 2007 article by Anne Silbert and Willem Buiter, has come to be called "market making of last resort" (MMLR), it is fair to ask why the identity of the counterparties should be so restricted. Silbert and Buiter, writing in 2007, assumed the Fed could be able to deal with "just about any institution, organisation or individual" under its powers under section 13(3) of the Federal Reserve Act in "unusual and exigent circumstances". This of course harkens back to Bagehot's recommendation in "Lombard Street".

In his January 2021 speech, Andrew Hauser makes the important distinction between traditional LOLR activities which involved backstopping the funding liquidity of banks and the broadened focus of backstopping market liquidity, when severe dysfunction threatens financial stability. The traditional LOLR activities, which involved central banks taking credit risk of their debtors had, as he notes, been accompanied by "an extensive prudential regulatory regime requiring banks to take greater ownership of managing their own risks, and setting quantitative minima for liquidity buffers". In contrast, MMLR operations target market liquidity and seek to restore market functioning. And, as he shows, central bank interventions in crisis situations are increasingly taking the form of MMLR:

Chart 4: Central bank balance sheet responses to the Covid-19 shock during 2020
Changes in components of central bank balance sheets since end-Feb 2020 (as % of 2019 nominal GDP)

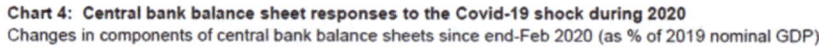

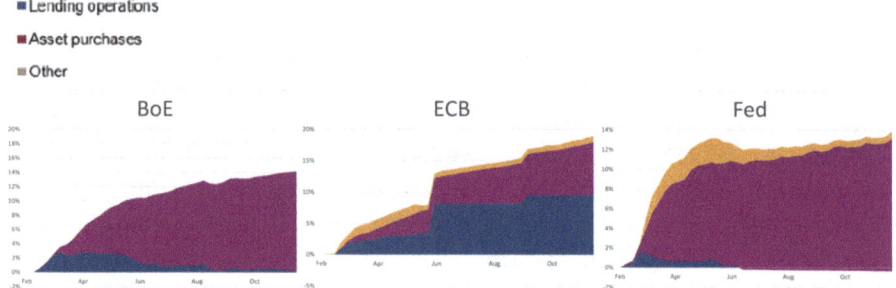

Sources: Bank of England, Bureau of Economic Analysis, European Central Bank, Eurostat, Federal Reserve Board, ONS and Bank calculations.

(a) Bank of England lending operations shown here: Indexed long-term repo, Contingent term repo facility, US dollar repo operations, Liquidity Facility in Euros, Term Funding Scheme and Term Funding Scheme with additional incentives for SMEs. Bank of England asset purchases shown here: Asset Purchase Facility and Covid Corporate Financing Facility.
(b) ECB lending operations: Lending to euro-area credit institutions related to monetary policy operations denominated in euro. ECB asset purchases: Securities held for monetary policy and other purposes.
(c) Federal Reserve lending operations: Repurchase agreements, Loans and Net portfolio holdings of TALF II LLC. Federal Reserve asset purchases: Securities held outright. Section of chart lying below the zero line from mid-2020 reflects a decline in repo outstanding relative to end-February.

Fig. 5: Central bank balance sheet responses to the Covid-19 shock during 2020. Changes in components of central bank balance sheets since end-Feb 2020 (as % of 2019 nominal GDP).

The ECB Working Paper No. 2805 of April 2023 discussed above concludes that whereas ECB lending programs had some trickle down effects, direct purchases were much more effective. Thus I believe that seeking to import the prerequisites for LOLR assistance to individual market actors into MMLR operations directed at restoring market liquidity makes much less sense, especially where the financial institutions subject to the prudential regulatory regime make up only a fraction of the holders of government securities. To limit access to central bank intervention to that small part of the market would seem self-defeating.

The distinguished authors of the January 2023 Report of the Advisory Scientific Committee of the European Systemic Risk Board (ESRB) on the topic "Stabilising financial markets: lending and market making as a last resort" come to a comparable conclusion for MMLRs, i.e. that central banks should be able to purchase "from a wide range of counterparties," (p.6) and note that in contrast to LOLR activities, "the MMLR does not need to know the identity or the financial soundness of the seller." (p. 20).

This corresponds to a remark Claudio Borio made at the conference that we are experiencing what he called a seismic fundamental change from looking at credit risk to collateral as a basis for a transactions. Concerning moral hazard the authors make the interesting observation that moral hazard already exists in the case of systemically important markets, based on central banks' prior interventions, even if the central banks do not have an established policy or program to intervene. Put another way, "constructive ambiguity" as it was once practiced by central banks, gains nothing in terms of preventing moral hazard in the Treasuries market. Their central point is worth citing at length: "an ad hoc structure ... means retaining most of the moral hazard costs while sacrificing the benefits of a thought-out, credible facility that reduces the likelihood and scale of any necessary interventions." (p. 8)

As noted above, I think an important distinction should be made between traditional LOLR interventions which targeted maintaining the liquidity of individual financial institutions and MMLR interventions targeted at maintaining the liquidity of entire markets. An individual institution might be tempted to engage in more risky behavior by the possibility of a bail-out, but a market isn't. It is the result of the interaction of market actors who have multiple motivations and business models, as Sarah rightly observed at the conference. It might be objected that repos, whilst structured as purchases are, in effect secured lending by another name and that, therefore we are dealing with a LOLR rather than a MMLR function and thus that all considerations applicable to LOLR programs should apply to repo programs, including the concern for moral hazard. I think that is to ignore what the purpose of the intervention is, which is not to benefit the particular counterparty by preserving it from insolvency, but rather to preserve the market from collapse. I also find the arguments of the authors of the ESRB paper cited above convincing.

But if we insist that moral hazard has a role to play in the discussion, my touchstone remains Larry Summers' September 23, 2007 short opinion piece entitled "Beware moral hazard fundamentalists", written to analyse the Long Term Capital Management rescue, in which he urges us to ask three questions about central bank interventions: "First, are there substantial contagion effects? Second, is the problem a liquidity problem or does it involve a problem of solvency? Third, is it reasonable to expect that the action in question will not impose costs on tax payers? If the answer to all three questions are affirmative, there is a strong case for public action." Asking all three questions in the MMLB context results, I believe, in affirmative answers. Yes, allowing the Treasury market to seize up will result in contagion. Yes, it is a liquidity problem. And yes, it is reasonable to expect that buying Treasuries especially as part of a repo transaction, will not impose costs on taxpayers.

Thus, I contend that not using the time between periods of market stress to design a system to deal with the next stress episode in a way which prevents it from developing into a full blown crisis, will do less to deter moral hazard than a thoughtfully designed program such as an expanded Fed standing repo program could accomplish. Plan beats no plan.

As this article was going to press in September 2023, the Bank of England (the "Bank"), in the person of Andrew Hauser, announced an initiative to do just that. Recognizing that in recent crisis situations banks did not (or could not) on-lend to NBFIs in sufficient size and that it is unrealistic for the private sector to self-insure against the most severe system-wide liquidity shocks, he announced an initiative to expand the Bank's liquidity provision to some parts of the NBFI sector. In a first step insurance companies and pension funds would be involved, while the Bank studied the possibility of expanding the initiative to further sectors of the NBFI world over time. In doing so, he emphasized the Bank's statutory authority to protect and enhance the stability of the entire UK financial system, encompassing banks, non-banks and markets. While expressing the usual central bank reservations about requiring recipients to have "appropriate ex ante resilience" and noting the operational challenges which would arise for the Bank from a much enlarged group of eligible counterparties, the fact that he is considering what types of NBFI need to be included to maximize policy efficiency and whether there may be ways to reach firms not subject to formal liquidity resilience requirements while still meeting the Bank's backstop principle goal, represents a significant leap forward in central bank thinking in the area. (pp. 3, 4, 9 and 14)

Conclusion: Key Attributes of MMLR Interventions

To summarize, my contentions are as follows:
- There was a time where constructive ambiguity and hastily cobbled together interventions could be relied upon to rescue markets in a crisis. That time is past. Markets are too large and move too quickly so that a plan/facility designed and announced in advance provides constructive clarity and primes hectic improvisation under pressure.
- The plan/facility has to give market makers the confidence to do their job knowing that they will not be left holding the bag on unsaleable assets.
- The plan/facility should be designed so that it is not attractive to use in normal circumstances, but does not generate stigma if used in a crisis, thus avoiding creating moral hazard in normal times, but recognizing that moral hazard considerations are largely out of place at the height of a crisis, when the proverbial house is on fire.
- The plan/facility should be designed so it has an exit which does not bloat the central bank's balance sheet and leave the central bank/treasury/taxpayer holding the bag, and the unwinding should not affect the market.

- Not all markets are important enough to merit setting up such a plan/facility, only the most important ones, such as those for the sovereign debt upon which all other debt markets are built, so Treasuries (and UK gilts).
- We have been used to thinking about such central bank interventions as involving a central bank acting as lender of last resort and rescuing individual financial institutions, but in the current financial world, such interventions are increasingly taking the shape of a central bank acting as market maker of last resort and are intended to stabilize a systemically important market as a whole. This involves not only a change in tools from loans to securities purchases, but also a change in focus and mindset.

The design that to my mind comes closest to meeting these criteria is the Fed's SRF standing repo facility for Treasuries, agency debt and agency mortgage-backed securities established by the Fed as recommended by the Group of 30: (a) it focuses on the most important US dollar market in the world; (b) given the size of the Treasuries market, there is no one other than the Fed, with the backing of the Treasury, with a balance sheet large enough and the credibility to do the job; (c) the Treasury market is the key to the stability of the financial markets so that maintaining it is surely within the central bank's mandate; (d) designing it as a repo facility means that the intervention creates the necessary liquidity on the front leg, but should unwind itself without either leg of the transaction (the purchase or the repurchase) causing the serious gyrations in the market that actual purchase and sale transactions would and, if there is a default, the Fed is left with US government obligations, not collateral of (more) dubious value. These characteristics correspond to the list of "desirable attributes of a framework to stabilising financial markets" in the ESRB report cited above, which includes buying from all sellers. So, the design is there. What needs to be changed, as a first step, is only the eligible counterparties, which needs to be broadened as much as possible, as per the ESRB report.

The counter argument that central banks should not extend their facilities to institutions which are not subject to prudential regulation and supervision puts an impossible burden on the currently eligible counterparties whose balance sheet size and regulatory positions limit what they can reasonably be expected to do. They were not able to stem the tide in March 2020 and will not be able to in a future crisis. While the current SRF facility can be expected to help them stand up more than they did in March 2020. The ECB's Working Paper No. 2805 indicates that this happened in the EU when the ECB announced additional bridge Long Term Refinancing Operations (LTROs) for EU banks, that paper also notes that lending programs are nowhere nearly as effective as direct central bank intervention. This risks exposing the entire market, including those supervised and regulated institutions to needless instability and thus the potential for needlessly large losses before the central bank finally bows to the normative power of financial reality and has to intervene, again, in an ad hoc way, to avoid a meltdown of the market and thus of the balance sheets of its regulated and supervised flock which hold the securities involved.

However, as noted above, expanding the eligible counterparties of the Fed's repo facility is only a first step, albeit an important one. The more complete solution would involve expanding the program into a purchase or market maker program. This would allow a fuller participation by the MMFs, who already make up the bulk of eligible counterparties under the Fed's existing reverse repo program.

References

Baklanova, Victoria, Isaac Kuznits, Trevor Tatum, *Primer: Money Market Funds and the Repo Market*, U.S. Securities and Exchange Commission, February 18, 2021

Breckenfelder, Johannes, Marie Hoerova, *Do non-banks need access to the lender of last resort? Evidence from the fund runs, Working Paper Series No 2805*, April 2023, European Central Bank

Breeden, Sarah, *Risks from Leverage: how did a small corner of the pension industry threaten financial stability?* Speech given at ISDA & AIMA, Bank of England, November 7, 2022

Buiter, Willem, Stephen Cecchetti, Kathryn Dominquez, Antonio Sánchez Serrano, *Report of the Advisory Committee No. 13*, European Systemic Risk Board, January 2023

Duffie, Darrell, *Still the world's Safe Haven? Redesigning the U.S. Treasury Market after the COVID-19 Crisis*, Hutchins Center, Brookings Institution, June 2020

Financial Stability Board, Global Monitoring Report on Non-Bank Financial Intermediaries, December 2022

Financial Stability Board, Policy Proposals to Enhance Money Market Fund Resilience, Final Report, October 11, 2022

Fleming, Michael and Claire Nelson, *How Liquid Has the Treasury Market Been in 2022*, Liberty Street Economics blog, Federal Reserve Bank of New York, November 15, 2022

Group of Thirty, *U.S. Treasury Markets, Steps Towards Increased Resilience*, July 2021

Hauser, Andrew, *From Lender of Last Resort to Market Maker of Last Resort via the dash for cash: why central banks need new tools for dealing with market dysfunction*, Speech given at Reuters, London, Bank of England, January 2021

International Monetary Fund, Global Financial Stability Report, April 2023

Liang, Nellie and Pat Parkinson, *Enhancing Liquidity of the U.S. Treasury Market under Stress*, Hutchins Working Paper #72, Brookings Institution, December 2020

Office of Debt Management, U.S. Treasury, Treasury Presentation to TBAC, Fiscal Year 2022 Q3 Report

Silbert, Anne and Willem Buiter, *The Central Bank as the Market Maker of Last Resort: From lender of last resort to market maker of last resort*, Vox EU, August 13, 2007

Summers, Lawrence, *Beware moral hazard fundamentalists*, Financial Times, September 23, 2007

IV. Regulated Financial Service Providers

Andreas Dombret and Oliver Wünsch

The Risks from false Illusions in financial Policy Making

Introduction

This text is to appear in the book reporting on the yearly ILF conference on the future of the financial sector that took place in January 2023 to discuss where the next financial crisis might come from. What sounded like a more academic exercise back then has since become reality, as two events have shaken the financial world: i) the collapse of the comparably small, regional Silicon Valley Bank (SVB) that sent shockwaves through the U.S.-domestic and international financial system and that prompted the U.S. authorities to establish bazooka-sized backstop facilities; and ii) the demise of Credit Suisse, the globally systemically important bank (G-SIB) that underwent a shot-gun marriage with the other Swiss G-SIB UBS in light of fears that any alternative strategies to deal with a bank run unprecedented in speed and scale would threaten global financial stability.

One might wonder whether these events, which have not been on the radar back in January (although some will claim they have), have fundamentally changed our risk assessment from the perspective of today. The emerging geopolitical environment, such as due to the Russian war in Ukraine, comes with new strategic challenges for the Western world. The latter used to dominate financial markets and policy making in recent decades built on the premise of free and liberal capital flows. Policy priorities such as the greening of the economy require vast amounts of financing, and many countries struggle with demographic developments that call into question the sustainability of social security systems and economic welfare.

To answer this question, we need to take a step back. Risk assessments, as well as the design of regulation, are based on assumptions. If the assumptions do not reflect reality, the outcomes of risk assessments and any decisions based on them will turn out to be less effective, monitoring frameworks will prove partially blind, and

Note: Dr. Andreas Dombret is former member of the board of the German Bundesbank and the ECB's Supervisory Board. Dr. Oliver Wünsch is former member of the International Monetary Fund's Monetary and Capital Markets Department and former Head of Strategy of the Swiss Supervisor FINMA. Both authors have significant private sector experience. They currently hold the positions of Global Senior Adviser and Partner, respectively, at Oliver Wyman, and focus central banking and capital markets issues globally. The authors thank Céline Kharma and Hélio Vale for their contributions to preparing this article as well as several reviewers for their insightful comments on earlier drafts.

https://doi.org/10.1515/9783111340937-013

policies as well as any risk-related regulation might turn out to be of limited effect or even be harmful.

In this paper, we are looking at several of the underpinnings of our current policy framework and argue that some of the important assumptions might in fact have turned out to be illusions and require a more structural review of financial and regulatory policies.

Number one: The Illusion of Liquidity

Financial intermediation is often about maturity transformation. Banks in particular fund long-dated loans and investments with deposits and wholesale funding that on average have a much shorter tenor. Maturity transformation allows banks to be profitable when they take in deposits at a lower rate than they are charging on their loans, akin to a simple carry-trade strategy. Banks operate under the assumption that most of the funding that is due can be rolled over or replaced in the market. No bank would survive the withdrawal of all funding that clients would be legally entitled to draw, since most of it is trapped in long-term loans.

Our current financial system has several "safety features" to prevent that situation from arising. First, risk management and related regulatory requirements aim at ensuring a bank remains solvent, therefore removing reasons for depositors to withdraw their funds based on concerns over the viability of a bank. This solvency pillar has been substantially strengthened in the aftermath of the Great Financial Crisis (GFC), such as by several elements of the Basel III reforms.[1] Second, liquidity rules compel banks to hold a certain amount of their assets so that they can liquidate them immediately, thereby putting a cap on maturity transformation, also with the Net Stable Funding Ratio (NSFR) implicitly setting a limit on the maturity gap.

On top of those bank-by-bank buffers, a mutualised safety net had been established decades ago[2] and has been subsequently reinforced. Central bank-provided Emergency Liquidity Assistance (ELA) enables banks to turn non-cash assets (such as bonds or less-quality assets) into cash at the "discount window" with the central bank, in case it is not able to liquidate non-cash assets in the market.[3] Financial systems also feature deposit guarantee schemes (DGS) that step in covering a portion of a bank's deposits if a bank were to fail on solvency grounds.[4] Such help can be extended by means of liquidity support where the DGS provides funds to allow for a

1 Basel Committee on Banking Supervision (2011)
2 The U.S. Federal Deposit Insurance Corporation (FDIC) was established in FIXME.
3 Dobler et al. (2016)
4 Moretti et al. (2020)

rapid pay out of depositors in cash while the recovery and sale of the failing bank's assets takes more time. It can also take the shape of solvency support, where any shortfall from asset recovery is borne by an ex-ante built fund and ex-post contributions of remaining banks. To cover for worst-case scenarios, DGSs enjoy an explicit or implicit public (sovereign) backstop, significantly boosting its capacity, only limited by the strength of the sovereign as debtor and the currency.

The DGS cannot provide an unlimited guarantee. Intended at providing reassurance mostly to less sophisticated depositors and for cases involving smaller, less sophisticated banks, the guaranteed amount is usually capped, for example at EUR 100,000 in the European Union (EU) or USD 250,000 in the U.S. Above this amount, deposits are uninsured, and in the U.S. such deposits currently represent about 40 % of all bank deposits. Banks with large proportions of uninsured deposits, such as SVB (90 % of uninsured deposits) and First Republic (66 % of uninsured deposits), are therefore particularly vulnerable to deposit flights.

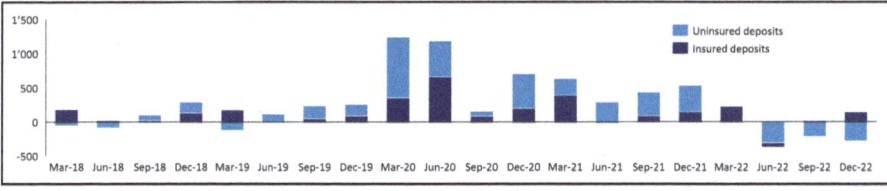

Fig. 1: Quarterly Change in Deposits in all FDIC[5]-Insured Institutions 2018–2022, USD BN
(Source: FDIC, Total deposits declined for the last 3 quarters of 2023, with a total decline of USD 143BN between Q3 and Q4, entirely driven by a reduction in uninsured deposits, as insured deposits increased).

It is for this reason that the post-GFC Basel III reforms placed significant emphasis on liquidity by requiring firms to hold sufficient liquid assets to sustain outflows for 30 days during times of stress and better matching the duration of their assets and liabilities. Those liquidity requirements become more costly for banks in a changing interest rate regime, as many high-quality liquid assets (HQLA) bought at the behest of the regulator will fall in market value with rising rates. Safe government bonds bought a year ago for example will now trade at larger discounts than those issued at higher rates today and are therefore worth less when banks are forced to sell them to meet depositors' demands. This chain of events is the direct result of the transmission mechanism of monetary policy, and particularly ill-regulated environment and badly managed banks that did not prepare for the interest rate lift off

---

5 Federal Deposit Insurance Corporation, www.fdic.gov

were particularly vulnerable.[6] Central banks in several countries and currency unions have amassed a large amount of sovereign debt by building up large long positions in government bond markets as result of quantitative easing. Banks in turn had to navigate such environment of excess liquidity and low interest rates, often building up large holdings of safe assets following risk-return considerations in a low-interest rate – large money supply environment and regulatory requirements. Further exacerbated by the central banks' "forward guidance" the general belief was that interest rates were unlikely to rise markedly and swiftly, and that the liquidation value of those instruments was therefore safe, which has proved untrue and generated harmful consequences.[7] Hence, while Basel III liquidity rules have succeeded in making banks hold larger buffers, this came with the side effect of increasing banks' exposure to interest rate risk (of course, banks are exposed to interest rate risks from other parts of their balance sheet as well).

The system built around maturity transformation then, by design, is prone to requiring (and raising the expectations of) public support to bridge the gap in stress situations. Such support measures have been created in several important economies. The ECB established the so-called "Transmission Protection Instrument" (TPI)[8] that would allow the ECB to intervene in the market to protect yields of specific Eurozone countries in case spreads between bond yields would increase so much that they would constrain the ECB's ability to implement a common monetary policy for the Eurozone. The sheer existence of the TPI can be considered as one of the factors allowing the ECB to implement recent rate hikes in combatting inflation, limiting the risk of hikes causing debt sustainability issues for certain Eurozone countries. Indirectly, the TPI is also protecting banks, some of which hold large amounts of local sovereign bonds in Eurozone countries considered economically weaker and therefore attracting less foreign private sector demand for their public debt. In the U.S., the Federal Reserve has created the "Bank Term Funding Program" (BTFP), allowing banks to repo U.S. Treasury securities at face value for cash, irrespective of their current market pricing.

The effect of such measures could be considered as a "bail out", especially as some financial market participants have enjoyed windfall profits as result of the interventions. This is often a cause for public outcry, as government funds are perceived to be persistently and unfairly extended to banks with poor risk manage-

---

6 Board of Governors (2023)

7 While banks can prevent the recognition of such "mark to market" valuation adjustments, by classifying tem as "hold-to-maturity" positions, this will only help to the extent the bank does not actually need to sell the assets, as such transaction would take place at the (lower) prevailing market value.

8 ECB (2022)

ment policies under the guise of maintaining financial stability. However, the "price" of such interventions could also be regarded as the "price to pay" by central banks and sovereigns to compensate for the distortive effects of central banks' balance sheet expansion, yield control efforts and high public indebtedness – all in the context of the incentives set by the regulatory framework of low to zero risk weights for sovereign exposures and the treatment of the latter as HQLA. As a result, today uninsured deposits have in reality to be considered implicitly backed and protected by the government, as any imposition of losses on depositors is seen as being too risky for financial and economic stability and would itself disturb the transmission of monetary policy.

Liquidity requirements can only reduce the risk of the system failing and requiring emergency government assistance. There is no simple approach to this problem as any approach addressing the issue completely would prevent commercial banks from performing maturity transformation and would therefore upend significant elements of today's banking business models and the concept of "fractional reserve banking" as such. Alas, a simple strengthening of liquidity requirements, such as an increase of the Liquidity Coverage Ratio (LCR), alone will not help as there is still the risk of a stress scenario exceeding the assumptions underpinning the calibrations, requiring the consideration of more radical solutions.[9]

At theoretical level, such solutions could for example be the introduction of pure payment banks: tightly regulated banks that only provide access to the payments system without taking any credit or maturity risks. These banks earn a safe return by simply investing the deposits in a master account with the central bank and thus cannot fail or suffer a run. This would effectively segregate customers unwilling to hold uninsured deposits in "traditional" banks and avoid the problem of systemically important banks holding large amounts of uninsured deposits prone to run risk. Attempts to create such payment banks have however not been successful so far. For example, the U.S.-based "TNB" ("The Narrow Bank") is yet to become operational, importantly as the Federal Reserve has so far not admitted TNB to its facilities. In 2018, the unsuccessful "Sovereign Money" initiative in Switzerland proposed to only allow the Swiss National Bank to create deposit money, thus insuring all bank deposits through backing by the central bank.[10] The 2012 work of IMF economists analysing Irving Fisher's "Chicago Plan"[11] had led to intense discussions at the time, albeit limited to academic circles. The appetite for such more radical solu-

---

9 It should be noted, however, that U.S. regional banks like SVB had been exempted from Basel liquidity rules by policy decision. Board of Governors (2023).
10 Swiss National Bank (2018)
11 Benes/Kumhof (2012)

tions has been very limited. The current system was seen to "work". And any move away from fractional reserve banking might lead to stronger political influence on credit allocation decisions, thereby undermining a key pillar of a liberal market economy. Insofar as such responsibility would fall into the remit of central banks, such extended role could also further endanger their independence.

While we subscribe to these counterarguments, we cannot ignore that the environment has changed. Concerns over monetary and financial stability have caused policy makers to (again) provide blanket guarantees to financial market participants. The Covid crisis as well as the challenges related to climate change and greening the economy prompted governments to absorb significant risks based on broader macro-economic and policy considerations, and they became very active funding providers, either through direct grants or state-backed development banks. Finally, central banks have to various degrees become political actors, such as by backstopping governments or by considerations on how to support green financing objectives as part of their secondary mandate.

Even if more radical solutions might eventually not be pursued, approaches that have stronger structural effects than the Basel III reforms so far should be explored. For example, additional liquidity requirements reducing the maturity gap could be implemented in the form of requiring banks to be funded more in the long-term, increasing deposit and wholesale maturities to match the tenor of long-dated loans. This could entail a review of the design and calibration of the NSFR. This would imply customer deposits earning a higher return, under the condition that they cannot be withdrawn before a pre-determined tenor, perhaps not even at a penalty rate. Such requirements would make parts of the banks' balance sheet closer resemble money market funds, and other parts closer to investment vehicles. For the former, stricter liquidity rules already apply such as a more substantial liquidity buffer in the event of rapid redemptions, and mechanisms to impose the cost of their redemption on redeeming fund investors. In the end, the solution might be somewhere in the middle. They will be costly to implement, though such increased cost might be seen as an ex-ante insurance premium as opposed to today's ex-post bail-outs. They might also provide a further stimulus toward the development of a capital market in Europe.

Finally, Non-Bank Financial Intermediation (NBFI, formerly "Shadow Banking") has gained importance over recent years. The March 2020 turmoil exposed the weaknesses of NBFIs, as withdrawals in Money Market Funds (MMFs) heavily exacerbated financial fragility, highlighting the need for stronger resilience in the NBFI sector. Banks remain heavily interconnected with NBFI providers, as there are funding relationships in both directions. At the same time, NBFIs usually do not have access to the central bank "discount window", which makes any issues at NBFIs crystallize in the formal banking system due to the interlinkages between the two. Liquidity risk considerations and rules therefore need to consider the NBFI sector and its links to the banks as well.

Banks enjoy a substantial privilege of having access to central bank facilities. In turn, central banks rely on banks in implementing monetary policy and providing lending to the economy. Efforts to minimise risks might therefore also involve a discussion on how the risks (and benefits) are distributed between banks and the broader financial sector, central banks and ultimately the sovereign.

Number two: The Illusion of loss Absorbency

One lesson from the GFC was related to the issue of not being able to expose bond holders and equity holders of banks to losses. Authorities saw themselves unable to enforce losses on any creditors as they feared wide-spread ramifications on the trust in the broader financial system and therefore preferred to stage large-scale bailouts. Banks even shied away from applying contractual clauses in their bond documentation that would allow them to withhold coupon payments, citing concerns on the negative impact of such measures on market confidence and ratings.

The post-GFC solution was to establish a clearer creditor hierarchy, creating an unmistakable understanding on which claims might be at risk in case a bank faces financial troubles. This included stronger requirements of the Basel Committee on Banking Supervision (BCBS) on capital instruments („capital quality"),[12] in particular related to hybrid instruments, as well as "Loss-Absorbency Requirements" as per the Financial Stability Board's resolution framework.[13] Most notably, large banks are now required to issue additional debt that can be bailed in by the resolution authority if other means to cover losses are exhausted. Holding such bail-inable debt is mandatory for G-SIBs (Total Loss Absorbing Capital; TLAC)[14] and is also needed for D-SIBs in some countries, including in the EU (MREL).[15] The objective was to reduce any hurdles and potential spill overs when such claims would need to be touched in a crisis scenario, such as by writing them down.

Events around SVB and Credit Suisse have shown that despite the upfront legal clarity provided by current frameworks, contagion concerns might still deter authorities from imposing losses on creditors, regardless of what legal frameworks and bond documentations provide for. Such concerns are not only rooted in legal risks (such as the fear of cross-defaults which constrained the authorities' room to man-

---

12 Basel Committee on Banking Supervision (2019)
13 Financial Stability Board (2011)
14 Financial Stability Board (2015)
15 Single Resolution Board (2023)

oeuvre during the GFC and which should have been contained as result of legal changes in context of the resolvability initiatives[16]). This is since bail-in is not only a tool to shore up the capitalisation of a bank, but rather are a loss-transfer tool. For political or economic policy considerations decision makers might decide to not trigger the conversion or write-down of loss-absorbing bonds. Cases include the government-orchestrated rescue of the Italian regional banks „Banca Popolare di Vicenza" and „Veneto Banca", where junior bonds had been sold to non-qualified investors that the authorities did not want to expose to losses consistent with the EU Bank Recovery and Resolution Directive (BRRD), despite a "failing or likely to fail" declaration by the ECB and a negative "Public Interest Assessment" by the Single Resolution Board (SRB).[17] In the case of SVB, it is said that one of the reasons for not hitting uninsured depositors was to protect the cash holdings of technology investors and companies, suspecting that otherwise the availability of financing to the West Coast technology ecosystem could be negatively impacted. Finally, contagion considerations are of utmost importance. Imposing losses on the creditors of one bank could trigger runs on banks that are perceived as being vulnerable as well. A tool aimed at plucking a capital gap in one bank might cause systemic liquidity ramifications that are considered being graver than the bail-out of a failing bank that was supposed to be avoided as one of the main objectives of the GFC's regulatory reforms. While one might argue that loss absorbency could still hold in idiosyncratic crises, such isolated failures are the exception, and most of the bank failures happen in context of macroeconomic vulnerabilities, which come with broader fragilities and therefore contagion risk.

There are three important conclusions: First, loss-absorbency might not work in systemic crises, and government-led support measures might be required to limit broader economic damage. It will again depend on the fiscal and monetary capacity of governments and safety nets to determine whether there is enough capacity to fend off crises. And although substantial progress has been made on establishing clearly delineated safety nets, one might wonder whether their capacity is big enough to cope with systemic scenarios. For example, at this time the Eurozone would not have the formal facilities and powers to extent liquidity at a scale and under the circumstances that were deemed necessary to deal with the cases of SVB and CS.[18] Second, as soon it becomes consensus that loss-absorbency only applies in non-sys-

---

16 ISDA (2015)

17 One of the subordinated bond investors committed suicide, creating a huge backlash against the decision and prompting the Italian authorities to avoid further bail-ins at all cost.

18 In the case of Credit Suisse, the Swiss authorities provided guarantees and liquidity backstops in an amount of more than EUR 200 bn. This significantly exceeds the capacity of the Banking Union's backstop (SRF and ESM backstop) of EUR 148 bn. Moreover, without a centralised deposit guarantee

temic and idiosyncratic scenarios, banks that do not enjoy the benefits of being "too big to fail" acquire a stigma in good times and become vulnerable to runs in bad times. Considering that such smaller banks form a group of firms that in total must be considered systemic (even if each firm on its own is not), so that all fears of contagion as well as the policy consequence of preferring bailouts to protect stability as well as the constraints involved (namely the sovereign-bank-loop), would apply equally. Third, as soon as government backstops are required, decisions that impact all or some classes of creditors become inherently political, which comes with risks for investors that are difficult to assess ex ante and might provide incentives to exit certain exposures or not enter them in the first place.

These conclusions are hardly new. In fact, they have been the starting point for the post-GFC reform considerations. Taking into account the experiences of recent bank failures, a review should analyse what measures would be needed to make loss-absorbency even more credible and executable, as implementation of resolution measures for a large bank or a group of mid-sized banks seems to be harder than already expected and comes with contagion risks. The recent repricing of AT1 instruments after the events in March 2023 could however be a good sign, insofar as investors realise the nature and risk of loss-absorbing capital instruments.

Number three: The Illusion of monetary Policy being independent of financial Stability

Monetary stability and financial stability are two separate areas of consideration with cleanly separated individual goals which, in the conventional macro-economic view, have no trade-off relationship or conflict of interest. Monetary stability, or price stability, consists of maintaining a stable increase in consumer price index over the medium term, while financial stability consists of maintaining asset price stability and avoiding banking crises. In the conventional view, it is argued that the two will tend to promote and reinforce each other in the long run. Historically, this has often been the case, as banking crises typically occurred during recessions following periods of high inflation.

However, recent history demonstrates that this relationship can break, and a trade-off between monetary stability and financial stability can exist. In such cases, central banks should consider the impact of their policy decisions on both areas. The primary responsibility of the central bank is monetary policy, and it is essential

---

in the Banking Union (EDIS), there will be continued dependence on the sovereign backing in each country for their local DGSs.

that it remains their main and independent mandate. This does not, however, mean that the central bank should throw the financial sector and all its stakeholders (i.e., most of the economy) under the bus in its fight against inflation. Rather, it should take measures against the built-up of financial stability risks that might unduly constrain its monetary policy conduct in the future, as well as consider the impact of monetary policy on financial stability at all times.

Recent rapid rises in interest rates and monetary policy tightening are creating stresses in the financial system that caused multiple bank failures and general market turmoil, as some business models are not able to adapt to the changing market conditions. Further tightening monetary policy could unmask additional weaknesses in the industry, particularly for small banks, as well as in the non-bank financial sector. This raises questions as to the risk incurred if central banks follow a pure and independent monetary policy view focused on fighting inflation. In such cases, a clean separation between monetary and financial stability goals is much more difficult to achieve. Rate setters at the ECB pushed to maintain this clean separation during their March 2023 meeting, pressing ahead with additional rate rises, despite rising tensions in the financial markets.

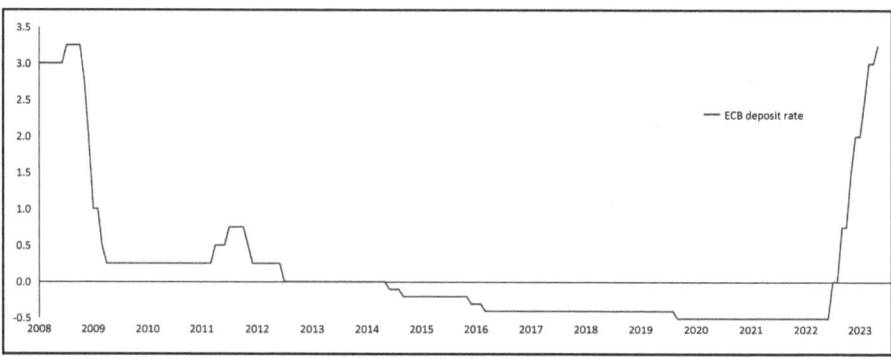

Fig. 2: ECB Deposit Rate 2008–2023, in % (Source: ECB).

Several options are available to central banks to manage potential conflict between price stability and financial stability. Ex-ante structural elements of capital and liquidity regulation (see above) as well as cyclical macro-prudential tools can be implemented,[19] although the latter might be difficult to target, are challenging to design and calibrate given gaps in the understanding of transmission channels and could attract political pushback. As described above, interventions like the TPI or

---

[19] Claessens (2014)

funding backstops could be required to gain and retain room to maneuver on monetary policy without creating excessive damage to financial stability. Optimal monetary policy should allow deviations from the targeted inflation rate in the short term when it creates strains in the financial system, to preserve price stability in the long term. In any case, however, price stability should remain the uncontested primary objective for a central bank to pursue, considering the damage of de-anchoring inflation expectations and protracted episodes of elevated inflation cause to the economy and to the confidence society and markets have in the monetary system.

Number four: The Illusion of financial Liberalism?

Many papers have been written on the extent to which regulation is consistent with a free market economy. We will not replicate this debate here, although we need to highlight that increasingly important players in financial markets cannot be regarded as liberal economies. Rather, we want to highlight the re-emerging connection between politics and finance. Over centuries it was common for the sovereign to use financial institutions to pursue political objectives, often coming with exorbitant benefits for the financiers. The Bank of England was founded in 1694 to provide the financing for the rapid expansion of King William III's naval fleet. This created dependencies into both directions: In 1523, Jakob Fugger, one of the most powerful financiers in history, sent a dunning to emperor Charles V demanding immediate repayment of an overdue loan with interest and without further delay. While finance and politics have always been intertwined, the last thirty years let this interconnection fade into the background, and political intervention into the financial system was limited. Rather, politics was paying close attention to the views of "the markets" in assessing which policies should be pursued. Only recently, the reaction of financial markets to the announcement of the British "Mini Budget" back in October 2022 led to an immediate collapse of the Truss government when investors dumped UK sovereign debt and the Bank of England had to intervene.

Going forward, we might see more intervention of politics into financial markets, directly and indirectly. Typical regulatory measures to make the system sounder and more stable will be joined by legislative action and market interventions that gear the financial system toward promoting political objectives. These could include rules that prohibit business relations with certain countries, corporates and individuals or make such relations prohibitively expensive, perhaps labelled as "friendshoring", also as to provide a competitive advantage to business that is politically favoured. While some elements of sustainability aim at ensuring financial institutions include climate-related aspects into their risk assessment, others might more directly interfere with financing decisions in line with political priorities. The

EU's discussion on whether nuclear power is to be considered as "sustainable technology" shows how science can often not play the role as an independent and fact-based referee. Depending on future developments, more drastic interventions could be considered, such as capital controls or measures of "financial repression," such as demanding that social security and insurance funds increase allocations toward sovereign securities so as to manage borrowing costs for the state. All these ideas are not new and have been or still are in place in many countries, including the developed world. However, as the debate on "Modern Monetary Theory" showed, this toolset has supporters in liberal market economies. What some might call "market distortion" is regarded a targeted intervention to pursue justified policies by others.

The consequences for the financial sector can be profound, as the category of "political risk", i.e., the impact of political decisions on asset valuations and business prospects, re-emerge as a truly relevant factor in advanced economies. This is especially challenging given the typical investment time horizon spans many years and decades and is therefore much longer than the time horizon for which political decisions are taken. It adds complexity that such political risks are not only attached to the assets. Rather, regulation might restrict investors and financiers from holding certain investments, constraining the deployment of capital or even requiring divestments of assets currently held on unfavourable terms. Combined with the added challenges of cross-border business, effective management of political risk and a good understanding of the evolving long-term policy environment will become an even more important success factor in international finance for private firms as well as central banks, regulators, and supervisors. Likewise, policymakers will need to keep an eye on the impact of their actions on macro and financial stability, which requires an ongoing and strong dialogue of all institutions involved as well as creating an environment of predictable policy decisions that market participants can rely on in the longer term.

Conclusion

Strategic and tactical decisions of financial market participants are based on assumptions, as is the regulatory framework and the tools, methods and processes to implement it. Recent events have demonstrated that some fundamental assumptions underpinning financial policies might need to be reconsidered, as work continues to further improve the stability and resiliency of the financial system. What has become more important in recent years is that policy shifts and actions by official institutions have an increasing impact on financial markets and participants. The very accommodative monetary policy in key economies has enabled the build-up of substantial leverage in the private and public sector and has fuelled asset bubbles. A reversal, for example due to the fight against inflation, is going to be costly for some or many, in particular when considering contagion effects. From a broader economic and political stability perspective, it could be considered as being too costly, in the end resulting in a wholesale public insurance for financial risk taking.

The same approach applies to other aspects of financial policy, such as measures to provide the substantial amounts of financing necessary for the global green transition. Policy and lending decisions to be taken and incentives provided to market participants come with costs and risks, and there will be a push for a public insurance against it. In sum, financial market participants will increasingly rely on implicit or explicit public backstops, creating moral hazard. More importantly, there is a high likelihood that the governments' ability to afford such backstops could be overwhelmed. High and increasing public debt ratios combined with increasing cost of debt provides clear warning signals, while approaches like the "Modern Monetary Theory" claiming a central bank could finance increased spending by monetizing sovereign debt have been debunked by recent inflation dynamics, if they ever had any validity for countries with no international reserve currency at all.

References

Basel Committee on Banking Supervision (BCBS 2011): Basel III: A global regulatory framework for more resilient banks and banking systems
Basel Committee on Banking Supervision (2019): Definition of Capital (CAP)
Benes, J., Kumhof, M. (2012): The Chicago Plan Revisited, International Monetary Fund Working Paper 12/202
Board of Governors of the Federal Reserve System (2023): Review of the Federal Reserve's Supervision and Regulation of Silicon Valley Bank
Claessens, S. (2014): An Overview of Macroprudential Policy Tools, International Monetary Fund, Working Paper 14/214
Dobler, M. et al. (2016): The Lender of Last Resort Function after the Global Financial Crisis, International Monetary Fund, Working Paper 2016/10
European Central Bank (2022): Combined monetary policy decisions and statement, 21 July 2022
Financial Stability Board (2011): Key Attributes of Effective Resolution Regimes for Financial Institutions
Financial Stability Board (2015): Principles on Loss-absorbing and Recapitalisation Capacity of G-SIBs in Resolution
ISDA (2015): ISDA 2015 Universal Resolution Stay Protocol
Moretti, M. et al. (2020): Managing Systemic Banking Crises: New Lessons and Lessons Relearned, International Monetary Fund, Departmental Paper No. 2020/003
Single Resolution Board (2023): MREL Policy 2023
Swiss National Bank (2018): Arguments of the SNB against the Swiss sovereign money initiative (Vollgeldinitiative)

Torry Berntsen

A "Five C" Approach to Managing Risk

Proactively navigating the evolving Risk Landscape

Although every year brings challenge and change, the past few years seem to have brought more than their fair share of crises, both natural and man-made. In recent months, we have seen the failure of Silicon Valley Bank – the second largest bank failure in US history, Silvergate Bank and Signature Bank – a US regional bank. Equally, we have seen the process set in motion for Credit Suisse to be acquired by UBS, all whilst the recovery from Covid-19 is still fresh in the mind and ongoing human tragedies continue to unfold in places such as Ukraine, Turkey, and Syria.

On this basis, CEOs around the globe are looking at how the risk environment is evolving, and how well prepared their teams and organisations are. Navigating this landscape is not guaranteed and complex, however, with a clear focus on a few key principles – the "Five Cs" – then the path ahead is more straightforward.

An evolving risk environment

Since the global financial crisis of 2007–8, in general terms, banks' approach to risk – including from a capital, credit and compliance perspective – has become far more rigorous. The benefits of this approach were illustrated through the sector's resilience during the Covid-19 pandemic and the market volatility that we have experienced over the past year. However, as we have seen recently, not everyone gets this right.

Banks therefore cannot be complacent, and leaders need to be constantly aware that the risk environment continues to evolve, and things can change quickly. Geopolitical risk is an obvious area of change and a focus for CEOs globally. For a bank like Standard Chartered that operates in many of the world's most dynamic countries, this risk gains an additional dimension, both to ensure the safety and well-being of our staff, and to meet the often rapidly changing needs of our clients in these markets.

Cyber risk and financial crime are areas where we spend a great deal of time and attention as a bank, particularly given our international footprint and diversity of markets in which we operate. Likewise, the need to comply with regulations around the world can be challenging for an international bank where geographic specific regulations may contradict or diverge. There are also industry changes taking place, such as the growth of shadow banking and the non-regulated banking sec-

https://doi.org/10.1515/9783111340937-014

tors as well as cryptocurrency, which still hold some areas of concern, particularly across consumer protection and financial conduct. Banks also have a major role to play in tackling climate risk, an issue that is of primary importance to the markets in which we operate, and which are vulnerable to the effects of climate change.

An inward-looking approach to Risk

While these macro and global issues are familiar and widely discussed, many companies face considerable internal challenges that are less frequently acknowledged. For example, like many industries, we've seen workforce attrition in the banking sector over the past couple of years, as well as moves across banks. Workforce mobility can, of course, be positive, by injecting new ideas and perspectives. On the other hand, we need to think about how we ensure continuity of experience for clients and consistent levels of expertise and service offering. Maintaining and building culture and identity as an organisation also becomes more challenging in the context of changing personnel.

The "Five Cs" of Managing Risk

Banks need to remain vigilant to changing risk dynamics. This applies not only in the boardroom, but a risk-aware culture needs to extend across the organisation as a whole, both upwards and downwards. I encourage my team to adopt a 'Five Cs' approach to doing this:

Communication – Throughout my career, I have found the most worthwhile and productive relationships, including with regulators, supervisors, colleagues, and partners, are those characterised by regular, proactive communication centred on honesty. By ensuring a culture based on open communication when times are good, difficulties are easier to overcome at times when trust and transparency may be tested. As the saying goes, a problem shared is a problem halved.

Collaboration – Senior executives are faced with a myriad of risks which can seem overwhelming. Many are dealt with using the standard "risk register" approach and through operational processes, and hence not always requiring a great deal of senior leaders' time. But some of the risks I've mentioned so far: cyber, financial crime, climate, prudential, as well as risks around disintermediation and digital disruption, require a strategic approach to policy, priority, and investment – spanning multiple departments and experts. Collaboration is therefore key. While we can make progress in addressing these risks, we will not 'solve' them; likewise, they will continuously evolve, so as a bank, and a wider industry, we need to remain vigilant and look not just for 'quick fixes' but focus on longer term and systemic approaches to risk, utilising all relevant resources and insights.

Continuous education – I have mentioned the importance of a risk-oriented culture, which may sound obvious, but many of the people now in, or moving into positions of responsibility may not have directly experienced high inflation or interest rates during their professional lifetimes. The evolution of new risks, such as from the ESG and digital agendas, also means upskilling our people is important to mitigate their impact. As such, we cannot forget the importance of continuous education and sharing of experiences across teams, organisations, and the wider industry. I'm not advocating everyone to look in the rear-view mirrors in order to make decisions, however, as Winston Churchill succinctly put it, "those that fail to learn from history are doomed to repeat it".

Co-ordination – Regulatory compliance is a necessary priority for senior leaders in international financial services organisations, both to ensure that the company retains the necessary permissions to do business in each country, and as part of our belief in and commitment to a well-managed robust industry. This can be more difficult when regulations in each country appear to diverge, or where regulations may have unintended consequences. Co-ordination between industry and regulators, and co-ordination between regulators is essential to ensuring that new regulations achieve the desired behaviours and outcomes, and do not create unwarranted or unintentional compliance burdens for companies operating internationally.

Creating value – Finally, it is easy for senior executives at banks and other financial services providers to spend significant time, effort, and attention on managing existing risks, such that they forget the business itself and the potential impact of systemic risks on the horizon. Banks need to deliver value for clients, shareholders, and community stakeholders. I'm not advocating growth at all costs, however, not investing in creating value is at least a big a risk as the issues I mentioned earlier. Equally, we need to grow our people and foster talent – this involves making commitments to build more inclusive teams that live and breathe our organisational culture. Furthermore, we need to develop long-term trusted client and regulatory relationships and deliver the solutions that help our clients to grow and flourish.

Bringing it all together

The future of regulated financial service companies in general is bright. Banks continue to provide essential services to society. To manage risks effectively, and build more robust, agile, and resilient organisations, senior leaders should not dampen their ambitions; rather, they should be thinking about how they can achieve these ambitions in a way that brings their entire organisations and their regulators with them – aligning on purpose, culture, and talent. By doing this, banks and financial services providers will find themselves in a stronger position to understand, prioritise, and mitigate their risks, and take opportunities as they arise.

This article is an updated version to one that appeared on www.thebanker.com in April 2023

José Manuel Campa

Higher Interest, Inflation and lower Output: Challenges for the EU Banking Sector

The recent failure of US bank Silicon Valley Bank (SVB) and the acquisition of Swiss bank Credit Suisse (CS) by Union de Banques Suisse (UBS) have reminded us that banking is based on trust. On the one hand, a combination of management oversights with poor risk management of the interest rate risk, and the high concentration risk in its funding mix precipitated the downfall of the US lender. On the other hand, ongoing concerns on the sustainability of Credit Suisse's business model coupled with recurring concerns on its governance and high conduct risk have been instrumental in the fall of one of the global systemic financial institutions. Depositors' and investors' trust in both banks was lost causing an acute confidence crisis in a handful of days. Both events have triggered heightened volatility in bank equity markets, not witnessed since the invasion of Ukraine, and it has also impacted the spreads of banking bonds, showing that contagion effects and spill over effects should also be closely and actively monitored.

While materially different, these cases should work as cautionary tales on our limited ability to assess how risks will materialize into financial instability. It also shows that failure of a bank, even if mid-sized, can spread through the financial system and trigger a loss of confidence in the banking sector. These failures shed a new light on a number of issues that will be with us going forward. Mainly: i) how the increase in interest rates after more than a decade of ultra-low rates will filter through the financial sector; ii) the likelihood and speed of deposit runs in the digital age; and, iii) our ability to ex-ante design a regulatory framework that will properly help us in addressing the challenges of a crisis when and where it arises.

EU Banks have built up Resilience

During the past fifteen years banks in the European Union have transformed their governance, balance sheets and risk management. The regulatory framework has also been substantially strengthened and supervision has become more intrusive, risk-based and forward looking. This transformation was not easy and required a great deal of effort not only from banks, but also from regulatory authorities, the supervisory community as well as strong political will. As a result, the EU banking sector is much more resilient today than it was fifteen years ago, with substantially higher capital and liquidity positions.

https://doi.org/10.1515/9783111340937-015

EU banks have increased their capital positions resulting at the end of 2022 in an average CET1 (fully loaded) ratio of 15.3 %. This compares with 11.5 % reported in 2014[1]. This capital level provides a capital headroom above regulatory requirements (i.e., Overall Capital Requirements – OCR – and Pillar 2 Guidance) of almost 500bp. EU banks also reported an average leverage ratio of 5.5 %, comfortably above the regulatory minimum. The improvement in EU banks' capitalisation is widely based with even lower ends of the distribution reporting well above regulatory minimums.

Liquidity held by banks is also ample. The average liquidity coverage ratio of the EU banking sector is above 164 % with the lower end of the dispersion (the 5th percentile) at close to 140 %. This should be sized against the regulatory minimum of 100 %. Still, what is most important, at least during a period of heightened uncertainty, is the mix of high-quality liquid assets (HQLA). For European banks this is dominated by cash and reserves at central banks, which make up more than 55 %. The net stable funding ratio (NSFR) was also comfortably above regulatory minimum, and it was reported at 125 %. Available stable funding (ASF) is well diversified, with notably almost half of it contributed by retail deposits which tend to be rather sticky.

The laborious and lengthy effort to improve asset quality and address structural deficiencies that were impediments to its profitability have also contributed to this effort. European banks reported around EUR 350 billion of non-performing loans (NPLs) as of end of 2022, which compares to more than EUR 1 trillion NPLs a few years ago. The NPL ratio decreased from 6.5 % at end 2014 to 1.8 % at end 2022. EU banks have also improved their loan origination standards which may shield them from rising credit risk.

In addition, we have a more fully-fledged regulatory framework. The EBA's single rulebook is a prime example of this, as it aims at providing a single set of harmonised prudential rules for financial institutions throughout the EU, helping create a level playing field and providing high protection to depositors, investors, and consumers.

Changes in the economic Environment and contagion Risks may challenge Banks' Resilience

Banks' core business was for many years under pressure due to low or even negative interest rates. Yet, increasing interest rates have helped to improve their profit-

---

1 Right after the Global Financial Crisis in 2009, the CET1 ratio of EU banks was 9 %.

ability last year through increasing widening margins and improvements in net interest income. European banks reported an average return on equity of 8.1 % at the end of 2022 which was the highest level for many years. Strong profitability can be the first line of defence for rising provisioning needs in the current macroeconomic environment.

Before the full recovery from pandemic effects, the European economy has been challenged by another supply shock due to the Russian invasion in Ukraine. The tensions in supply chains due to the pandemic have been exacerbated by the war, the subsequent energy crisis, and the abrupt inflationary pressures. In order to tackle inflation, central banks across the world have responded with faster-than-expected interest rate rises accompanied with monetary tightening of their balance sheets. What was expected to be a rather short-term inflation spike has proven to be stickier. Inflation and increasing interest rates impact economic growth and impairs customers' ability to service their loans. It may also act as a deflator of assets (debt, equity, house prices) being held by banks or their customers.

In the current context and looking forward it is expected that EU banks will be confronted with material risks. The increase in interest rates that has in the short run helped profitability through enhancements of the banks' net interest margin will have wider effects on the banks' medium term outlook. First, the normalization of monetary policy and higher rates will affect banks' borrowing costs. Rising rates will also impact the value of financial assets as well as real estate markets. Finally, the tightening of financial conditions will ultimately impact economic activity, and reduce the credit worthiness of those firms and households that find themselves with excessive leverage.

Vulnerabilities in the financial sector are likely to come from those areas most likely to be affected by the new macroeconomic environment. Those sectors and firms where credit growth and leverage have increased are most likely to be vulnerable. The growth of nonbank lending and financial activity is an area of concern. The range of activities included under this category is very broad, with many different business models and sectors being included. Nevertheless, the growth and lack of transparency in many of these activities are reasons for concern. Additionally, those business models, such as buy now pay later, that have relied on low interest rates for their recent growth will need to redesign their strategies to a future with positive rates.

The impact of these vulnerabilities on banks' outlook and financial stability will depend, as usual, on each institution's business model. Credit risk remains on top of the list for potential vulnerabilities in European banks. In general, exposure to those sectors of the economy where lending has grown in the past few years, leverage is high, and business sustainability may be challenging are key areas of concern as deterioration in asset quality will be most likely in those circumstances.

In fact, there are already signs of deterioration in the asset quality. For example, banks now allocate a higher share of loans in stage 2 and they have increased provisions for performing loans. The share of stage 2 loans is 9.4 %, which is higher than the pandemic peak, which was characterised by extreme volatility and low visibility from banks' point of view. Another area of concern are the rising insolvencies, which are picking up at a steady rate in some EU countries. They, however, remain lower than pre-pandemic levels.

EU banks have significant exposures to loans collateralised by residential and commercial real estate. The commercial real estate sector has a procyclical behaviour and has therefore concentrated a lot of investment in the previous years, benefiting from the low-rate environment. The pandemic particularly impacted this segment. In fact, it was one of the segments that made extensive use of Covid-19 related support measures, such as moratoria on loan repayments. Teleworking and other changes in working conditions are also raising questions on the long-term attractiveness of such investments. Pockets of risks could be exacerbated in this segment as higher interest rates add pressure. CRE exposures have already one of the highest NPL ratios (3.7 % at end 2022), as banks still struggle to clean-up legacy assets from previous crises. This could quickly deteriorate considering the upcoming challenges to the sector among which a rise in construction costs, lower demand amid already empty premises and changes in work practices, or climate transition risk.

During the pandemic and its aftermath, demand for housing had accelerated rapidly, also helped by historically low interest rates and the liquidity accumulated during the pandemic. The growth in mortgage loans halted during the second half of 2022 as interest rates rose and banks tightened credit standards. There are already some indications that house prices began to correct in some countries of the European Union. This could impair consumer confidence and their overall expenditure, dampening economic activity further. Coupled with the rising non-performing loans volumes, banks will also be challenged by diminishing collateral valuation, as mortgage loans are collateralised, the value of collateral will also decrease and could potentially reduce the recovery value in case of default. In addition, this risk prevails even more in countries where households bear of interest rate risk via variable-rate loans. In such cases, monthly payments can increase substantially in a very short timeframe, putting at risk the solvency of part of the household loan book. Although risks stemming from these exposures are material, there are several factors that will probably mitigate the impact on banks. Loan to value ratios have been decreasing, as banks adhered to stricter and more prudent lending standards in recent years.

Unsecured retail loans are also at the forefront of concerns. In fact, there is already a marginal increase in volumes of consumer credit NPLs. Consumer credit loans are particularly sensitive to economic growth and especially unemployment rates and they are usually the first to react in economic downturns.

Small and medium size enterprises (SMEs) are also particularly vulnerable as they are not only challenged by rising interest payments, but also struggle with higher energy costs. In addition to this, the challenging situation in capital markets has led larger firms to seek funding from banks. This raises the risk of crowding out SMEs as banks tighten their credit standards and limit the expansion of their balance sheets.

As discussed above, banks' profitability has benefitted from increasing rates and widening margins, yet there is rising concern about their liquidity management and funding cost. Focus on liquidity and funding needs started picking up gradually in late 2022 and further intensified in the beginning of 2023. The recent banking turmoil in United States followed by the events at Credit Suisse have brought these issues to their most dramatic materialization.

Banks have managed to front load funding needs during the early months of the 2023, taking advantage of investors' appetite for better yields backed by positive momentum due to increasing bank profitability. Despite this active start of the year, the maturing of Targeted Longer-Term Financing Operations and the need for some banks to meet their MREL targets must be kept in mind. EU banks also have a diversified asset and funding mix. On the latter EU banks have a greater reliance on retail deposits (around 30 % of total liabilities is household deposits) which have proved very stable and around 17 % are deposits from NFCs. EU banks have also the ability to execute securities financing transactions such as repurchase agreements (repos) to avoid fire-selling their assets should they need liquidity. As of end 2022, EU banks had only 25.8 % of their assets encumbered.

The increasing interest rates have emphasized the importance of prudent management of interest rate risk. Debt securities with accounting treatment as held to maturity (or at amortised cost) have come at the centre of attention following the failure of SVB, as among other failures, it had also failed to limit the interest rate risk on its sovereign debt portfolio. EU banks report more than EUR 1.5 trillion of debt securities at amortised cost, which is around 5 % of total assets. If these securities offer fixed interest rate, an increase in interest rates affects their net present value and therefore their market value falls. The difference between the market value and the booked value of these assets, being held until maturity, does not need to be reported through the banks' profit and loss account.

As indicated above, EU banks' liquidity position is comfortable, with over 50 % of their high quality liquid assets being held in either cash or reserves in the central banks. However, considering the turmoil in funding markets following the demise of SVB and CS, volatile markets may continue to test banks' ability to obtain market funding at reasonable costs. Additionally, banks are likely to confront harder competition for customers' deposits. So far, indications show that deposit betas in European banks have remained low. Nevertheless, banks will likely need to increase the remuneration rate of deposits to retain them, therefore generating higher cost to maintain a solid deposit base.

As part of the regulatory framework and the management of interest rate risk, European banks need to comply with the EBA guidelines on interest rate risks for banking book (IRRBB). Last Autumn, the EBA published two final draft Regulatory Technical Standards (RTS) specifying technical aspects of the revised framework capturing IRRBB positions. The final draft RTS on the IRRBB standardised approach specifies the criteria to evaluate the risks arising from potential changes in interest rates that affect both the economic value of equity and the net interest income of an institution's non trading book activities. The final draft RTS on IRRBB supervisory outlier tests (SOT) specifies the modelling and parametric assumptions and the supervisory shock scenarios to identify institutions for which the economic value of equity would decline by more than 15 % of Tier 1 capital, as well as to evaluate if there is a large decline in the net interest income, that could trigger supervisory measures. The EBA is committed to closely monitor the implementation and application of these guidelines.

We cannot underestimate other Sources of Risks

The recent banking turmoil has taught us several lessons. Perhaps, the most important is that any risk can have a significant impact on the banking sector, therefore none can be overlooked. So far, I have focused on the most salient risks in the balance sheets of banks, mainly credit, market and liquidity risks. In this final section, I would like to highlight the need to assess thoroughly and deal effectively with risks such as conduct risk, cyber and data security risk, fraud, and financial crime.

I would like to focus on cyber risks, which are particularly high on the risk map for the EU banking supervisors. Significant cyber-attacks incidents have risen in the past months with 10 % of banks answering in our RAQ that they faced at least one major successful cyber-attack. Fortunately, none of these events have had large material impacts or systemic consequences. But we should not be complacent. Banks, but also supervisors, are continuing to build-up knowledge and resilience on this topic. Incoming DORA requirements are also important to foster cyber resilience, including information and communication technology (ICT) risk management, testing of ICT systems, and cyber resilience testing.

Geopolitical risk also affects the smooth operations at the short-term and strategic planning for the long-term of the banks. Geopolitical risk is entirely exogenous to the banking sector, but it remains paramount that this risk is mitigated, both for the resilience of the bank and of its customers. Part of the difficulty lies in the fact that until realised, geopolitical risk is uncertain, diffuse and often poorly measured. Geopolitical risk mitigation lies therefore in preparedness and sound procedures to be activated in case risk materialises.

There are two major types of geopolitical risks that warrant banks to set up appropriate procedures. The first is the case where a country in which an EU bank is established or has exposures to is embroiled in a conflict. This happened in the aftermath of Russian invasion, with banks being led to dispose of businesses and subsidiaries in Russia to safeguard their clients and other activities. Some banks were fast, other kept on struggling with solving this issue. The second case is the risk for a bank to be impacted in its day-to-day operations (due to pandemic-like disruption, cyber-attacks, etc.). To tackle this risk, preparedness on cyber risk should be acute, as explained before, and banks should also be mindful of their dependency to companies within a country identified as having geopolitical risk which are acting as third-party providers for core business functions.

Finally, one of the major challenges for EU banks stems from climate transition risk. Climate related incidents are expected to become more frequent and more intense. They are linked to increasing mortality rates and have sparked aggressive wildfires. It will induce in the long run important shifts in banks' exposures allocation. This challenge bears a significant reputational risk if it is not met with the appropriate management actions and diligences. Banks need to enhance their information gathering, risk modelling and management of these activities to ensure they properly manage their exposures to climate-related risks.

We need to remain vigilant, and Supervisors will be on the Forefront

Although it's perhaps early to fully analyse and assess the consequences of the recent banking turmoil we could infer some early lessons. First, we can't overlook that banking is an industry based on trust and confidence is key for its smooth operation. I trust that the regulatory, the supervisory framework and the improvement in the risk management safety nets put together in the years following the financial crisis, has contributed to fostering confidence in the EU banking sector. The ability to generate profits which will translate in capital generation and capital distribution to shareholders, is also a necessary condition to bring confidence to markets and build up investors' trust.

This endogenous resilience is however not entirely sufficient, and the recent cases of failures have highlighted yet again that supervisory initiative remains a major component of the global resilience picture a banking sector can draw. The importance of contingency planning, and stress-testing for preparing banks to the worst possible outcomes in a widespread negative scenario cannot be overemphasized. Under the 2023 EU-wide stress test launched by the EBA, the severe scenario is based on a narrative of hypothetical heightened geopolitical tensions associated with high inflation and higher interest rates which materialise into having strong adverse effects on private consumption and investments, both domestically and globally. The stress test exercise provides additional evidence of the resilience of the banking sector under very adverse scenarios.

Stuart Graham
Key systemic Risks faced by global Banks

The global banking system is in much stronger shape than in 2008/09. However, recent events at Silicon Valley Bank and Credit Suisse show that vulnerabilities remain. Higher for longer interest rates may yet lead to further vulnerabilities emerging. This article considers some of the major potential systemic risks for the banks. As well as the obvious concerns around interlinkages with non-bank financial institutions, we at Autonomous Research are also worried about the strain on banks' balance sheets from a potential stagflationary environment. We also see tail risks in the Bank of Japan's eventual exit from Yield Curve Control. Finally, sovereign debt sustainability also remains a major concern – especially in a stagflationary environment.

The global Banks are in much better Shape than in 2008/09

Most commentators agree that the global banking industry is in much better shape than going into the Great Financial Crisis in 2008/09. For example, European banks' tangible common equity/asset ratios are currently above 5%, which compares to 3.0% in 2007 and 4.2% in the early 1990s. We at Autonomous Research have estimated that the European banks' CET1 ratio, which now stand above 13.5%, would have been below 5.0% on similar supervisory standards back in 2007.

The banks also have much stronger liquidity ratios. The GSIBs run with 5x the liquidity buffers they held back in 2007. The industry has also made enormous progress in reducing the volume of bilaterally cleared OTC derivatives. The large GSIBs have reduced their volumes by -70% since 2007 on average.

Nonetheless, recent events have shown that the global banking industry can still be vulnerable under certain circumstances. Most importantly, deposit outflows can occur at speeds which were previously unimaginable. This probably means that the Liquidity Coverage Ratio (LCR) needs to be recalibrated. Assuming 10–12% outflows of uninsured retail deposits over a 30 day period is likely too optimistic given what we have just seen at some US regional banks and Credit Suisse (20%+ in a day). In the extreme scenario where 100% outflows of uninsured retail deposits would be assumed in the calculation of the LCR, Autonomous Research has estimated that the LCRs of the largest European and US banks would decline from 145% to 95%.

https://doi.org/10.1515/9783111340937-016

The Risks from Stagflation

Forward curves are signalling investors' belief that central banks will successfully slay inflation and then be able to cut interest rates. However, this may prove to be wishful thinking and another path of stubborn inflation requiring yet higher rates for longer is entirely plausible. Although we are unlikely to see either inflation or interest rates at 1970s levels, a review of that period can highlight some key risks for the banks in a stagflationary environment.

Inflation erodes the economic value of banks' equity. The 1970s was a period of constant strain on banks' capital ratios. The US banks allowed their equity/asset ratio to fall from 5.4% in 1970 to 3.9% in 1979. Under today's supervisory framework, such a decline in capital ratios would not be tolerated. Moreover, in the 1970s the banks were not required to mark their securities portfolios to market (thereby flattering their stated capital ratios). Today's tougher accounting standards would create additional challenges for the banks. Unrealised fair value losses on both banks' held to maturity securities and loan books due to higher interest rates could become so large that – as in the case of Silicon Valley Bank – they begin to unnerve investors, depositors and bond holders. As at end 2022, unrealised fair value losses on banks' loan books were equal to 33% of tangible book value at US banks and 20% at European banks. Some US and European banks with large fixed rate mortgage books are already seeing unrealised fair value losses on their loan books approach or even exceed 100% of CET1 capital. "Higher for longer" rates could lead such unrealised fair value losses to increase still further.

Although such fair value losses are highly theoretical for 99%+ of the time, they could become a reality if (i) a bank's liquidity situation is sufficiently bad that it needs to sell such assets or (ii) in the event of a takeover (when under both US GAAP and IFRS a buyer would need to fair value all assets and liabilities, irrespective of their prior accounting treatment).

Global banks' real ROEs suffered during the 1970s and valuations came under significant pressure (mid-single digit P/Es and P/BVs of ~0.5x were not uncommon). In such an environment, it became very difficult for banks to access fresh capital.

The economic crises of the 1970s led to significant "bank-bashing" from politicians. The banks were also subject to significant financial repression via price controls, dividend restrictions and enforced "national service" (for example, the UK's so-called lifeboat during the secondary banking crisis). Although hard to imagine today, there were repeated calls for the nationalisation of banks in the UK in the 1970s.

The 1970s was obviously a particularly extreme period of stagflation. Any read-across should be made with great care. That said, for at least a decade, bankers have been learning to live with ultra-low rates. Their balance sheets have not been constructed with stagflation as a base case.

The Risks from Non-Bank financial Institutions (NBFIs)

At Autonomous, we have written what seem like an endless series of reports over the last five years detailing the possible risks (both direct and indirect) for global banks from the NBFIs. Like most commentators, we worry about the NBFIs' size ($68trn per the Financial Stability Board), growth rates (9 % CAGR over the last decade) and opaque nature.

We believe there are both direct and indirect risks for the global banks from the NBFIs. The direct risks relate to the banks' financing of NBFIs. In so far as the NBFIs could incur large losses in a recession, this could lead to loan losses for the banks themselves on their exposures to the NBFIs. The indirect risks relate to market turmoil, which could lead *inter alia* to (i) mark-to-market losses on the banks' holdings of similar credit assets, (ii) "bad volatility" in banks' sales & trading results and/or (iii) depressed origination revenues due to dislocated markets.

In terms of direct risks, the NBFIs are highly interconnected with the banks via financing flows of $6–7trn in both directions. US banks have provided $2trn of credit to NBFIs, EU banks €2.6trn while Japanese banks have provided at least $1trn. Data on individual banks' exposures to NBFIs is very difficult to find and compare. Autonomous Research estimates that the leading global US, European and Japanese banks have exposures to NBFIs equal to on average 165 % of CET1 capital. In some cases that figure is as high as almost 400 % of CET1 capital. Over the period 2019–2022 the large global banks' exposures to NBFIs have grown by a cumulative +25 %.

With regards to indirect risks, the banks own many of the same assets as the NBFIs. Focusing on the $5.4trn of US sub-investment grade corporate credit outstanding, Autonomous Research estimates that $1.4trn of this is owned by banks, $1.3trn by institutional investors with the vast bulk of the remaining $2.7trn being owned by a variety of NBFIs. The banks are acting as "arms dealers" to some of these NBFIs via, for example, warehouse lines for CLOs and subscription lines of credit for Private Equity firms. In some cases, the banks in the US and Japan are also significant investors themselves in highly rated CLOs.

The obvious danger is that the NBFI sector as a whole has pursued the same "hunt for yield" strategy over the last decade. Problems in a small part of the NBFI sector could potentially spread and therefore lead to broader problems for asset markets relatively quickly.

The Risks from the Japanese banking System

The Bank of Japan has been warning about large interest rate risk in the banking book (IRRBB) at domestic banks for many years. This feels like a potentially very dangerous set-up at a time when the central bank may finally be exiting Yield Curve Control. A disorderly exit from YCC could lead to a major IRRBB shock for Japanese banks, with potential spill-overs into global markets. We have already seen such interest rate turmoil before, with the so-called VAR shock in the Japanese market in June 2003 when yields on 10Y JGBs rose +70bps in a month and +120bps in three months.

Of the major Japanese banks, we at Autonomous Research worry the most about Norinchukin given its size ($850bn of assets) and very high IRRBB (equal to a 40% hit to CET1 capital in a parallel +100bps rates shock scenario). For context, this compares to <10% at the three Japanese megabanks. With a CLO portfolio of almost $50bn, Norinchukin is referred to as "the whale" in the global CLO markets. Large Japanese banks own $150bn of CLOs which is a similar level to both US banks and US insurers.

More broadly, Japanese banks are major financiers of global NBFIs. For example, BIS statistics show that of the $1.1trn of international bank financing of NBFIs based in the Cayman Islands, $485bn comes from US banks, $400bn from Japanese banks and then the next largest lenders are Swiss, French and Canadian banks at around $50bn each. The Japanese banks are also major financiers of NBFIs in the US ($465bn versus for example $150bn from Swiss banks, $115bn from French banks and $70bn from German banks).

A disorderly exit from YCC could create an IRRBB shock for Japanese banks which could cause them to de-risk more generally. This could then reverberate around global markets as they retrench in their financing of NBFIs.

It is these indirect risks which worry us most for the global banks. International banks' direct exposures to Japanese borrowers are modest. We at Autonomous Research estimate that leading global banks' exposures to Japanese borrowers are equivalent to only 20% of CET1 capital (with a few international banks in the 50–80% range).

The Risks from sovereign Debt Sustainability

In recent months, sovereign debt sustainability has not featured highly in investors' minds. For example, the spread between Italian and German 10Y government bonds remained below 200bps throughout the market turmoil of March 2023. However, a stagflationary environment could put more pressure on sovereign debt sustainability. In any case, consensus forecasts would suggest that the "debt snowball" maths for the US, UK and Italy should begin to deteriorate again in 2024. Optimists will argue that the ECB's anti-fragmentation Transmission Protection Instrument (or TPI) should stave off any bond market pressure on EU sovereigns but this tool has yet to be deployed and tested.

The good news is that the sovereign-bank doom-loop has been weakened somewhat. Back in 2012, a 100bps widening in Italian sovereign debt spreads would have depleted Italian banks' CET1 ratios by 90–100bps. Now, because of a combination of smaller portfolios, shorter durations and more assets being held to maturity (and therefore not marked-to-market for capital purposes) that same sensitivity would be only a -20bps hit to Italian banks' CET1 ratios.

The less good news is that Covid-19 caused a new corporate nexus to be added to the sovereign-bank interlinkages via government loan guarantee programmes. In some EU markets 15–30 % of bank's domestic corporate loan books are currently guaranteed by domestic sovereigns. This has created a new feedback loop between certain sovereigns and the European banks.

Kerstin af Jochnick
Fostering stable Banks in the Union

Introduction

When we met in Frankfurt for the conference at the turn of the year, there was broad consensus amongst participants that one of the main challenges to banking activity stemmed from the macroeconomic and financial environment prevailing at the time. In this regard, some of us noted that while the effect of the rise in interest rates associated with the normalisation of monetary policy by major central banks was meant to be beneficial for the global banking sector when seen in aggregate terms, its distributional effects would still matter. In turn, this meant that, in relative terms, one could expect to see 'winners and losers' across individual banks associated to the rise in interest rates, including on account of size and business model considerations.

However, conference participants also agreed that the banking sector remained resilient overall and that the reforms enacted in the aftermath of the Great Financial Crisis by global policymakers and regulators in the Basel setting had served banks well. In this regard, there was broad recognition that such reforms had been instrumental for banks to withstand the test of large and unexpected external shocks taking place in quick succession in recent years, first with the outbreak of the COVID19 pandemic and then with the fallout stemming from Russia's war of aggression in Ukraine.

The events during recent months, and in particular the market turmoil triggered by the failure of Silicon Valley Bank in the United States, have largely proven this assessment to be correct. In the remainder of this article, I will first elaborate on the current state of the European banking sector. Thereafter, I will discuss the potential lessons to be had from the recent market turmoil. Lastly, looking beyond the recent events, I will outline the challenges which banks need to tackle in a medium-term context and the issues which we as supervisors have high on our agenda.

The current State of the European Banking Sector

The European area banking sector remains resilient from both a capital and a liquidity perspective, despite Russia's war of aggression in Ukraine and the market turmoil triggered by the failure of Silicon Valley Bank in the United States in March. The Common Equity Tier 1 (CET1) capital ratio of significant banks, that is those banks which are directly supervised by the ECB, stood at 15.3 % at the end of 2022,

https://doi.org/10.1515/9783111340937-017

while the liquidity coverage ratio (LCR) stood at 161 %, well above both regulatory requirements and pre-pandemic levels. At the same time, asset quality remained stable, with a non-performing loan (NPL) ratio of 1.8 % at the end of 2022, compared with 2.1 % at the end of 2021. The normalisation of monetary policy has also continued to support European banks' profitability, with a return on equity of 7.7 % in the fourth quarter of 2022, mostly driven by growing net interest income, the contained cost of risk and a slight increase in cost efficiency. As of the time of writing (June 2023), banks and analysts alike expect the profitability outlook to remain equally positive this year, as confirmed by results published so far for the first quarter of 2023.

It is important to underline that, from an ECB perspective, we don't see a direct read-across from recent events in the United States to the banks under our supervision. In particular, the business models of the banks we supervise do not share the same unique features as those of the regional banks that have come under stress in the United States. Our banks tend to rely on a more diversified depositor base and, more specifically, do not exhibit the combination of extreme dependence on volatile funding sources, especially uninsured deposits, and material unrealised losses in securities portfolios held at amortised cost.

In this context, one should also keep in mind that the perimeter of regulation in Europe is also different to that in the United States. I would like to mention two examples in this regard. First, in the case of regional banks in the United States, there was a possibility not to reflect on capital the depreciation of assets held in the available-for-sale book. Such banks did not map the unrealised losses on the available-for-sale assets into capital. In contrast, this is not an option for banks here in Europe, so everything in the available-for-sale book goes to capital through fair value through other comprehensive income. This important difference helps to explain why, as recently documented by the IMF in its April 2023 Global Financial Stability Report, the median impact of banks' unrealised losses in terms of capital is much higher in the United States (more than 250 basis points) than in Europe (less than 50 basis points). Second, here in Europe, all of our banks are subjected to the liquidity coverage ratio (LCR), whereas the affected banks in the United States did not actually have the application of the LCR. In turn, this aspect exacerbated the problem related to the comparative magnitude of unrealised losses in US and European banks, as mentioned above.

From a European perspective, therefore, at the ECB we would argue that loosening our rulebook compared to the Basel 3 standards would reduce the resilience of the European banking sector and could expose our banks to the same weaknesses we have seen in other jurisdictions. This shows how important it is to minimise the deviations from the Basel standards in the upcoming Capital Requirements Regulation (CRR III)/Capital Requirements Directive (CRD VI) legislative framework.

Lessons from the recent Market Turmoil

Notwithstanding the important differences between the US and European banking landscape to which I referred to above, the events in recent months have been a reminder of the challenges posed by a rapidly-adjusting monetary policy and interest rate environment in a setting in which debt from various counterparts is still at very high levels. From a supervisory perspective, while the process of monetary policy and interest rate normalisation has been beneficial for the European banking sector as a whole, the recent events have pointed to the continued need to monitor risks related to rising interest rates and liquidity and funding across individual entities. These risks have been a point of supervisory attention for us for some time now, and they will continue to be going forward as they are an integral part of our supervisory priorities for the coming period. Let me outline the salient initiatives in this regard.

First, our supervisors started to assess the risks and vulnerabilities associated with a rising interest rate environment in the second half of 2021 when the first signs of inflationary pressure emerged, thus well before the recent market turmoil. Interest rate risk and credit spread risk in the banking book, counterparty credit risk and the credit risk arising in segments of the lending business such as leveraged finance and commercial real estate were all supervisory priorities in 2022. In all these areas, targeted reviews of risk management practices at banks have been complemented by dedicated on-site inspection campaigns, some of which are still ongoing.

Second, concerning interest rate risk in the banking book more specifically, we regularly assess how the economic value of banks is affected by changes in interest rates and credit spreads. Furthermore, we performed deep-dive analyses of banks' modelling practices as regards behavioural items, such as sight deposits and loan repayments, their credit spread stress-testing practices and their use of derivatives for hedging interest rate risk. Our targeted reviews and on-site inspections also extended to residential real estate exposures and exposures to energy and commodity traders. In addition, we are focusing increasingly on how banks are applying IFRS 9 with a view to better understanding and assessing the way banks provision for risks.

Third, as regards banks' asset and liability management strategies, we have identified a need to focus on the sustainability of banks' funding plans in view of the normalisation of monetary policy and the forthcoming phasing-out of extraordinary central bank funding facilities. Our supervisors have reviewed the targeted longer-term refinancing operation (TLTRO) exit strategies of selected banks that showed a material reliance on this funding source and were more vulnerable to increases in market funding costs. This targeted review will be complemented later this year by a broader analysis of banks' liquidity and funding plans and, where appropriate, targeted on-site inspections in order to identify weak practices and the more vulnerable institutions and to take the necessary supervisory actions where needed.

Recent market developments, in particular the observed speed of transmission of information and financial decisions by depositors and other market players, confirm that increased attention needs to be paid to the liquidity and funding risk outlook of the banking sector as monetary policy shifts to a new regime. Let me say upfront, however, that there is often a sort of 'knee jerk' automatic reaction in the aftermath of a crisis which leads policymakers to the perceived need to jump the gun and enact regulatory reforms. We at the ECB don't think that this should be the case this time around. There might be areas in which we want to review and maybe fine-tune the calibration of some of our requirements, but in general, as mentioned in the introduction to this article, we think that the overall framework underpinning activity in the banks under our supervision has shown to be robust.

Therefore, while we are convinced that the rulebook designed in response to the global financial crisis is not in need of major changes, however, we welcome the intention of the Basel Committee on Banking Supervision and the Financial Stability Board (FSB) to assess whether any lessons can be learned from the events we have recently witnessed. We are thoroughly assessing the lessons and reform proposals recently published by US authorities. The ECB is participating actively in the international work in this area. A thorough analysis is thus required, and we should avoid the temptation to prejudge the findings. However, areas of focus include some elements of the calibration of the LCR and the extent to which assets held at amortised cost, which may be difficult to sell without suffering losses when liquidity needs arise, can qualify as high-quality liquid assets. In addition, it may be beneficial to explore how factors such as high deposit base concentration and a predominant reliance on uninsured deposits could be dealt with in the Pillar 2 framework. More broadly, the question of the minimum scope of application of the Basel standards may also need to be discussed, and further reflection on the role of digital banking and social media in accelerating deposit outflows may be needed.

Beyond the remit of prudential regulation and supervision, another issue highlighted by recent market events is the transparency of credit default swap (CDS) trading. These markets are characterised by low liquidity and high opacity. As CDS spreads may also be used by institutional and corporate depositors as triggers for withdrawals, sharp price changes in this market have the potential to become highly destabilising for banks and wider securities markets. Enhancing transparency in this market is something that might need to be tackled at global and European level.

The supervisory Agenda going forward

Looking beyond the events in recent months and the associated risks in the near-term, we as supervisors also need to maintain our focus on the medium-term challenges that banks are facing, such as the impact of climate change as well as digitalisation. Concerning climate change, we intend to follow-up on the results of the various reviews of climate-related and environmental risks that were conducted in 2022. We are also urging banks to further develop their risk management frameworks and reduce data gaps. Banks have received individual letters setting out the steps to be taken in order to be fully compliant with our supervisory expectations by the end of 2024. As regards digitalisation, in 2022 we conducted an extensive survey to better understand the state of play of the digital transformation and the use of innovative technologies of the banks we supervise, and to prioritise our supervisory activities around this. This year we follow-up on these results by performing targeted reviews and on-site inspections on digital transformation to shape supervisory expectations in the years to come.

Separately, from a narrow supervisory perspective, we will continue to work towards improving our processes and strengthening the effectiveness of our risk-based supervision. Let me mention a couple of on-going initiatives in this regard. First, as of this year, supervisors will apply a new risk tolerance framework to strengthen our focus on strategic priorities and key vulnerabilities, with more flexibility in planning activities based on a multi-year approach as part of the Supervisory Review and Examination Process (SREP). Second, the European Commission and the European Court of Auditors have recently published the results of their respective reviews of the overall application of the SSM Regulation[1] and of the audit of the ECB's operational efficiency in supervising banks' management of non-performing loans[2]. These reports recognise the success of the ECB in establishing effective supervision and include some recommendations on how to further enhance its processes. Work on the implementation of these recommendations has already started. In addition, we recently published the results of an external assessment of the SREP, drafted by a group of external high-level experts[3]. Here too, the report acknowl-

---

1 See "REPORT FROM THE COMMISSION TO THE EUROPEAN PARLIAMENT AND THE COUNCIL on the Single Supervisory Mechanism established pursuant to Regulation (EU) No 1024/2013", European Commission, 18 April 2023.
2 See "Special report 12/2023: EU supervision of banks' credit risk – The ECB stepped up its efforts but more is needed to increase assurance that credit risk is properly managed and covered", European Court of Auditors, 12 May 2023.
3 See "Assessment of the European Central Bank's Supervisory Review and Evaluation Process – Report by the Expert Group to the Chair of the Supervisory Board of the ECB", ECB, 17 April 2023.

edges the success of ECB Banking Supervision in establishing itself as an effective and respected supervisor and provides recommendations on how to further enhance the efficiency and effectiveness of our work, leveraging on what we are already doing. We will start implementing some of the report's recommendations as early as in the 2023 SREP cycle and will take the report into account in a review of supervisory processes planned for 2024.

Conclusion

Overall, developments in recent years, including those related to the market turmoil in recent months, point to the importance of well-capitalised banks, prudent supervisors and strong institutions, respectively. The collective efforts by all parties concerned has meant that banks have thus far coped well with the many challenges it has faced. However, this should not lull us into a false sense of security. We know from our experience with crisis management that past success may not necessarily be a reliable bellwether for future performance. In order to further strengthen our collective resilience to potentially adverse developments in the future, we at the ECB are thus calling for the prompt implementation of the Basel III regulation and the completion of the European banking union project.

Luiz Awazu Pereira da Silva

The broad Context in January 2023 for financial Stability and the Risks in a poly-crisis World

Since early 2022, we have been in a cycle of global monetary policy tightening due to inflation that started to rise in mid-2021. At times like these, financial disturbances – even financial crises – are always a possible known risk, since the low-for-long interest rate environment over the preceding decade heightened these vulnerabilities. What could go wrong? There are some areas where we can see the vulnerabilities – ie the known risks, but also some that we can't readily identify – ie the unknown risks. The main task for policymakers is to use their instruments to minimise the known risks and do their best to guess the unknown risks – and plan ahead for how they would respond if these risks were to materialise.

Let me elaborate on these points. The banking industry finds itself in an environment of policy tightening, which inevitably raises concerns about potential financial crises. What could go wrong in this poly-crisis context? There are both known and unknown risks. To effectively address them, it is crucial to identify the known consequences and, while differentiating them from the unknown ones, prepare ourselves for them.

As a result of the cumulative effect of the monetary tightening cycle, it is natural that the global economy is currently experiencing a soft patch. The robust post-Covid growth is tapering off, and we are starting to feel the contractionary effects of tightening monetary policy. However, we are still grappling with high inflation, which is slowly eroding household incomes in real terms and creating uncertainty. Additionally, the lingering impact of elevated energy prices, although somewhat reduced recently, continues to pose challenges. The debt levels of both households and corporations remain high due to the ongoing effects of the pandemic and are likely to produce strains in an environment of higher debt repayment costs.

These are the known challenges: there is a relatively good understanding regarding the known risks for the financial sector. But it is essential to also consider how the current economic situation will evolve, especially if the observed disinflation process prevents inflation targets from being reached, and persists longer than anticipated. Factors such as a still tight labour market despite cuts in real wages may necessitate further action from central banks to tighten financial conditions beyond current market expectations, and that might produce further deceleration where a risk of recession cannot be discarded.

In addition to these known risks, there are other reasonably well mapped risks that should be considered. The resurgence of energy prices, the uncertainties surrounding the war in Ukraine, and the possibility of a significant slowdown in Chi-

https://doi.org/10.1515/9783111340937-018

na's growth all have the potential to exert further contractionary effects. These issues could impact the stability of regulated institutions and other segments of the financial sector.

Moving on to unknown risks, policymakers must pay close attention in several areas. Geopolitical tensions worldwide continue to evolve, and these developments pose significant concerns. Financial institutions face vulnerabilities in terms of liquidity risks as they navigate tighter financial conditions despite progress in implementing Basel III. We observed some elements of these new types of vulnerability in the United Kingdom, with the stresses experienced by UK pension funds last September. Furthermore, non-bank financial institutions operating in less regulated market segments, such as money market funds and hedge funds, may face challenges associated with liquidity mismatches or hidden leverage.

The domain of prudential regulation highlights the increased systemic importance of central counterparties, leading them to strengthen their safeguards. However, these measures have made their clients more susceptible to liquidity shortages during times of market stress. The Bank for International Settlements (BIS) has repeatedly warned about these types of risk in non-bank financial institutions. Finally, the crypto universe represents another potential unknown risk. While we have observed signs of fragility, we hope that possible stresses and even collapses will not have a contagious effect on the traditional banking sector and produce a significantly negative impact on the real economy.

Another critical area that deserves attention is climate change. While it is often viewed as a long-term risk, we are witnessing the high cost and manifestation of short-term physical risks at a faster and more abrupt pace than previously thought. This, in turn, has the potential to affect financial stability due to the potentially large financial losses that these more frequent climate-related events can inflict.

Lastly, considering the current state of labour markets, it is noteworthy that, while nominal wages have grown, real wages remain in negative territory. We must consider the potential implications if social unrest were to arise due to a worsening inflationary picture and economic conditions. That could trigger a round of wage-inflation catch-up that, if passed on to consumer prices through mark-ups, increases the likelihood of inflation sticking at a high level, despite the disinflation process.

In summary, these are the known and unknown risks that could impact financial stability in our potentially poly-crisis world. The known risks encompass factors such as economic deceleration, inflationary pressures, energy prices, geopolitical uncertainties and China's growth trajectory. These risks, though challenging, provide a relatively known set of scenarios and outlook for the financial sector. However, policymakers must also contend with unknown risks, including evolving geopolitical tensions, liquidity vulnerabilities among financial institutions, the crypto universe and the accelerating physical risks of climate change. It is crucial to remain vigilant and proactive in addressing these risks to maintain financial stability in an ever-changing landscape.

Moving on to how to mitigate these risks. It is clear that our collective aspiration is to achieve successful macro financial stabilisation where monetary tightening achieves its goal with a minimum damage to activity, together with a smooth transition towards a net-zero economy. We must acknowledge that we are currently in a phase of transitioning from a period characterised by exceptionally low interest rates and ample liquidity to a world where interest rates will be higher, and liquidity will be significantly reduced.

This transition presents a classic challenge as tightening global financial conditions inevitably give rise to financial events. The exceptional starting points, coupled with the impact of Covid, geopolitical tensions and energy price fluctuations, make this situation particularly complex. A crucial element for the future is achieving successful macro stabilisation, leading to a swift reduction in inflation. Central banks are actively engaged in pursuing this objective, as we are well aware of the detrimental effects of inflation on social stability, investor confidence and sustainable growth.

On the regulatory front, it is vital to ensure that financial institutions are adequately supervised to ensure they are provisioned and capitalised to navigate this transition effectively. It is encouraging to note that the banking sector has strengthened its capital positions and improved capital quality, while also maintaining robust liquidity positions. However, it is imperative to pay attention to liquidity risks in the non-bank financial sector, mapping and understanding these risks as they unfold.

The emergence of unknown new risks must be highlighted, including cyber, crypto and climate-related risks. It is paramount that we effectively map and comprehend these risks to ensure the resilience of the financial sector in the face of the potential events that these factors might trigger. While we have tools at our disposal, such as strong capital buffers, the example of climate risk reminds us that we may need to rethink our existing risk models to adequately quantify and address these unique challenges. Linear models and normal distributions of risks may not capture the non-linearities, cascading effects and distinctive distribution patterns associated with these risks.

In addition to managing risks, it is important to consider the future. We need to think beyond risks and embrace a process of Schumpeterian creative destruction in our economies to address the need to decarbonise, which implies a transformation of our capital stock away from its existing carbon footprint characteristics. That process will require massive new investments and financing by both the public and private sector. This entails leveraging the opportunities presented by stabilisation processes, digitalisation, cyber security, cryptocurrencies and climate considerations. It is an opportunity for us to invest in our future in a sustainable and stable manner, fostering higher economic growth while maintaining a social consensus. We know that the transition to net zero and its accompanying and much needed policies have redistributive implications and we should be prepared to pre-emptively address them.

In conclusion, our collective efforts should focus on achieving macro financial stabilisation, fortifying the resilience of financial institutions, while comprehending and managing both known and unknown risks, and embracing innovation and sustainable growth. It is through these endeavours that we can navigate the complex challenges ahead, forging a path towards a more robust and resilient financial system and strengthening the odds of moving towards a sustainable and inclusive growth regime in the years ahead.